Devotional Strength and Praise for Every Day

a daily devotional

Patricia Phillips Kincer

Lavender Falls Printing

Copyright 2016 by Patricia Phillips Kincer

ISBN - 978-1-365-33571-6

Acknowledgements:

First of all, I thank my parents for their encouragement and for raising me in a Bible-believing home.

I would like to thank the different pastors who have fed me spiritually through the years.

Many Christian friends have spurred me onward to pursue the study of the Bible.

And I want to thank my husband for being so patient with me.

Thanks to Paulita for helping me format my devotional.

To my children, you've always been supportive of my endeavors.

To my associate and good friend, Pat Carpenter, who helped me find and organize the scriptures for this devotional, I am grateful for your help.

My brothers and sisters have always been there for me when I needed them.

To the members of my church, both current and former, thanks for nurturing my teaching and studying of the Bible.

I pray a blessing on all of you who read and study this devotional.

DEVOTIONAL STRENGTH AND PRAISE FOR EVERY DAY

INTRODUCTION

This calendar of daily devotions has been a dream of mine for over thirty years. I have worked on it for almost that long while taking many sabbaticals. I started the devotions while I was still working. I have been retired more than twenty years and have finished the book at last.

Many of the devotions are urging people to come to Jesus. They are invited to accept Him and live for Him. The Bible is a book of invitations to enter into a personal faith with our Savior. Jesus invited all people to come to Him and receive rest. I believe we can have rest in a life that is filled with turmoil if we put our trust in Jesus. There will be peace in the storm.

My hope is that you will read and identify with the devotions in some way. I have included a place for prayer requests as well as a place to give praises every day. The praises may be as simple as a phone call from a child or a friend. It might be sunshine or rain. The Lord wants our praise, and we should praise Him for all things, whether simple or complex.

The devotions include extra reading from the Bible, which is meant to increase your faith and help you each day. All the readings are taken from the New International Version (NIV) of the Bible, unless noted.

By spending twenty or thirty minutes on devotions in the morning with the Lord before work or your busy day, I believe your day will go smoother.

You may not agree with the things I've written, but I base my belief on the Bible. We can disagree and still love Jesus and His teachings.

May the Lord Jesus Christ bless you and make your life complete.

In Christian Love,
Patricia Phillips Kincer

JANUARY

January 1
Read I Timothy 2:1-7

I Timothy 2:1

"I urge, then, first of all, that requests, prayers, intercession and thanksgiving be made for everyone."

Prayer is such an important part of the Christian life. We often neglect this part of our Christian ministry. We first came to know Christ through prayer, by asking for forgiveness. It is important that we continue in prayer. We can minister to the many needs of people through prayer. We may not be with the people physically, but through prayer our spirits are there lifting up their needs.

There are four types of prayer mentioned in verse one:

1. Requests are humble pleading prayers before God for some important need or request for God's help. These are prayers of supplication, which are prayed in intense earnestness.

2. Prayers are all types of prayer, collectively. They may be constant prayers in the heart and mind, routine prayers at church or home before bed or upon arising.

3. Intercessions are prayer presented to God on behalf of other persons. It is standing in the gap for the needs of others. It is interceding for a specific person's need.

4. Thanksgiving is giving praise to God for His loving kindness, His goodness, His blessings, His forgiveness, and everything we receive from Him.

Prayer is a powerful way to accomplish God's will in the world.

DAILY PRAISES	**DAILY PRAYER REQUESTS**
1.	1.
2.	2.
3.	3.
4.	4.
5.	5.

January 2
Read John 17:1-26

John 17:11

"I will remain in the world no longer, but they are still in the world, and I am coming to you. Holy Father protect them by the power of your name—the name you gave me—so that they may be one as we are one."

Jesus is our Mediator. He prayed to the Father for each of us to be kept by Him. He cares for each of us in a personal way. He desires that each of us be faithful to Him while we are in the world. He wants us to take the opportunities He provides for us to be a witness for Him. He wants us to obey His will. He has prayed and interceded to the Father that we would be faithful and true. He wants us to stand sure and firm in the last days. He is able to help us stand if we will keep our eyes on Him and follow Him alone.

We can each come boldly to Christ for our sins and all our needs because He is mediating for us. We are to come with confidence and faith because we are loved by the Father and His Son. We shall rejoice by coming to Christ and there are no limits on the fullness of joy or the magnitude of answered prayers through our Mediator.

DAILY PRAISES	DAILY PRAYER REQUESTS
1.	1.
2.	2.
3.	3.
4.	4.
5.	5.

January 3
Read II Corinthians 8:1-12

II Corinthians 8:9

"For you know the grace of our Lord Jesus Christ, that though He was rich, yet for your sakes He became poor, so that you through His poverty might become rich."

Christ is our example. He took on the nature of mankind in humility and poverty to be our example. We are to learn from Him. He is meek and lowly in heart. He gives rest to the weary, tired souls. He furnishes us with a spiritual mind as He had. He gives us joy in the time of confrontation. Because He endured suffering and confrontation in this world, so can we. We will not only endure, but be an overcomer as He is. We are not to live after the lust of the flesh, but follow the will of God. He loves us so much that He gave His life so we could have His spiritual blessings and riches.

God is Lord over all. He is everywhere. Our riches are obtained through Jesus. Often we think of our riches as material possessions. Through life in Jesus we can have so much more than material riches. Jesus is our life, our Savior, our joy, our comfort, our happiness, our strength, our love, our boldness, our victory, and our freedom.

Let us become rich in the Lord. Let us be obedient as He teaches us in all richness to glorify and honor Him. He has provided sufficient grace for every need. No matter what position we are in, there is always more grace. Do not underestimate the power of God's grace.

DAILY PRAISES	**DAILY PRAYER REQUESTS**
1.	1.
2.	2.
3.	3.
4.	4.
5.	5.

January 4
Read I Corinthians 15:35-58

I Corinthians 15:52
"in a flash, in the twinkling of an eye, at the last trumpet. For the trumpet will sound, the dead will be raised imperishable, and we will l be changed"

The resurrection of the bodies of the saints of God is a wonderful thought. We are assured by Christ that those who have died in Christ shall be resurrected at His coming. Their bodies which went into the ground, at burial, as diseased, maimed, and infected will come forth pure and undefiled when the trumpet of God sounds. Oh, what good news! What rejoicing! How we should be praising God for this promise of an uncorrupt, pure body one day.

Praise God because we have the promise of seeing those who have died again. Jesus promised to raise His followers at the last day. Death is the last enemy we must conquer and through Jesus, we can conquer death, as Jesus did. When the dead are raised they will have a spiritual body, a perfect body, and a glorified body.

After the dead are raised, the living saints will be caught up in the clouds to meet those arisen with the Lord. What a glorious thought! What a wonderful meeting in the air! This is to be a comfort to all Christians. This world is not the end of life. We will live forever somewhere. Let it be in Heaven with our loved ones.

DAILY PRAISES	**DAILY PRAYER REQUESTS**
1.	1.
2.	2.
3.	3.
4.	4.
5.	5.

January 5
Read Psalm 85

Psalm 85:9
"Surely his salvation is near those who fear him, that his glory may dwell in our land."

The Lord has promised divine deliverance for those who truly trust in Him when trials and persecutions come to them. Jesus hears the groaning and prayers of His children. He stands ready to save us from those snares the enemy sets in our path. We should have faith and know the Lord will help us endure persecutions and afflictions through faith, longsuffering, charity, and patience until the moment of deliverance.

The beginning of wisdom is to fear the Lord, to stand in awe of Him and His great works as we worship and glorify Him. We are to dwell in the Lord, by keeping our eyes on Him and off of trouble and sorrow. He is our deliverer. If we dwell on the problem instead of the deliverer, we will not be able to see the victory of the Lord. He is near to deliver us. Focus on Jesus. Look for the good in each situation. Concentrate on what good can be accomplished in your trouble or conflict.

We are not to fear humans and what they can do to us. We know that God is on our side and we will flourish as we go forth praising and fearing Him. As we worship and praise we can expect God to bless our nation and provide protection for our country as we put God first and honor Him for our blessings.

DAILY PRAISES	DAILY PRAYER REQUESTS
1.	1.
2.	2.
3.	3.
4.	4.
5.	5.

January 6
Read Galatians 2:15-21

Galatians 2:16

"Know that a man is not justified by observing the law, but by faith in Jesus Christ. So we, too, have put our faith in Jesus Christ that we may be justified by faith in Christ and not by observing the law, because by observing the law no one will be justified."

When we are united with Christ we must die to the world and serving the world. We are made alive in Christ Jesus through faith and grace. We are to submit to the righteousness of Jesus and to live by faith.

We are made rich in faith by studying the Bible and spending time in prayer. We must believe the Word of God, for it will be counted unto us as righteousness. When we have faith in God we also have peace with Him through Jesus Christ.

We must count the things of this world as loss to know the excellence of the knowledge of God all things which we will ever need are in Christ. If we have faith and believe He will supply all our needs. We are to walk after the Spirit and not after the flesh. The things of the world, the flesh, will vanish away and decay. They will all pass away. They will eventually elude us, but the things of faith, the Spirit, the righteousness of God, will last eternally and forever.

Live each day unto the Lord through faith.

DAILY PRAISES	**DAILY PRAYER REQUESTS**
1.	1.
2.	2.
3.	3.
4.	4.
5.	5.

January 7
Read I Chronicles 16:7-36

I Chronicles 16:11

"Look to the Lord and his strength; seek his face always."

Humans long for a relationship with God. There is an empty feeling in the soul until we come to know Jesus Christ.

God is also seeking all men and women to be saved and to turn to Him for eternal life. God desires that all living people seek his face and His strength. He is so near to us. He will come in and abide with us if we will only let Him.

If we will only ask Him to enter our heart and replace the sin that dwelt there, He will receive us gracefully as we come to Him confessing. We will be born again in His Spirit. Let us lift up our souls to the Lord. Let us seek Him while He may be found. Let us continue to praise Him and adore His Holy Name. Let us make prayers and supplications to Him without ceasing.

Always give praise to God as David did in today's prayer. He is worthy of all our praise.

We are to delight in the Lord. He takes away all fear and doubting. We have confidence and reassurance through Him. By seeking the Lord and resting in His strength, mercy, and grace we shall live with Him forever.

DAILY PRAISES	DAILY PRAYER REQUESTS
1.	1.
2.	2.
3.	3.
4.	4.
5.	5.

January 8
Read I Timothy 3:1-16

I Timothy 3:16

"He appeared in a body, was vindicated by the Spirit, was seen by angels. Was preached among the nations, was believed on in the world, was taken up in glory."

The great mystery of the Christian life is that we cannot live it on our own. We are not sufficient in ourselves to live it. We have to depend on the sufficiency of Jesus to help us. We are made sufficient only by His mercy and grace through the Spirit of God.

Everyone is called to live for Christ by being born again of His blood and Spirit. Jesus became man to experience life as we experience it. He suffered pain, disappointment, and persecution as we do. He was ministered to by angels throughout His earthly life, as we are.

He died for our sins and rose again, so that we could have Salvation and be free from sin. Because He ascended into Heaven to be our Mediator, one day we will also be raised to meet Him in the air and forever be with Him in His glory.

It is amazing when we realize what God has done to save us from sin. He loves us so much. Let us never take this Salvation for granted or become careless about our Christian living. Be proud to be on the winning team. Shout forth His praises.

DAILY PRAISES
1.
2.
3.
4.
5.

DAILY PRAYER REQUESTS
1.
2.
3.
4.
5.

January 9
Read I John 2:15-27

I John 2:15

"Do not love the world or anything in the world. If anyone loves the world, the love of the Father is not in him."

We are not to conform to this world because world here, is being referred to as the realm of Satan. We are to have our eyes and our affection on things above. The devil is in control of the earthly world. That is why our minds should be on Heavenly things rather than on things in the world. We all know that this earth and the things in it are going to pass away. Why put your love and trust in something that will burn up?

Those who do the will of God will abide forever with Him. So let us not follow that which is evil, but that which is good. We know to follow God, for His ways are righteous and good.

The Lord is able to keep us above reproach as we live in the world. He will keep us from evil if we will put our trust in Him. We have obtained mercy and grace from God. We are no more of this world, but of God. We are followers of God, and through patience and faith we will inherit the promises of God.

DAILY PRAISES	**DAILY PRAYER REQUESTS**
1.	1.
2.	2.
3.	3.
4.	4.
5.	5.

January 10
Read Colossians 2:6-19

Colossians 2:9-10

"For in Christ all the fullness of the Deity lives in bodily form, and you have been given fullness in Christ, who is the head over every power and authority."

Jesus performs the works of God in our lives when we come to Him. Jesus is all sufficient. He is all we need. We can be complete in Him if we will only trust Him to be our head, our hands, and our guide.

When we come to Jesus and repent, we are accepting Him, who paid the price for our sins with His own blood. We receive justification because Jesus took our place of sin on Calvary and died for all. We are cleansed by His blood and are raised from sin to Holiness. His grace is sufficient for us to live this life. Jesus is our model. We are sanctified by Christ and therefore live a holy life. He gives us peace and comfort through His Holy Spirit. He cares about our daily duties and problems. Jesus is over all. He will cause us to triumph over every hindrance in this life then give us tranquility and triumph in death. He will take us home to Heaven when our time on earth has ended. We will have Eternal life forever.

Praise God for making a way for us to be complete through Jesus Christ, His Son. Who would not want to live forever, with a new body, in a mansion prepared especially for you, praising and glorifying our Lord throughout all eternity.

DAILY PRAISES   **DAILY PRAYER REQUESTS**
1.   1.

2.   2.

3.   3.

4.   4.

5.   5.

January 11
Read Philippians 2:1-11

Philippians 2:1-2

"If you have any encouragement from being united with Christ, if any comfort with His love, if any fellowship with the Spirit, if any tenderness and compassion, then make my joy complete by being like-minded, having the same love, being one in spirit and purpose."

As Christians, we are to dwell in unity as the body of Christ. The body is to be single-minded, one toward another as we are toward Christ. We are to receive one another as Christians, as Christ received us. We are to love each other as we love Christ and as Christ loves us and the church. We are to have compassion on our Christian brothers and sisters, as Christ had compassion and mercy on us. We are to show courtesy to our fellow Christians, preferring them before ourselves.

The above instructions are from the Word of God. They may appear hard to live by, but if the mind of Christ is in us, as it should be, we will be filled with joy as we obey the Word of God. We will see prayers answered as never before when we unite in love and become single-minded toward God and each other. Let us enter into the joy of the Lord by uniting together with others right now.

DAILY PRAISES
1.
2.
3.
4.
5.

DAILY PRAYER REQUESTS
1.
2.
3.
4.
5.

January 12
Read Isaiah 42:10-17

Isaiah 42:16

"I will lead the blind by ways they have not known, along unfamiliar paths I will guide them; I will turn the darkness into light before them and make the rough places smooth. These are the things I will do; I will not forsake them,"

When we need guidance we can pray a prayer of praise to the Lord as Isaiah did in Isaiah 42. Our Lord is always there. He knows everything we need. If we commit our ways to Him, He will lead us in the correct pathway. He will direct and counsel us in ways we did not know or expect. It may be something that we do not understand at the time. Remember, the Lord knows the best path for us and we will not go wrong as long as we let Him lead us. He loves us so much that He keeps His eyes on us. He supplies us with wisdom, if we only ask. He is always ready with a bountiful blessing, giving to us so generously. He instructs us along the pathway of life and carefully watches our progress.

Often when we are seeking guidance, we find ourselves in places that we never knew existed. But God is working out the best path for our lives. He knows what we need, even before we ask.

He will make the darkness light as we trust in Him and seek His will for our lives. Trust him to guide you.

DAILY PRAISES	**DAILY PRAYER REQUESTS**
1.	1.
2.	2.
3.	3.
4.	4.
5.	5.

January 13
Read Colossians 1:3-14

Colossians 1:9

"For this reason, since the day we heard about you, we have not stopped praying for you and asking God to fill you with the knowledge of His will through all Spiritual wisdom and understanding."

When we know God personally through His Son, it is our duty to pray for others. We are given the Spirit to help us pray.

The deep things of God can be revealed to us by His Spirit. We have Christ in us and His Spirit manifests the Spiritual things to us. As we walk worthy of the Spirit, obeying Him in all things, we will receive understanding of this life and the eternal life to come.

When we are fruitful Christians, others will see and be saved. We are to minister to others so that comfort, healing, and peace can come into their lives. Give foods to the hungry, clothes to the naked, and love and care for all people in our world.

Jesus is our example. It is our privilege and responsibility to learn all we can about Jesus Christ, as He gives us wisdom and knowledge to impart.

DAILY PRAISES	**DAILY PRAYER REQUESTS**
1.	1.
2.	2.
3.	3.
4.	4.
5.	5.

January 14
Read I Peter 3:8-22

I Peter 3:13

"Who is going to harm you if you are eager to do good?"

God assures us of Divine favor if we follow and obey Him. The Lord will not forsake His people. It pleases Him to make us His chosen people. The Lord keeps His hand upon us and establishes us in places to honor Him. The Lord is our strength. He is especially near in the times of trouble. Our meditation should be on the Lord and what He has done for us. As we meditate on Him we receive His sweet benefits. We are told to be happy in the Lord. We are to rejoice in Him because He has promised to protect and sustain us from all our enemies.

We are a blessed people. We have sins forgiven. We are personal ambassadors for Jesus Christ. We are privileged to share His love, goodness, mercy, and grace with the world. We possess the Kingdom, although to the world, we may appear poor, but our inward person is wealthy in Christ. Our confidence is in abiding in Jesus. He is our comfort and strength. We have the assurance of His protective care.

Usually people are not harmed for doing acts of kindness. We should be enthusiastic for doing good to honor Christ. Rejoice that we are honored to be followers of Christ and to do His work.

DAILY PRAISES	**DAILY PRAYER REQUESTS**
1.	1.
2.	2.
3.	3.
4.	4.
5.	5.

January 15
Read II Corinthians 5:1-10

II Corinthians 5:7
"We live by faith, not by sight."

Do you remember when you were young and your parents promised you something? You could hardly wait until the promise was fulfilled. You were so happy to get the promised item or event.

It is our duty to believe the promises in the Bible. They were recorded by prophets of God, who were inspired with the Holy Spirit. These promises are not fairy tales or make believe stories. The promises are real. So as we trust in Jesus and walk with Him in faith, we wait for the promises to be fulfilled.

We did not have the privilege of seeing Jesus in the physical body, as the disciples did. Yet we must believe and trust His Word with all our hearts. We are to lean toward Him and His wisdom and knowledge as we trust Him to meet our needs.

Example after example is given in the Bible of those who trusted Jesus and walked in faith with Him. We read of miracles performed by Jesus and His followers through faith.

We walk in faith, believing that Christ is the Son of God. As we believe in our hearts, He will do what He promised in His Word.

We cannot always see an example in reality or understand the things that happen in our lives. But we have to step out in faith and keep our eyes on Jesus believing Him. We will be happy if we just let our faith soar and keep the love of Jesus as He commanded.

DAILY PRAISES	**DAILY PRAYER REQUESTS**
1.	1.
2.	2.
3.	3.
4.	4.
5.	5.

January 16
Read John 17:20-26

John 17:24

"Father, I want those you have given me to be with me where I am, and to see my glory. The glory you have given me because you loved me before the creation of the world."

Jesus prayed for all believers to be with Him throughout eternity. He wants us to have a close relationship with Him so that we may enjoy the Home He has prepared for us in Heaven. We decide to serve Him. We make our commitment to go with Him. It is our free choice. He wants everyone to be with Him.

Jesus was betrayed by one of His close associates. One who had walked and talked and listened to Him daily. The one who betrayed Him made the choice of betrayal. Judas chose to let Satan influence Him for money. The money didn't satisfy him.

The question should be asked; will you sell out to Satan? Will you betray Jesus for a few dollars, a little sin for a while or deny Him?

We have a right to experience Jesus because He prepared the way for us. He glorified the Father through obeying His will. We need to let the Spirit confront us and do as the Spirit bids us in order to make progression in our walk for Jesus. Jesus speaks to us through His Spirit, the Word, and through worship. Remember He prayed especially for you.

DAILY PRAISES	**DAILY PRAYER REQUESTS**
1.	1.
2.	2.
3.	3.
4.	4.
5.	5.

January 17
Read Romans 8:1-17

Romans 8:1

"Therefore, there is now no condemnation for those who are in Christ Jesus."

Those that are in Christ and live according to His Word are free from condemnation. How can we live free from condemnation? Jesus promised and gave us the Holy Spirit to be our Comforter, friend and guide. The Holy Spirit remains in the world since Jesus ascended. He is with every Christian. He helps us overcome our weaknesses. He guides us into growing, maturing Christians. He gives us the ability to witness and be strong when we would be weak. He leads us into worship in our homes and churches.

These are just a few of the ways the Holy Spirit helps us to be free of condemnation. We must seek to walk after the Spirit. We are able to walk in the Spirit because we have been justified by grace and faith through Jesus Christ our Lord. The love of Christ flows to us and through us that we might joy in the Lord whom we have received.

Today is the day to give praise to the Lord for all you have received from Him. Joy in Him!

DAILY PRAISES	**DAILY PRAYER REQUESTS**
1.	1.
2.	2.
3.	3.
4.	4.
5.	5.

January 18
Read Colossians 3:1-17

Colossians 3:15

"Let the peace of Christ rule in your hearts, since as members of one body you were called to peace. And be thankful."

It is our desire to live a peaceful life in all godliness and honesty. As Christians we are a light to the world and it is our responsibility to strive for peace in our lives. Peace at home with our spouse and children. Peace at work with our boss and co-workers, and employees is a goal we must seek. Peace in the community with our neighbors, business associates, and friends will help to shine a bright light.

Jesus gives us peace. We are to let it rule our hearts and follow that peace with all people. The Bible tells us, "Blessed are the peacemakers for they are called the children of God." Christ gives us the attitude of peace to replace the attitudes of bitterness or quarrelling. The peaceful attitude is to rule our lives.

There is so much to be thankful for in our lives. We are thankful for knowing the Lord, by being born again. We are thankful for the peace in which we live with family and friends. We have peace within our own body. We are thankful for fellow worshippers who desire peace as they pray for our nation as well as the world. There are so many blessings to be thankful for that we receive from the hand of the Lord. Above all let us be thankful and give praise for the peace which rules in our hearts.

DAILY PRAISES	**DAILY PRAYER REQUESTS**
1.	1.
2.	2.
3.	3.
4.	4.
5.	5.

January 19
Read Hebrews 7:11-28

Hebrews 7:25

"Therefore He is able to save completely those who come to God through Him, because He always lives to intercede for them."

No one can come to the Father, except through Jesus, the Mediator. The Father loves us, because He gave His Son, Jesus, that we could be saved. Jesus is now sitting at the right hand of the Father making intercessions for us. Here are some of the things Jesus has done for us. I will use them in a personal sense.

1. I was lost and He found and saved me.
2. I was dirty and He washed and cleaned me.
3. I was brought low and He lifted me.
4. I was naked and He clothed me.
5. I was hungry and He fed me.
6. I was weary and He brought comfort to my soul.
7. I was confused and He made my path straight.
8. I was depressed and He made my spirit joyful and glad.
9. I was sick and He healed me.
10. I was on my way to hell and He rescued me and gave me Eternal Life.

We do not need another mediator, when we have Jesus, who is perfect and complete. Jesus can do all that we need doing. He is to be praised and glorified for all that He has done. I praise His Name above all names. Glory to God in the Highest! Praise to Jesus the Son of God!

DAILY PRAISES
1.
2.
3.
4.
5.

DAILY PRAYER REQUESTS
1.
2.
3.
4.
5.

January 20
Read Mark 16: 9-20

Mark 16:15

"He said to them, "Go into all the world and preach the good news to all creation."

What good will it do people to gain the whole world and lose their soul? As believers, we have the responsibility and privilege to carry the Gospel to others.

We are given the command to "GO"! For some of us it does not mean to leave our homes or families. We are called to spread the gospel wherever we are. We can spread the Gospel at work, at school, in our neighborhood, at play, or in the grocery. We can witness in various kinds of services for people.

The days are too short for us to mind our own business and ignore others' needs for Christ. We need to care for others and desire that they are saved. Christ cared for everyone and He is our example. He cared enough to die for sinners. Surely we can care enough to make a small effort to get the Word of God to the lost. We have found, in Christ, what the world needs. We want to share it. God will help if we go in sincerity and faithfulness.

Are we doing our part for Christ? Are there other ways we could serve the lost or helpless for Jesus? Where would Jesus have us go and what should we be doing?

Don't be shy or ashamed to mention Jesus to anyone. Just look what He has done for you.

DAILY PRAISES | **DAILY PRAYER REQUESTS**

1.

2.

3.

4.

5.

January 21
Read Matthew 18:10-14

Matthew 18:12

"What do you think? If a man owns a hundred sheep, and one of them wanders away, will he not leave the ninety-nine on the hills and go to look for the one that wandered off?"

Christ compared sinners to lost sheep in this parable. God does not want anyone to be lost. Jesus is instructing us, as Christians, to go get those that have left the faith. It is wonderful to pray for those who have left, but the most effective thing we can do after praying is to go searching for them. Let them know that God loves them and you do too. Tell them you love them and care for them as well as what happens in their lives.

I really believe the church should bind together in unity and bombard those who go astray with visits of love. Let us set up a program where we can be in touch with the lost sheep. Let us search and seek until that lost one is found and returned to the church.

We give up too easily. We are too quick to write people off because they mess up or miss the mark. What if Jesus lacked patience with us, as we do with others?

The Bible clearly tells us that if two or three agree together we will be able to reach the lost ones. Let us rejoice and praise God for the return of the lost ones to Jesus and the church.

DAILY PRAISES	**DAILY PRAYER REQUESTS**
1.	1.
2.	2.
3.	3.
4.	4.
5.	5.

January 22
Read Psalm 91

Psalm 91:1

"He who dwells in the shelter of the Most High will rest in the shadow of the Almighty."

The Lord is our defense and protection. We have the guarantee that if we live a righteous life we do not have to fear because the Lord is our shield and strength.

To dwell with the Most High, we must first accept Jesus as our Savior. Then we walk with Him, obeying His commands. We have to trust Jesus for keeping us. We are to read the Word daily and communicate with Jesus. We are to be in prayer and meditation with our Lord. We should let the Spirit lead us.

We have assurance that He is our refuge and strength. He will deliver us in the time of trouble. He will cover us with His Spirit for protection from the enemy. The Lord will give us strength during the trial. We will be able to endure and overcome when the enemy comes against us.

Let us realize that the Lord is with us. We are not to be afraid of what people can do to us. We are to put our trust in the Most High God and realize that He is on our side. We have safety in the Lord. Just like an earthly father looking out for His children, the Lord looks out for us.

DAILY PRAISES	**DAILY PRAYER REQUESTS**
1.	1.
2.	2.
3.	3.
4.	4.
5.	5.

January 23
Read I John 5:1-15

I John 5:15

"And if we know that he hears us—whatever we ask—we know that we have what we asked of him."

God is the Eternal One. He even transcends all our thoughts. Through the Son our prayers are taken to God. Through the union of God and His Son the power of prayer has its beginning. Our strength and comfort are in knowing that the Father and Son have eternal fellowship. Our prayers become a reality to God. Through the Trinity we can approach Him with our needs and concerns. If we have a childlike faith to believe, when we pray, our prayers are heard and answered according to the will of God.

It is the will of God that we should love and serve Him with all our souls, heart, and mind. It is His will that we grow in the knowledge and wisdom of His Word.

We must **act**, by praying. We must **believe** through faith. We must be **sincere** through persistence. We must **be repentant of sin** through the blood of Jesus. We are **to pray in simplicity** as Jesus taught. We have to **be patient** for answers, as they are often delayed for various reasons. We must pray in **humility** because we are unworthy except through Jesus. We must pray according **to God's will** and not our selfish will. We must believe and receive.

DAILY PRAISES　　　　　**DAILY PRAYER REQUESTS**

1.　　　　　　　　　　　　1.

2.　　　　　　　　　　　　2.

3.　　　　　　　　　　　　3.

4.　　　　　　　　　　　　4.

5.　　　　　　　　　　　　5.

January 24
Read II Thessalonians 2: 13-17

II Thessalonians 2:13

"But we ought always to thank God for you, brothers loved by the Lord, because from the beginning, God chose you to be saved through the sanctifying work of the Spirit and through belief in the truth."

God has chosen each of us to serve Him. He chose us to be redeemed and to bring forth fruit in His Name. He has chosen us that we would magnify and glorify His Name through holiness.

We are the workmanship of Jesus. Created to love Him and walk in His commands. Walk in love, as we go through the world, as Jesus walked. There is nothing we have done or can do to earn Salvation, other than to believe on Jesus Christ as our Savior. Salvation comes through faith in Jesus. We must believe the written Word of God.

God desires holiness in our lives. Through Him we can live holy and pleasing to Him. He chose us from the beginning of inception. We can choose Him by putting our trust in Him. If we have faith in God, we will cease to worry, because faith puts worry aside. We can have a bright outlook when we rest in faith. The future looks wonderful through faith.

Praise God for fellowship with other believers who also walk in faith with us. Together, through unity, the Lord's work will be accomplished.

DAILY PRAISES	**DAILY PRAYER REQUESTS**
1.	1.
2.	2.
3.	3.
4.	4.
5.	5.

January 25
Read Colossians 3:1-17

Colossians 3:16

"Let the word of Christ dwell in you richly as you teach and admonish one another with all wisdom, and as you sing psalms, hymns and spiritual songs with gratitude in your hearts to God."

When we have the Word of Christ in us we should be joyful people. It makes us want to sing praises to our King. In fact, when we are born anew, it puts a new song in our hearts. It makes us want to sing aloud unto God, our strength.

The Lord desires us to make a joyful noise before Him through singing praises to Him. He is worthy to be praised and we who are thankful for His redeeming grace should be willing to praise Him continually for all He has done to deliver us from our sinful condition.

We are blessed by our Lord. Why would we not be glad and melodious toward Him, as well as everyone else? We help others when we have a song in our hearts. It uplifts others spirits when we can testify of God's goodness and mercy. We should continue with gladness in our hearts and talking of the wondrous works of the Lord.

Are you sad, non-smiling, and fretful in your daily walk as a Christian? Where is your joy? Do you dwell on the negatives of life?

Our joy is often stolen by the devil when we concentrate on the negative side of living. Turn to the positive side of life and receive joy and life in the fullness of the Holy Spirit.

DAILY PRAISES	**DAILY PRAYER REQUESTS**
1.	1.
2.	2.
3.	3.
4.	4.
5.	5.

January 26
Read Mark 9: 14-32

Mark 9:23

"If you can?" said Jesus. "Everything is possible for him who believes."

Through faith much is achieved. We have the promise that if we believe all things are possible. For faith to be achieved we must be living according to the Bible and ask God according to the instructions in the Word of God. If we abide in Christ and Him in us, we will not ask amiss.

Do we have that unquestioning belief when we pray for a need? You see, unbelief limits God. We have to trust Him and believe His Word in obedience.

The more we are filled with His Spirit, the more faith we will exert. Faith can grow in a climate of love. When we are filled with the Spirit we will be filled with love. We are now ready for those great achievements to take place through faith. Faith and love work hand in hand.

We had to exert faith to believe to be saved. The faith that delivered us from the power of sin can also work to accomplish other achievements. Through faith we have security and comfort, as well as healing and other needs. In faith we believe for everlasting life with Jesus. By faith our illnesses are healed. If we have faith our children will be saved. Through faith all things are possible. Keep believing in Christ and see his hand at work in your life.

DAILY PRAISES	**DAILY PRAYER REQUESTS**
1.	1.
2.	2.
3.	3.
4.	4.
5.	5.

January 27
Read Hebrews 13:1-15

Hebrews 13:2

"Do not forget to entertain strangers, for by so doing some people have entertained angels without knowing it."

As Christians, we are to be given to hospitality and kindness. In the world today it is rare to see hospitality given freely, due to the evil and distrust we have for each other. If we are truly trusting in the Lord, when the opportunity to show hospitality arises, Jesus will take care of us and keep us from evil. He has greater power than the power of Satan.

As we have been ministered to, we are to minister to others without spite or expecting to receive a reward. Remember our reward will be given to us when Jesus returns and gathers us to Heaven.

Suppose you refuse someone in need and that someone just happened to be an angel. How would you feel? Probably, not too good, if you really knew it was an angel. We should also feel badly about not ministering to the needs of hurting, living humans.

You need to understand that as Christians we are ambassadors of Christ. We are to show kindness and hospitality to everyone we come in contact with. It is not just those we go to church with or our friends and relatives, but strangers who are hurting and have real needs. We have so much to give by the Spirit of the Lord. He is not a selfish God. If He had been selfish, where would we be today? Let us not be selfish with the love of God. Let us share the love as Jesus shared Himself with us. Continue to give love to others as Christ gave to us.

DAILY PRAISES
1.
2.
3.
4.
5.

DAILY PRAYER REQUESTS
1.
2.
3.
4.
5.

January 28
Read Hebrews 4:1-13

Hebrews 4:12

"For the Word of God is living and active. Sharper than any double-edged sword, it penetrates even to dividing soul and spirit, joints and marrow; it judges the thoughts and attitudes of the heart."

The Word of God is powerful. It is not just a book written for lucrative purposes or for someone to have a job. It is the Book inspired by the Spirit of God as the Spirit worked through humans to record the words that would be handed down for thousands of years. The words in the Book are real to us today, as they were when the prophets were recording them long ago.

It is important for us to read and study the Word of God. We get our spiritual food from God's Word. We get filled when we feel empty. The Spirit speaks to us through the Word to comfort, teach, and to drive home an important message.

The Word of God will not return to Him void. It will accomplish its purpose. We are to be knowledgeable in the word so we can be witnesses for Him. We are to spread this powerful message throughout our part of the world.

The Word of God is powerful so that it penetrates our hearts to remind us to walk according to His Word daily. It is the light. It is pure. It is for all people. It is the truth. We can put our trust in the truths of the Bible. The truth will lead us and guide us by its light. We have hope through the Scriptures. We know that nothing is hidden from our Lord. He knows all about us. He is a forgiving Savior. Trust Him.

DAILY PRAISES   **DAILY PRAYER REQUESTS**

1.   1.

2.   2.

3.   3.

4.   4.

5.   5.

January 29
Read II Corinthians 9:6-15

II Corinthians 9:6

"Remember this: Whoever sows sparingly will also reap sparingly, and whoever sows generously will also reap generously."

The Lord requires liberality in giving. There are many different ways of giving. I believe we are commanded to, at least tithes our wages to the Lord. I believe we should be able to tithe our time also. Our time is precious. The time we spend for the Lord will be well worth our reward. If we think we do not have the time to give to the Lord, how do we know, He will have the time to give us when we really have trials and sickness.

It is serious business to serve the Lord. We must take the entire Word of God. His Word tells us to give and help others. When we help others physically, we are giving our time to God. The same is true when we visit those in hospitals, nursing homes, jails, or other facilities. We give our time when we prepare food for others that are sick or hurting.

Let us not give grudgingly but rejoice as we are able to give in any capacity. God loves a cheerful giver. By giving we will be happy and have a joyful heart. It is a delight to make others happy and see their reactions when we give in cheerfulness.

God made the plan of Salvation so easy that a child can understand it. Simply trust Him and believe on Jesus with your heart and serve Him. Give others a hand any way you can. You will be blessed.

DAILY PRAISES
1.
2.
3.
4.
5.

DAILY PRAYER REQUESTS
1.
2.
3.
4.
5.

January 30
Read Romans 5:1-11

Romans 5:1

"Therefore, since we have been justified through faith, we have peace with God, through our Lord Jesus Christ,"

Peace is one of the greatest attributes we can have after we receive salvation. When the world around is tumbling down and everything is going wrong, we can have peace through Jesus. The peace of God means so much to us. Words are not available to describe the serenity of the peace of God.

The source of our peace is God. We can keep peace through Jesus, as He promised us. He instructed us not to be troubled, but to let our hearts be flooded with peace. The Holy Spirit gives peace to us as we live for Jesus and walk in the spirit.

I can testify that it is possible to have peace when your heart is breaking. When our eighteen-year-old daughter was killed instantly and accidently, my heart was broken into two parts, but my soul had peace because I knew where she was going and someday I will join her in Heaven.

Having peace through God means we are living and growing according to God's Word. When we have peace we can enjoy he Lord. We are not to be afraid or restless, but to be content in safety and assurance in Christ.

By being filled with the Spirit, we have access to God's grace and peace. First we must believe, in faith, to receive peace. This peace is free to those desiring to obtain it. It is received through God, the Father, Jesus, the Son, and the Holy Spirit. After we are reconciled to Jesus, we secure peace by faith.

We are to follow peace with all people. We are to have peace in our hearts and be able to live with ourselves as well as others.

DAILY PRAISES	**DAILY PRAYER REQUESTS**
1.	1.
2.	2.
3.	3.
4.	4.
5.	5.

January 31
Read I John 2:1-14

I John 2:3

"We know that we have come to know Him if we obey His commands."

There is a connection between knowing God and obeying God. If we know Him, we desire to obey Him and keep His commandments. We are required to obey Him according to the Bible.

It is comfortable to know deep within our hearts that we do know the Lord and keep His word. How reassuring it is to follow Jesus.

There will be rewards for being obedient to the commandments of the Lord. He will deliver us from trials and tribulations if we are faithful to Him. He will provide our needs and much more as we are faithful to honor Him. He will give us knowledge and wisdom as we listen and walk with Him. If we do the will of the Father, we will be rewarded in Heaven someday.

It is so important to know, without a doubt, that we are saved and walking with Jesus. It is as simple as giving your heart to Jesus and obeying His commands. Let us not delay in giving ourselves to Jesus and following His Words. Make haste in setting your hearts in obedience to God. Through Jesus our lives will show the integrity that He gives us to do what is right. Our lives will show that we do know Him.

DAILY PRAISES	**DAILY PRAYER REQUESTS**
1.	1.
2.	2.
3.	3.
4.	4.
5.	5.

FEBRUARY

February 1
Read Philippians 2:1-18

Philippians 2:5

"Your attitude should be the same as that of Christ Jesus:"

Jesus Christ is our example. We need to strive to understand how Jesus felt about situations. To realize what Jesus would have done under the same conditions, we are working under, we are to have His attitude of self-sacrificing, love and humility toward others. He said we could do the things He did. He is the Author and Finisher of our Salvation. Through Him we can do all things.

Let us consider Jesus, who was rich and became poor for our sakes. He took upon Himself the form of a physical person. He suffered much pain and humiliation in the flesh from sinners and hypocrites. He did not grumble or complain. He was not faint or weary in His mind. He kept His mind on God. He is our example.

When we complain and feel discriminated against or are humiliated for no reason, let us fix our mind on Jesus and think of all He endured for us. Help us to not complain, when we are persecuted. Let us perceive those persecutions as spiritual growth to prepare us for the Kingdom of God.

DAILY PRAISES	**DAILY PRAYER REQUESTS**
1.	1.
2.	2.
3.	3.
4.	4.
5.	5.

February 2
Read Psalm 62

Psalm 62:8

"Trust in Him at all times, O people; pour out your hearts to Him, for God is our refuge." Selah

I am so glad I am on God's side. I am ecstatic that He chose me and I accepted Him. I can trust Him at all times. I know that if my heart is right and I am serving Him, He hears my cry for help.

I remember a time, on my job when I felt like I was being unfairly treated or "picked on" by my boss. As I prayed, I asked Jesus to give me something for reassurance. That very morning, as I was to report to the office of my boss, the Spirit gave me Psalm 62:7-8.

I read and reread these verses. I read from four different translations to get every bit of information I could from the Word of God. I made copies of these verses. I taped them in my closet, in my desk, and on my work materials. I was able to walk into that office with reassurance. I was confident.

The meeting went smoothly, the problems which had appeared so gigantic, decreased as we talked. So you see the reason I trust in the Lord. He never fails. I go to Him continuously. He always hears and answers. His answer may not be what I want to hear or the way I want it to be, but I know He will answer perfectly and just right for me. God is to be trusted. We can rely on Him for help with all our needs. The needs may be real or fantasized, but whatever they are, we have a God who cares and will meet us if we call on Him.

DAILY PRAISES	**DAILY PRAYER REQUESTS**
1.	1.
2.	2.
3.	3.
4.	4.
5.	5.

February 3
Read I Thessalonians 4:13-18

I Thessalonians 4:17

"After that, we who are still alive and are left will be caught up together with them in the clouds to meet the Lord in the air. And so we will be with the Lord forever."

Do you want to go to Heaven? What are you doing to prepare? When you plan a trip, you must make the proper preparations for traveling. This trip to Heaven requires some planning, also. First you must make a decision in your heart that you want to go on this trip. Next you must send in a reservation, by inviting Christ into your heart. Then you begin to learn all you can about the route you will travel. You study the map, Bible, about the place you are going. You begin to get things taken care of at home. You set all things in order by making everything right according to the Bible. You begin to pack for your trip. In packing for this trip, you will need to do all you can for Christ. You may be a witness to others. You may teach a Sunday school class or other Bible study. Do whatever you are called to do. Listen to the Holy Spirit as He guides you toward your planned trip.

No, we cannot work our way to Heaven. The more we love, the more we will do for the Lord. We will be happy as we see our plans progressing for our trip.

Have you made your reservations for Heaven? It is never too early to start. Is your position in church, anything other than a pew warmer? There is something for everyone to do. Most of all we must prepare our hearts by deciding to go to Heaven. Keep studying and learning about the trip you will take when Christ returns to gather His children.

DAILY PRAISES
1.
2.
3.
4.
5.

DAILY PRAYER REQUESTS
1.
2.
3.
4.
5.

February 4
Read II Corinthians 6:14-18

II Corinthians 6:14

"Do not be yoked together with unbelievers. For what do righteousness and wickedness have in common? Or what fellowship can light have with darkness?"

The devil is determined to destroy the family system in this last day. We have a defense against him and it is our faith in our Lord Jesus Christ.

As Christian families, we belong to God and are set apart from the world. We must love sinners and be their friends. We are to tell them and show them the love of Christ. We must display the love that Christ has for them.

Marriage is one type of being unequally yoked together. There can be other ways, such as business partners. We are to involve ourselves in relationships that will cause us to grow not hinder our relationship with Christ.

Today people seek escape from pressures within the family by turning to drugs or alcohol. There is no solution outside of Christ. There is no alternative or sure cure other than Jesus. Jesus can and will make every person whole, who has gone astray and has become addicted to things in the world.

The world expects Christians to accept their morals and values, instead of standing for Christ. The Bible tells us to turn away from the world's attitude and stand on what the Bible teaches. The home is a powerful influence in the world. Pray for homes to stand in this evil day, so that Biblical values may prevail. Pray that Christians will not be unequally yoked, but seek the Lord's will in their joining themselves to partners whether in marriage or business.

DAILY PRAISES	**DAILY PRAYER REQUESTS**
1.	1.
2.	2.
3.	3.
4.	4.
5.	5.

February 5
Read Matthew 12:22-37

Matthew 12:37

"For by your words you will be acquitted, and by your words you will be condemned."

Words make up an expressive language. Communication would be very difficult without words. How do we use words? Do we use them to inflict pain or heartache or to produce love and adoration?

In the last judgment every person will be judged by Christ. The books will be opened and every word we have spoken will be there before us and Jesus. We will give an account as to how we used each word. God will reveal every secret thing, whether it is good or bad. In Matthew 12:36 and 37 Jesus tells us that we will give an account of our careless words.

Let us concentrate on our words and speak out of the goodness of our hearts. We should speak good treasures of comfort and joy, life and hope, love and peace. Let us refrain from idle words and piercing words which we will be accountable for on our judgment day.

Let us speak the message of Christ to the world in love. We are to spread the Good News about Jesus. Words of life are words that will be justified. Let every word that goes out from your heart be an expression which reflects Christ in your life and you in Him. We can win others by our message in words. We will be rewarded for our message of words in love through the Spirit.

DAILY PRAISES
1.
2.
3.
4.
5.

DAILY PRAYER REQUESTS
1.
2.
3.
4.
5.

February 6
Read Titus 2:1-15

Titus 2:11

"For the grace of God that brings salvation has appeared to all men."

Praise God because His grace is sufficient for all people. He has included every race, tribe, and color in every country. He has extended His grace to those who will accept Him.

Those who accept Him are then cleansed from every sin. Their guilt and sins are gone. They no longer live in fear or shame, but in joyfulness because Jesus has washed their sins away. He casts our sins as far from us as the East is from the West. Praise God! Our sins will no longer be remembered. They will never be brought up again. Praise the Lord!

Oh, what a wonderful promise and invitation to all people. Why wouldn't everyone accept this invitation? Come and be cleansed and filled with the Spirit of the Living God. His Spirit and cleansing is for all.

DAILY PRAISES	**DAILY PRAYER REQUESTS**
1.	1.
2.	2.
3.	3.
4.	4.
5.	5.

February 7
Read Ezekiel 28:11-19

Ezekiel 28:15

"You were blameless in your ways from the day you were created til wickedness was found in you."

God was speaking to Ezekiel about Lucifer, who was corrupted by sin. Lucifer was created as a beautiful and brilliant perfect angel. He was Son of the Morning. His heart was lifted up and corrupted because of his beauty and brightness. He desired to receive the praise due God, for himself. He rebelled against God and was cast out of Heaven by God.

Lucifer has not given up the fight against God. He, with his demons, is going to and fro upon the earth seeking to destroy every person.

Satan, Lucifer, is receiving the praise he desires through a lot of music which carries the occult messages. He is destroying our youth through drugs, alcohol, sex, pornography, and witchcraft. All of these things magnify the devil. It is time for us to stand up and fight against these evils.

Let us awake and realize that we are in a spiritual warfare. We need more of God to fight and defeat the enemy. The Bible gives us authority to come against the devil in this world. We need to stand against evil through the blood of Jesus. We can and must stand firm in the Lord. We will be victorious if we do not compromise. In the Name of Jesus rebuke the devil and his evil deeds. The devil cannot stand against the blood of Jesus. Say, "I rebuke you, Satan, through the blood and the Name of Jesus, you are defeated."

DAILY PRAISES	**DAILY PRAYER REQUESTS**
1.	1.
2.	2.
3.	3.
4.	4.
5.	5.

February 8
Read Proverbs 11:16-31

Proverbs 11:25

"A generous man will prosper; he who refreshes others will himself be refreshed."

The Bible commands us to share with the poor. For those who give out of an abundant heart, not seeking any return, will receive the blessings of God.

There was a certain widow who gave all she had to the treasury. It did not appear to be very much, compared to what the rich men were giving. Jesus said that she had given more than any of them because she gave everything she had, while the rich men did not miss the portion they gave.

This is a good comparison with our God, who gave His Only Son. His son, Jesus Christ, gave His life for all people. He was willing to be hanged on a tree in humiliation and mocked by the multitudes, so we could have Salvation. We are blessed and have life because Jesus died and rose again.

As we give to others out of a pure heart, with a pure motive, we will receive blessings. We cannot out give God. Try Him and see what He will do.

DAILY PRAISES
1.
2.
3.
4.
5.

DAILY PRAYER REQUESTS
1.
2.
3.
4.
5.

February 9
Read Mark 11:20-26

Mark 11:24

"Therefore I tell you, whatever you ask for in prayer, believe that you have received it, and it will be yours."

There are conditions of acceptable prayer. The Bible tells us we must have our sins forgiven.

We must pray in Christ's Name. We must pray in faith, putting our trust and belief in Him. Without faith it is impossible to please the Lord. Our faith must not waver but be steadfast and sure. We must know that the Lord hears us when we pray.

We pray in sincerity from our hearts and soul. The Lord is near all that call upon His Name in true worship.

We are told to pray in righteousness. The eye of the Lord is upon the righteous. He will hear them. We are to keep His commands and do those things pleasing to the Lord to receive the desires of our hearts. By keeping His commands and obeying we will be righteous.

Pray in humility and patience. After we pray we are to wait to hear from the Lord.

We are to pray with perseverance. We are to continue to seek God's will in any situation until we get an answer. It may not be our answer, but an answer according to God's will. The answer may be, "yes', "no", or "later". But whatever the answer we must be willing to accept God's answer. All things work together for the glory of God. We need to seek the Lord's will instead of our own.

DAILY PRAISES
1.
2.
3.
4.
5.

DAILY PRAYER REQUESTS
1.
2.
3.
4.
5.

February 10
Read Proverbs 14:1-16

Proverbs 14:14

"The faithless will be fully repaid for their ways, and the good man rewarded for his."

How sad when people who have served the Lord begin to go astray and forget God. They begin to take the blessings of the Lord for granted. They lose the desire to attend church and fellowship with other Christians. They become more interested in the natural and material things than in spiritual things. Often times working and toiling on Sunday is more important than attending church. They desire to work more in order to buy more material possessions. Material possessions are necessary and nice, but they should not be put ahead of Christ.

Satan tempts people and they begin to give in to his ways. He knows all our weaknesses and tempts us all. We do not need to give in to his temptations. The power of God is greater and we have the victory to rebuke Satan and stand against him. The person who is feeling tempted and weak should look in the Bible and read. Then pray to stand against the devil's assault.

When people give in to the devil, they no longer have a burden for the lost. They become insensitive to the Spirit of God and slowly their hearts harden to the Lord's call. They let their daily and family devotions slip away for one reason or another.

Take a quick look at yourself. Evaluate where you are with the Lord. Are you moving forward or slipping backwards? We cannot stand still. If we do, we will get stagnate. Be on your toes for God. If you have moved backward, repent, accept God's forgiveness and move forward with Jesus leading you. You can conquer anything with the Lord on your side.

DAILY PRAISES　　　　　　　　**DAILY PRAYER REQUESTS**

1.　　　　　　　　　　　　　　　1.

2.　　　　　　　　　　　　　　　2.

3.　　　　　　　　　　　　　　　3.

4.　　　　　　　　　　　　　　　4.

5.　　　　　　　　　　　　　　　5.

February 11
Read Jeremiah 2:11-25

Jeremiah 2: 21

"I had planted you like a choice vine of sound and reliable stock. How then did you turn against me into a corrupt wild vine?"

God created humans to serve Him. We are the branches of the vine. Jesus is the true vine and was sent to establish it. So each of us were to serve the Master and honor Him. We are to grow and produce fruit throughout the world.

We must begin where we are in Jesus. First of all, we have to be faithful in the small things. Then larger challenges will come our way. We can start with the people we normally come in contact with, such as the people at home or at work. Let them see Christ in us as we witness to them by our right living and the Word.

We cannot bear fruit or be a witness within ourselves. We must have Jesus and through the Holy Spirit let our lives shine in the world. If we pray earnestly, seeking His guidance, He will direct us. Without Him, we can do nothing. Jesus is the source and we must abide in Him to bear fruit.

Let us not go astray as the Israelites did and produce wild fruit. Let us bring forth fruit for the glory of God. The Lord will cause us to produce more and more fruit for His glory.

DAILY PRAISES
1.
2.
3.
4.
5.

DAILY PRAYER REQUESTS
1.
2.
3.
4.
5.

February 12
Read Psalm 18:1-24

Psalm 18:3

"I call to the Lord who is worthy of praise, and I am saved from my enemies."

To call upon the Lord is to act in faith. Faith is necessary in worshipping God. God is worthy of our praises. We were made in His image and to praise Him. We are to express our adoration to God. We are to honor Him because He is worthy. We are to praise Him with our total being. We are to praise Him in joyful singing. We are to praise Him with musical instruments, by playing and singing. We are to praise Him by extending hands upward toward Heaven. Offer Him praise by kneeling before Him and whispering His Name in reverence.

Why don't all people desire to worship God in praise? God inhabits the praises of His people. He enthrones Himself in our midst when we praise Him. God dwells in praise. He will guide and strengthen those who praise Him when things go wrong. Praise Him when things are fine. Praise requires humility and surrender to God. God is pleased with praise.

It would be good to take one day each week and rather than ask God for answers to prayers, spend time praising God for all answered prayers and for family and friends.

DAILY PRAISES	**DAILY PRAYER REQUESTS**
1.	1.
2.	2.
3.	3.
4.	4.
5.	5.

February 13
Read Ephesians 5:22-33

Ephesians 5:33

"However, each one of you also must love his wife as he loves himself, and the wife must respect her husband."

It is important to work toward marital happiness. The Bible gives husbands and wives a guide to follow. The fifth chapter of Ephesians is an excellent starting place.

First of all, love is important, as the husband is to love the wife as he loves himself and as Christ loves the church. This kind of love is unsurpassed. It is real. No woman could be unhappy and complain about her husband if she is receiving this kind of love. When the husband gives this kind of love, he will be the recipient of sacrificial love from his wife. God requires a supernatural love of husbands and wives. Both are commanded to love one another.

Secondly, communication between couples is extremely important. The Bible tells us to speak with truth in love. We should pray for wisdom and the leading of the Spirit in speaking with our mates about anything that is troubling us. Plan a time for talking, when both of you are relaxed. Do not lose your temper. Allow reaction time and commit the problem to the Lord. Remember the golden expressions, "I'm sorry" and "I love you".

Thirdly, it is important to have prayer together to the Heavenly Father. What an excellent means of communication. The time spent in prayer together is valuable time for both partners. How can you quarrel with your spouse whom you have prayed with every day?

DAILY PRAISES	DAILY PRAYER REQUESTS
1.	1.
2.	2.
3.	3.
4.	4.
5.	5.

February 14
Read John 6:25-40

John 6:27

"Do not work for food that spoils, but for food that endures to eternal life, which the Son of Man will give you. On him God the Father has placed his seal of approval."

Jesus is our bread of life. He is the one we are to pattern our lives after and follow. Jesus was sealed by God the Father. He was placed in a position to go forth and forgive sins. He responds to faith in His Name. Jesus has been given power to raise up the saints on the day of His return and to catch us away in the clouds to glory. These are all reasons we should labor for Jesus. This is life eternal.

I know Salvation is without price or without working our way into Heaven. But when we love Jesus, we desire to work for Him. We desire to see others saved and serving Him. We want to help win the lost world for the Kingdom of God.

Our service to Jesus is such a small amount to do for what our reward is going to be. Let us labor for the things that will last forever. The Heavenly things will never fade away. Oh, what a joyous thought! We will ever be in the presence of the Lord.

DAILY PRAISES	**DAILY PRAYER REQUESTS**
1.	1.
2.	2.
3.	3.
4.	4.
5.	5.

February 15
Read Mark 2:1-12

Mark 2:5

"When Jesus saw their faith, he said to the paralytic, 'Son, your sins are forgiven.'"

This man with palsy was in a hopeless condition, until he heard of Jesus. He was filled with unbearable pain, guilt, and shame. Four friends carried him to Jesus. The crowd made it look impossible to get to Jesus. By faith, the men lowered the man through the roof to the feet of Jesus. This kind of faith, in action, caused Jesus to forgive the sins of this man and heal him.

Jesus heals the inner person as well as the physical person. Jesus puts lives back together. Only Jesus can make the pieces of our lives fit together.

Jesus is the only hope for this life and life eternal. Everyone needs to come running to Jesus with the faith of those men who carried the man with palsy to Jesus.

Jesus paid the price for us with His own blood at Calvary. Each of us should believe what Christ says, seek Jesus, and be at His feet with our lives.

Speak your faith and let Jesus see that you really believe He will do what He says He will do. Let Him see your faith and it will grow immensely.

DAILY PRAISES	**DAILY PRAYER REQUESTS**
1.	1.
2.	2.
3.	3.
4.	4.
5.	5.

February 16
Read Romans 8:1-17

Romans 8:10

"But if Christ is in you, your body is dead because of sin, yet your spirit is alive because of righteousness."

It is by mercy and grace that we are saved by the blood of Jesus Christ. If we are saved we are dead to sin. Dead to the way we used to be, when we were at enmity with Christ.

We have decided on what relationship we want with Jesus. Flesh cannot please God. We must let the Spirit control our lives. We must make a place for the Comforter to live within our lives. It is necessary to listen to what the Bible says as He reveals Himself to us as He guides us along life's way.

Our spirit must be in the right relationship with God, before our needs are met. We are to put aside the flesh and let the Spirit control us. The Spirit will make us adequate and fill all of our needs. We must believe and be filled with the Spirit. He will enable us to stand all adversity. Spiritual mindedness is life in peace. The hope of Christ keeps us going. Rejoice in the hope that Jesus offers.

The Spirit glorifies Jesus and reveals to us what the Bible is saying as we read and study.

DAILY PRAISES
1.
2.
3.
4.
5.

DAILY PRAYER REQUESTS
1.
2.
3.
4.
5.

February 17
Read John 10:1-21

John 10:1

"I tell you the truth, the man who does not enter the sheep pen by the gate, but climbs in by some other way, is a thief and a robber."

Jesus is the source, the way, and the truth. Through Jesus is our only way to come to God. Those who seek another way to God are deceiving themselves. We must watch, pray, and read the Bible to insure that we are not being deceived and drawn away from Jesus.

Jesus is everything we need. He fulfills our every need if we will only trust Him and allow Him to be in our life. We can rely on Him. He is trustworthy and faithful. He will satisfy our souls spiritually and physically. The Bible assures us that our needs will be met if we put Jesus first and follow Him.

We are to follow Jesus willingly and joyfully to receive the benefits promised in His Word. We will be happy in Christ in this life and receive a reward in Heaven, if we walk in the Spirit.

DAILY PRAISES	**DAILY PRAYER REQUESTS**
1.	1.
2.	2.
3.	3.
4.	4.
5.	5.

February 18
Read I Thessalonians 4:1-9

I Thessalonians 4:9

"Now about brotherly love, we do not need to write to you, for you yourselves have been taught by God to love each other."

It is our duty as we live Christian lives to love one another. It is a God given grace to automatically love fellow Christians.

How will we witness to the world without love? We must be as Christ and love as He loved. Christ commanded us to love one another in John fifteen. If we cannot love our fellow human associates, family, and friends whom we see every day, how can we love Christ and God, whom we have not seen?

If we cannot show love and affection to people we know and worship God with, how can we go to Heaven without love? In Heaven there will be love. There will be no strife or petty differences or selfishness. We must put all attitudes aside that do not put the love of God first. It is important to return to our first love and abide in the light. Love covers a multitude of sins. Love is light. Let us love in word, truth, and in deeds.

Pray for love, if you are lacking in it. If we know God we have love for Him and for our family, as well as fellow Christians. We have a love to see sinners saved. We must not love their sin, but love their soul.

DAILY PRAISES	DAILY PRAYER REQUESTS
1.	1.
2.	2.
3.	3.
4.	4.
5.	5.

February 19
Read I Peter 3:8-22

I Peter 3:8

"Finally, all of you, live in harmony with one another; be sympathetic, love as brothers, be compassionate and humble."

Peter is urging all people to unite in love. To become as one mind in Christ to glorify Him, we must show love to one another. We are to feel toward one another as Jesus feels toward us. Oh, what unity and love, when we agree. As Christ receives and loves us we are to receive and love one another.

Think of the miracles which take place through love and unity in Christ. We live so beneath our privilege in Jesus because we do not abide in that love and unity.

Let your love flow to others as Jesus did. It will not cost you anything. It will fill you with joy unspeakable and full of glory.

Jesus will be glorified and lifted up as we show and live in love toward others. We are refreshed through love. We need each other. We need to be filled with joy, the joy of love. When you are filled with the joy of love, it will overflow you. You cannot hide this love. It bubbles forth and it is contagious. It grows and multiplies. Praise the Lord for love.

DAILY PRAISES	**DAILY PRAYER REQUESTS**
1.	1.
2.	2.
3.	3.
4.	4.
5.	5.

February 20
Read John 6:60-68

John 6:68

"Simon Peter answered him, 'Lord, to whom shall we go? You have the words of eternal life.'"

Jesus Christ stands at the door of each heart and knocks. He seeks each person out, so that all have the opportunity to accept Him and receive eternal life.

Some people turn Jesus away. Some tell Him to wait until a later date. Others tell Him that they will think about Him. Then there are those who accept Him and invite Him into their hearts to live and reign. He gives eternal life, also. Praise God for the gift of His Son and Eternal Life!

Those rejecting Christ must be most miserable. To whom do they turn for comfort and peace? My Savior provides the comfort and peace for me. It then becomes my duty to tell everyone I can about Jesus Christ. I love to tell about Heaven and how we have an appointment to go there some day where we can be reunited to our loved ones that have gone to Heaven.

I love to tell how Jesus comforts in times of trouble. I love to share how He delivers from all our daily cares and worries. I tell of how He saved me from sin, deceit, and violence that I might glorify His Name. He has filled me with His Spirit, which gives me wisdom and understanding. I am not perfect, but striving to do the will of my Savior from day to day.

There is no place else to go other than to Jesus. Jesus truly has the words to Eternal Life. It is His will for all who will come to Him and accept Him to receive this Eternal Life. Jesus is all we need. He has provided everything for us.

DAILY PRAISES
1.
2.
3.
4.
5.

DAILY PRAYER REQUESTS
1.
2.
3.
4.
5.

February 21
Read Isaiah 55:1-13

Isaiah 55:6

"Seek the Lord while He may be found; call on Him while He is near."

Every soul yearns for something to fulfill the needs of it. People go searching for all types of pleasure, business ventures, and personal satisfaction to try and fill this yearning in their soul. They may find things that satisfy for a short time, but they are never truly satisfied or happy until they meet and accept Jesus and He fills them with His love.

We are to seek the Lord and His strength continually. We are to lift our hearts and hands to the Heavens calling upon the Lord. We are to watch and pray continually without doubting. We are to get rid of anger before we retire at night, by asking for forgiveness. We are to commit our cares to Jesus and trust Him to take care of our needs. If we truly trust Him and believe as we follow His commandments, He will bring to pass what we have need of, according to His will.

Jesus wants everyone to seek Him. He made provisions for all who will come to Him. Now is the time to seek Him, because He is near. Ask Him to come into your heart, if you have not done so yet. Now is the time.

DAILY PRAISES   **DAILY PRAYER REQUESTS**
1.   1.
2.   2.
3.   3.
4.   4.
5.   5.

February 22
Read James 4:1-12

James 4:2

"You want something but you don't get it. You kill and covet, but you cannot have what you want. You quarrel and fight. You do not have because you do not ask God."

Is there a war going on inside you? Do you desire things unattainable? Are you fighting with family, friends, or business associates? Are the doors closing everywhere you turn? James says we have not received our desires, because we have not asked properly.

War is an offensive word to God. That is, countries at war, people at war, and we at war within us. God is displeased with warring. He came that we might dwell in peace. There is no need to have turmoil and adversity inside when God gives peace and comfort. All we have to do is ask, believe, and receive. There are some prerequisites to asking, believing and receiving. We must be born again, obeying the commandments of Jesus, believing the written Word of God for faith, and ask Him for all things that we need.

We must be patient to await the outcome from God. While we are waiting we can be at peace. There can be calm in our souls rather than war and conflict. Let the Spirit of God take away the war inside you and bring peace and love.

DAILY PRAISES   **DAILY PRAYER REQUESTS**

1.   1.

2.   2.

3.   3.

4.   4.

5.   5.

February 23
Read Colossians 1:15-23

Colossians 1:21, 22

"Once you were alienated from God, and were enemies in your own minds because of your evil behavior. But, now he has reconciled you by Christ's physical body through death to present you holy in his sight, without blemish and free from accusation-."

God has made the initiative to reconcile everyone to Him. He sent His son to live and minister among people, to die on the cross for the sins of all and He was raised that we might live eternally.

We cannot save ourselves. We do not have the power, but because Jesus died and shed His blood to bear our sins we can be reconciled to Him.

We were once estranged from God and hostile toward Him. Because of our enmity with God we were performing wicked works. We were at war with Him. But when we repented all of that changed. God sought to reconcile us to Him so that we might lead a life of holiness with Him. We are to trust Him and be free from our wicked ways. Jesus promised deliverance form sins and our sins will not be remembered against us again. They will be cast as far away from us as the East is from the West.

Praise God that He searches for us and cleanses us and helps us to be new creatures through Him. We are to continue walking in faith because we are saved. We can look toward the future, which is our hope in Heaven. We are set on a solid foundation. Let us keep our eyes, heart, and mind, and soul on Jesus and follow His example according to the Bible.

DAILY PRAISES	**DAILY PRAYER REQUESTS**
1.	1.
2.	2.
3.	3.
4.	4.
5.	5.

February 24
Read I John 3:1-10

I John 3:1

"How great is the love the Father has lavished on us, that we should be called children of God! And that is what we are! The reason the world does not know us is that it did not know him."

Did you ever really think about the reason God sent His Son to earth? I trust you will spend some time thinking and meditating on the real reason Christ came to live among humans and to die on a cross for us.

Christ came to save people that He loved, from the influence of Satan. He came with divine powers to rescue sinners form the clutches of the devil. We are delivered from sin by believing on Jesus Christ. We know that the devil desires to destroy our soul. But each soul was created to praise God and for His glory. Jesus seeks to rescue souls from Satan's grasp.

Christ is in us. He gave us power over sin when we were born into Him. We have the power to rebuke Satan when he comes against us with temptations. We walk with God and He is in us filling us with His love and the Holy Spirit. He gives us power to cast out demons, which terrorize people's minds and hearts. The demons are against God, yet they know Him and recognize His power and fear Him.

Thank God for giving us His power. In the Name of Jesus the demons have to flee. Praise God for His love toward us.

DAILY PRAISES	**DAILY PRAYER REQUESTS**
1.	1.
2.	2.
3.	3.
4.	4.
5.	5.

February 25
Read Romans 6:1-14

Romans 6:14

"For sin shall not be your master, because you are not under law, but under grace."

When we trust in Jesus as our Savior, sin will not be able to control us any longer. We are redeemed by the mercy and grace of God. He gives us power, through His Spirit to overcome sin and those things which tempt us back toward sin. As long as we trust in God and believe in Him, He will deliver us and help us to overcome everything unlike Him. I am not teaching perfection in this world, but that Jesus will give us victory over sin and help us to be delivered from the power of sin.

Because we have come to Jesus and trusted in Him, we have blessedness and joy, knowing we have been saved from sin. We have security and peace because Jesus is our refuge and strength. We believe in Him for overcoming. We have hope for the glory of God, because we have access to Him through grace.

We have life eternal because we believe in Him. When we accept Jesus and live according to the Bible, putting our full trust in Him, we know without a doubt that we have eternal life. We shall never, never die, but live on in Heaven. Praise God!

DAILY PRAISES	**DAILY PRAYER REQUESTS**
1.	1.
2.	2.
3.	3.
4.	4.
5.	5.

February 26
Read II Corinthians 11:1-15

II Corinthians 11:14

"And no wonder, for Satan himself masquerades as an angel of light.

As Christians, we fight against the powers and principalities of Satan. Satan is in the deceiving business. He desires to take everyone to Hell with him. Hell was prepared for Satan and his angels. Satan knows that he is going there when his run is ended, eventually. On his way there through this world, he is making every effort to take all of us with him, to that undesirable place. He does not really care about us. He only wants us to worship him. He will deceive people by getting them to follow and serve him. Then he will destroy and kill them. The devil is a liar and a masquerader. Therefore, we must be careful of his sly methods of deceit.

The devil tempts people to sin against God. He even tempted Jesus, but Jesus used the Word of God against him. We should have knowledge of the Bible so we can use it when we are tempted.

No matter how good the devil looks and how promising his temptation may be it will eventually lead you away from the Lord, if you give in to the temptation. We are victorious over the devil by the blood of Jesus. Let us rebuke the devil by the blood of Jesus and in the Name of Jesus. Then praise God for the victory.

When Jesus was tempted by Satan, He said, "Away from me Satan! For it is written: Worship the Lord your God and serve Him only." Matthew 4:10.

DAILY PRAISES	**DAILY PRAYER REQUESTS**
1.	1.
2.	2.
3.	3.
4.	4.
5.	5.

February 27
Read II Timothy 1:3-14

II Timothy 1:13

"What you heard from me, keep as the pattern of sound teaching, with faith and love in Christ Jesus.

It is our duty to believe the Bible. We are responsible for reading, studying, and learning the Word of God. The more we get to know the Bible, the more we believe and trust and rely on the Lord. The more we know about the Word of God the more we can commit to Him and allow Him to be in control of our lives. He will help us to stand in times of trials and temptations. If we trust in Him, He will never cause us to be moved from our faith.

By believing, living, and praying the Word of God our household will be saved. Our joy will be full and we shall rejoice in our salvation and the salvation of our relatives and friends.

When we believe in Jesus, He puts a new song in our hearts to praise and glorify Him. Others will see our faith and be won to the Lord.

We must stand by faith on the Bible and believe all the promises in the Bible. Because we believe, we have joy, peace, and eternal life.

DAILY PRAISES	**DAILY PRAYER REQUESTS**
1.	1.
2.	2.
3.	3.
4.	4.
5.	5.

February 28
Read I Timothy 1:12-20

I Timothy 1:17

"Now to the King eternal, immortal, invisible, the only God, be honor and glory for ever and ever. Amen."

God is our Savior. We learn to worship Him in spirit and truth. We seek communication with God through the Son and Spirit. So we are in harmony with Him to worship. We have been given the Holy Spirit and it is through this spirit that we truly worship and commune with God.

When we worship in truth we are sincerely adoring and praising God for what He has done in giving us the Son and the Spirit. We are carnal people and do not know how to worship but through faith and trust we yield ourselves to the Holy Spirit which indwells us and teaches us to worship.

God loves us and He is waiting to teach us to worship Him. We are to rejoice that we have God's love through an overflowing of a life dwelling in Christ, we can worship Him. The spirit will flow through us and give us access to the Son. We can live a confident life in strength, prayer, and worship because we have a heart for true spiritual worship.

DAILY PRAISES	**DAILY PRAYER REQUESTS**
1.	1.
2.	2.
3.	3.
4.	4.
5.	5.

February 29
Philippians 2:1-4

Philippians 2:3

"Do nothing out of selfish ambition or vain conceit, but in humility consider others better than yourselves."

Pastors teach and share the good news from Jesus Christ. We, as His children are to tell others about Christ.

Visionaries dream of a greater impact in their life and their testimony for Christ. Some of us lead, others are administrators, and some are followers. We all have a duty to obey the Word of God and be a light to the world. We may be the only Bible some people ever read.

We are to help heal the brokenness of the body of the Church of Christ to make it stronger. We work together as a unit. God heals the family through the family of God. In the church we use our gifts to love each other, honor each other, keep an eye on each other for troublemakers and to carry each other's burdens.

The church is God's treatment center. Do you need encouragement? Do you need healing? Do you need a compassionate home? Whatever you need, you can find in the House of the Lord. Don't miss a place to find food for your soul.

DAILY PRAISES	**DAILY PRAYER REQUESTS**
1.	1.
2.	2.
3.	3.
4.	4.
5.	5.

MARCH

March 1
Read II Chronicles 7:11-22
II Chronicles 7:14

"If my people, who are called by my name will, will humble themselves, and pray and seek my face, and turn from their wicked ways; then will I hear from heaven, and will forgive their sin, and will heal their land."

This verse tells us how to have a revival and be refreshed from the Lord. We simply have to humble ourselves, pray, seek Jesus, and turn from our sins to experience a personal renewal in Christ. This kind of personal revival will result in peace from the Lord, blessings from God and his power of The Holy Spirit in our lives. By following this formula, we can have the most joy, the sweetest peace, and an overflowing measure of God's love and the quickening power in our everyday lives. We will be living a victorious life daily. We will be enjoying a life of obedience, faith, and happiness instead of an abnormal life of fear, unfaithfulness, and sadness.

As believers we must be faithful to do the will of God and enjoy His blessings, presence, and power always.

Let us maintain that high level of spiritual power and victory on a daily basis by glorifying God each moment.

DAILY PRAISES	**DAILY PRAYER REQUESTS**
1.	1.
2.	2.
3.	3.
4.	4.
5.	5.

March 2
Read Hebrews 4:14-16

Hebrews 4:16

"Let us then approach the throne of grace with confidence, so that we may receive and grace to help us in our time of need."

Each person is invited to come to the throne for their needs that God would show mercy to them. Every born again believer has a right to petition Jesus for needs and concerns. (The sinner will be heard when praying the sinner's prayer for forgiveness.)

Maybe we do not approach the throne because we feel like we don't know how to pray. Jesus will teach us if we ask Him and seek His face. We are aware of the mighty wonders accomplished throughout the Bible because of prayer. The promises are given to our generation if we will pray. The Lord still answers prayers for those who believe in

the promises of God.

We must submit ourselves to God, for His glory, in faith and full assurance in the Name of Jesus, believing we will have answers to our petitions. We must persevere and continue to trust Him. He has access to our hearts and teaches us by showing us our sins and giving us thoughts for intercession in the spirit of prayer within us.

DAILY PRAISES	**DAILY PRAYER REQUESTS**
1.	1.
2.	2.
3.	3.
4.	4.
5.	5.

March 3
Read Acts 16: 25-34

Acts 16:31

"They replied, believe on the Lord Jesus and you will be saved-you and your household."

Have you ever been born again? The Bible tells us that we are all sinners in Romans 3:23. We must believe on the Lord Jesus to be saved. We are to confess our sins and He will forgive us according to I John 1:9. Then we must be baptized in the Name of Jesus. We are to tell someone about our conversion and witness about Christ and what He has done in our lives as recorded in Romans 10:9. How simple it is: believe, confess, pray, be baptized, and tell others.

Jesus died on the cross to save us from our sins. He arose victorious from the grave. That is why He can forgive our sins. It is a gift. We only have to accept it and believe on Him and experience His wonderful promises.

Christians can use the scriptures with those they come in contact with to witness to them on how to be saved. Invite people to be born again. We are all to be a witness for Christ right where we are. We don't have to go to a foreign field. We are to witness at home, work, school, grocery, or in our community. Jesus told us to be a witness for Him.

Oh, what a personal cleansing from sin and restoration to fellowship with Jesus, when we accept him. We will have his peace. We do experience joy and can live victoriously by accepting the gracious provisions of Jesus.

DAILY PRAISES
1.
2.
3.
4.
5.

DAILY PRAYER REQUESTS
1.
2.
3.
4.
5.

March 4
Read Psalm 95

Psalm 95:6

"Come, let us bow down in worship, let us kneel before the Lord, our Maker."

God made us to praise Him. So many times in Scripture we are called to worship and praise God. There is no excuse for ignorance, because we are admonished often, in the Word, to worship Him in various ways. Everyone worships something. If we are not worshipping God, we are robbing God of the praise He deserves.

Christians worship to God is spiritual worship into the most Holy presence of God, who dwells within us through the Spirit.

Can't you realize how praise and worship pleases God? Don't you know it benefits humans to praise the Lord? God is calling His people to praise Him and worship Him today. A call has gone out to the entire world for individuals who will worship Jesus. We must not let anyone or anything hinder us from praising our God.

Often we spend too much time on temporal things that vanish so quickly. By spending more time praising and worshipping God we will find time to do the necessary things. You see, everything we own belongs to God. He has given us everything. We only own our soul and doesn't it make sense to give it to the Lord and let Him supply every need.

DAILY PRAISES	**DAILY PRAYER REQUESTS**
1.	1.
2.	2.
3.	3.
4.	4.
5.	5.

March 5
Revelation 13:1-10

Revelation 13:5

"The beast was given a mouth to utter proud words and blasphemies and to exercise his authority for forty-two months."

Today is the day of salvation. There is coming a day when it will be too late to receive Jesus. He is calling everyone today. He is standing at the door and knocking, seeking to enter in and abide with you. The Holy Spirit is convicting people of sins and urging them to give their hearts to Christ.

When Jesus takes the church away the Holy Spirit will be taken, I believe. Imagine a world without the Holy Spirit to intercede and a world without the Christians to love and to pray on behalf of others! How sad and how bleak it will be. There will be evil everywhere.

The Antichrist will slowly rise and gain power to take over the world. He will be an organizer in a world of chaos. He will have unity among political, religious, cultural, and industrial worlds. There will be a common trade system with one money system. He will be enthusiastic and call for worship of himself, eventually. He will set himself us as god. He will order everyone to take the "Mark of the Beast." Taking the "Mark" will mean damnation. Refusing the "Mark" will mean sure death.

Make sure you have received Christ in your life today and avoid this future happening. Read II Thessalonians 2 to find out more about the coming of the Lord.

DAILY PRAISES   **DAILY PRAYER REQUESTS**
1.   1.

2.   2.

3.   3.

4.   4.

5.   5.

March 6
Read Jeremiah 32:16-35

Jeremiah 32:27

"I am the Lord, the God of all mankind. Is anything too hard for me?"

God is speaking this to us. If we have a concern or a need He is able to meet it. All we have to do is believe, be obedient, have courage, portray boldness and be loyal to the Lord as He speaks to us in His Word. He may not provide the solution that our selfish, human spirit desires, but God has the correct solution. We may not always understand when God's answer is 'No' or when it is delayed, but rest assured it is the best answer. It is for our good. God knows and sees all and His ways are far above our ways. He is our perfect Father and all things are possible through Him.

What are those 'hard things' in your life? Those things which you feel that have no answer or which you feel cannot be helped. Bring them to Jesus. Lay them at His feet. Commit them to Him. He has power, far more than we can comprehend or even think to ask about. Let us realize the power of God! Nothing is impossible with God. Just believe. Let your faith soar as you commit your concerns to Him. He wants to work in our lives if we will only let Him. He is omnipotent and He reigns. Just believe and praise Him. Nothing is too hard for our Lord Jesus Christ.

DAILY PRAISES   **DAILY PRAYER REQUESTS**

1.   1.

2.   2.

3.   3.

4.   4.

5.   5.

March 7
Read John 16:17-33

John 16:33

"I have told you these things, so that in me you may have peace. In this world you will have trouble. But take heart! I have overcome the world."

Have you ever had afflictions, troubles, grief, trials, pain, diseases, misery, or hardships? Did you consider the source from where the problems came? The world is the source of all types of troubles. Let us consider the opposite side of the world. Have you ever had relief, alleviation, consolation, gratification, blessings, and pleasures? Where do the blessings come from?

Jesus overcame the world and so can we. We can overcome by putting our trust in Him and looking to Him as our example. It is natural to expect conflict in the world. Jesus had conflict and confrontation in the world. We are not greater than He, therefore we will meet conflict. Praise the Lord we can overcome the conflict by keeping our trust in Jesus. He will give us peace. We can have happiness and joy throughout our lives regardless of the problems. We are overcomers through Jesus.

Remember this verse when trials come to you. Say it often. Enjoy the peace of the Lord. Praise the Lord.

DAILY PRAISES	**DAILY PRAYER REQUESTS**
1.	1.
2.	2.
3.	3.
4.	4.
5.	5.

March 8
Read I Corinthians 6:12-20

I Corinthians 6:19-20

"Do you not know that your body is a temple of the Holy Spirit, who is in you, whom you have received from God? You are not your own; you were bought at a price. Therefore, honor God with your body."

As Christians we should value our bodies as a sacred place where God dwells, By the presence of the Spirit we can be helped through any temptations.

We need to be completely sold out to God and let the Holy Spirit control our lives. Praise God for the Comforter. We, as humans, do not know what is best for us, or what we need, but the Holy Spirit searches us and knows us better than we know ourselves. He prays through us making intercessions for the will of God in our lives.

To let the Holy Spirit control us, we must yield our stubborn will to God's will. God will not put anything on us that will be bad for us. The Lord loves us as dear children. We bring the bad things when we fail to obey or fail to listen to the Holy Spirit. We are to pray daily and communicate with God. We must read the Bible for food on which to grow and mature. It is necessary to be filled with the love of God, because God is love. Our duty is to produce the fruits of the Spirit in our lives as in Galatians 5:22-23.

The Holy Spirit will teach us if we are willing to learn and obey. Let the Holy Spirit rule in you. Be willing to sell out to the Lord completely. Do not let anything stand between you and the Lord.

DAILY PRAISES	**DAILY PRAYER REQUESTS**
1.	1.
2.	2.
3.	3.
4.	4.
5.	5.

March 9
Read I Thessalonians 4:13-18

I Thessalonians 4:16

"For the Lord himself will come down from heaven, with a loud command, with the voice of the archangel and with the trumpet call of God, and the dead in Christ will rise first."

As I meditate and contemplate the return of Jesus Christ, a smile comes across my face, my eyes begin to sparkle and tears of joy roll down my cheeks. At the shout of the voice of the archangel the saints which have died will come forth. Just imagine the victory and power coming from six feet under the ground, emerging from coffins and steel vaults!

My mind reflects back to that old song written by Claude Eely, "Ain't No Grave Gonna Hold My Body Down". How true that title is. If we have been born again, washed in the blood, nothing will keep us from rising to meet Jesus in the air.

I do not know if I will be dead or alive when He returns, but I know without a doubt, when He calls, "Patricia Kincer", I will rise to meet Him. I know that I will recognize His call where ever I am.

Just think what a reunion it will be as we alive saints reunite with those who have gone by the way of the grave. Think about meeting Jesus in the air! Joy overwhelms me when I think of meeting my eighteen-year-old daughter, my dad, my mother, my sisters and other relatives and friends. Praise God for the victory!

Everyone can be ready, as I am ready.

DAILY PRAISES **DAILY PRAYER REQUESTS**

1. 1.

2. 2.

3. 3.

4. 4.

5. 5.

March 10
Read Psalm 33:12-20

Psalm 33:18

"But the eyes of the Lord are on those who fear him, on those whose hope is in his unfailing love,"

God is to be reverenced and held in awe. He is a Holy God. We are to not to be wise in our own eyes but wise through the serving of God and worshipping Him. Our duty as humans is to fear God and keep His commandments. When we fear God we get wisdom and knowledge of Him. He gives us understanding.

Fearing God does not mean we tremble in a slavish fear, but we reverence Him in a Holy awe. He is the God that created the universe and all things within. We are to stand amazed at what He has done and who He is.

When we worship Him in the beauty of Holiness we are in reverence. He cannot teach us His way unless we respect Him. When we seek the Lord, He will give us the good things. He will bless us if we walk in His ways and serve Him. He will hear our cry and have mercy on us, when we call on Him.

Through the fear of God we have a place of refuge and a fountain of life. The fear of the Lord causes us to be satisfied in our soul. The fear of the Lord is our treasure. It is the stability of our strength, It gives us hope and mercy to all generations.

Keep His commandments and walk with Him through this life. He has prepared a Heavenly Home for those who fear Him.

DAILY PRAISES
1.
2.
3.
4.
5.

DAILY PRAYER REQUESTS
1.
2.
3.
4.
5.

March 11
Read Romans 12:9-21

Romans 12:21
"Do not be overcome by evil, but overcome evil with good."

Evil is all around us. There is no way to hide our heads in the sand and ignore it. We must be determined to overcome evil. We have to show love to those that would be our enemies, as well as those who persecute the way of the Lord. We will win people to Christ by loving them in spite of their evil ways. When we see those who hate us in need, we are to help them by providing food, clothing, love or other needs, whatever they may be.

It is important to show love as a Christian, by giving ourselves, our time, or materially. If we do not love, we are no different from the world. It is easy to love those who love us and are good to us. The real test is to love those who hate us and wish us ill will.

By loving and doing good we are heaping coals on the heads of our enemies. We are warming them through love. They will come around if we endure through love. Overcome that evil one with love.

DAILY PRAISES	**DAILY PRAYER REQUESTS**
1.	1.
2.	2.
3.	3.
4.	4.
5.	5.

March 12
Read I Timothy 4:9-16

I Timothy 4:15

"Be diligent in these matters; give yourself wholly to them, so that everyone may see your progress."

The Lord uses what we have learned from His Word and from experience to help us minister to others. When we are witnessing to others the Holy Spirit will bring to our attention those verses we have been faithful to memorize for the glory of God.

No person lives totally to themselves. There must be some type of communication and interaction with others. When we have the opportunity to share we should do it with zeal and excitement. God has given us the Spirit of love and power and a sound mind. We do not have the spirit of fear or shyness because we have Jesus. We are to share His love. We are God's instruments to bring about the salvation of others.

Can't you see how important it is, dear Christian friend, to share the Word of God with sinners and those with problems? In sharing you are saving them from Hell and destruction. Another name will be added to those in the Book of Life. By sharing, you are gaining an eternal home in heaven for someone else. You are enjoying the blessings and benefits of the Holy spirit in this life for yourself. You are also magnifying Christ in your life. He is worthy to be witnessed about and praised.

DAILY PRAISES
1.
2.
3.
4.
5.

DAILY PRAYER REQUESTS
1.
2.
3.
4.
5.

March 13
Read Psalm 92

Psalm 92:1

"It is good to praise the Lord and make music to your name, O Most High"

Everyone enjoys receiving praise and thanks for the things they do to help others by making their life easier and happier. If we, then in our human form enjoy praise and thanks, just think how much more our Lord enjoys praise and thanks from His people. He does so much for us. So many things that we don't even think about, occur each and every day. Think of how much He deserves our praise and thanks. No matter how much we do it is as a grain of sand in comparison to what God has done for us. Praise Him! Thank Him!

Dwell on the praise of God, who desires to bring deliverance. Praise Him for victory. God causes us to triumph. Pray-Read-Obey. God will bless us as we do. How rich we are through Christ.

Oh, how wonderful to call upon the Name of Jesus and we know He hears us. Oh, how wonderful the answer from Jesus. Give God the praise in everything. How magnificent to thank and praise the One who is responsible for our very existence and everything we have: family, health, food, shelter, jobs, friends, but most of all salvation. It is not a selfish act to praise God for blessings. It is an act of respect and reverence. Praise Him and thank Him right now.

DAILY PRAISES	**DAILY PRAYER REQUESTS**
1.	1.
2.	2.
3.	3.
4.	4.
5.	5.

March 14
Read I Corinthians 9:19-27

I Corinthians 9:24-25

"Do you not know that in a race all the runners run, but only one gets the prize? Run in such a way as to get the prize. Everyone who competes in the games goes into strict training. They do it to get a crown that will not last; but we do it to get a crown that will last forever."

Running is a very strenuous exercise. One must prepare the body for running the race. You must begin to train, slowly at first, then daily you gain more strength and stamina with which to run the race. Your body must be under subjection as you cannot abuse it, while preparing for the race. To be in the best possible shape one must undergo daily preparations. If you skip your daily training your progress will regress, therefore you have to go back and start over.

As Christians, we are in a race. We are racing against powers and principalities of the world. It is not our physical body racing, but our spiritual bodies. We must prepare just as the people who run the physical race. We are to train our souls and mind daily by going to the Bible, reading and learning from God. Next we have to come to the throne of God in prayer daily to meditate and seek Jesus. As we seek Him, we listen to what He has to say to us through His Word and meditation. We are responsible to witness to those who don't know Jesus. Our training is important and we should not skip a day. After all we are training for an eternal home in Heaven.

We will be rewarded at the end of the race if we stay well prepared. Let us run with patience and love so that we can reach the finish line with eagerness and vigor.

DAILY PRAISES	**DAILY PRAYER REQUESTS**
1.	1.
2.	2.
3.	3.
4.	4.
5.	5.

March 15
Read I Corinthians 1:18-31

I Corinthians 1:30

"It is because of Him that you are in Christ Jesus, who has become for us wisdom from God-that is, our righteousness, holiness, and redemption."

Today the world is filled with major problems. Jesus is our only hope. It is through God, who gave us Jesus that tasks are performed and major problems are solved.

Jesus has the power to forgive sins; to heal sickness; to raise up nations to honor Him or to tear down nations that ignore Him or put Him aside for other gods.

It is by faith that we are united with Christ and we are justified and declared righteous.

What have you accomplished? How will you be remembered? Have you allowed the spiritual blessings into your life? Jesus is the answer.

It does not matter what we accomplish in this life, if we leave Jesus out. Without Jesus we cannot have eternal life in Heaven. We should want to be remembered as loving God and people. Our responsibility is to care for others and do the things that glorify God. By desiring spiritual blessings, we will increase our faith in God. We have so much promised from God, but we have to step out in faith and claim those promises. God is to be trusted. It is so wonderful to know the love of Christ. He makes us to overcome all of life's problems. Through His grace we receive faith, wisdom, and righteousness. His goodness will penetrate your very soul and life.

DAILY PRAISES	**DAILY PRAYER REQUESTS**
1.	1.
2.	2.
3.	3.
4.	4.
5.	5.

March 16
Read I John 4:1-6

I John 4:4

"You, dear children, are from God and have overcome them, because the one who is in you is greater than the one who is in the world."

What dynamic words for the believer to rejoice about. By being born of God we have overcome the world and the things in the world. Because we have God, we can overcome every temptation of the world, flesh, and the devil. The devil is a powerful influence, but God is more powerful. With God on our side we can defeat every enemy. The Holy Spirit, which indwells, us provides the power we need to defeat the devil and all of his demons.

We are to be faithful to God and walk an upright life so that we do not miss out on the blessings from the Lord. He has so much for us. By studying the Bible. we gain spiritual victory. Through prayer we have a personal communion with God. By obeying Him, we receive the best in blessings. We can defeat the enemy because the Bible tells us that 'victory is ours'

Praise God, because He is greater than the other powers! Praise God, because we have the power to overcome the enemy through Jesus Christ!

DAILY PRAISES	**DAILY PRAYER REQUESTS**
1.	1.
2.	2.
3.	3.
4.	4.
5.	5.

March 17
Read John 16: 5-16

John 16:7

"But I tell you the truth: It is for your good that I am going away. Unless I go away, the Counselor will not come to you: but if I go, I will send him to you."

The Holy Spirit or Counselor or Comforter performs the works of God. He was from the beginning of creation with the Father and the Son. He is active in convicting people of their sins. He bestows spiritual gifts and blessings on people. He is active by living within our hearts to help us with our everyday life.

In the physical life, my husband is my helpmate. When I'm cooking those home canned green beans and cannot open a lid, I call on him to help remove the lid. When I am cleaning and cannot remove a heavy piece of furniture or reach high places, I depend on him to help me. And so it is with the Holy spirit. He is always with us to help us. When we are inadequate in our own ability to accomplish a task, the Holy Spirit aids us. He is the strength that we need. We are never alone. We always have the comfort, strength, height and power of the Holy Spirit.

Ask Jesus to help you rely more on the Comforter that you may be a blessing to others. Praise the Lord for the Comforter.

DAILY PRAISES
1.
2.
3.
4.
5.

DAILY PRAYER REQUESTS
1.
2.
3.
4.
5.

March 18
Read I Peter 4:12-19

I Peter 4:13

"But rejoice that you participate in the sufferings of Christ, so that you may be overjoyed when his glory is revealed."

I remember parts of a song from my youth which said, "This world is not my home, I'm just passing through." I now realize how true those words really are for the Christian. "This is just a dressing room for us," my Dad often said. It is a place to prepare for living eternally with Jesus. If we really look at the world and the spirit of evil with which it is filled, we recognize that we do not fit. We are not really accepted or we are treated as strangers.

The Bible tells us to rejoice anyway, because we belong to Christ. One day we will be ruling and reigning with Christ. Every persecution we suffer because of Jesus will be worth it when Christ returns to take us to Heaven. Our steadfastness in Christ will be rewarded. Our reward is in Heaven and not in this world. We must continue as ambassadors for Christ until His return. Many souls need to be saved. We are the light of this dark world. We are to love the world and minister to it. We are to do the will of God and not be afraid to commit our lives to Him.

DAILY PRAISES	**DAILY PRAYER REQUESTS**
1.	1.
2.	2.
3.	3.
4.	4.
5.	5.

March 19
Read Psalm 33

Psalm 33:6

"By the word of the Lord were the heavens made, their starry hosts by breath of his mouth."

God created the universe and all things in it. He prepared the foundation of the earth and the heavens. He formed the oceans and seas, the stars and all that is within the kingdom of the earth. Let us realize that the Lord who created the universe, also formed our bodies in our mother's womb. We are not accidents, but made by the Lord for the purpose of worshipping, serving, and praising the Lord. He created us to inhabit the earth and praise Him with our voice. He cares for each of us individually and personally. We are His people.

Yes, He is great, majestic, and powerful. Yet He is personable enough to indwell each of us with His Spirit. Through faith, we are to understand that God calls each of us by name. He is concerned about each facet of our lives.

The Lord is worthy to receive our praise and honor because He has created us for that purpose. He created us for His pleasure, to enjoy our companionship as we worship Him. Look at the earth and sky above and declare God's glory of His handiwork. His Spirit is everywhere to enhance and help us. Receive His help. Let the Lord breathe His Spirit on you.

DAILY PRAISES	DAILY PRAYER REQUESTS
1.	1.
2.	2.
3.	3.
4.	4.
5.	5.

March 20
Read Matthew 6:5-14

Matthew 6:6

"But when you pray, go into your room, close the door and pray to your Father, who sees what is done in secret, will reward you."

School children have a place to go and learn from a teacher. It is their privilege and responsibility to learn everything they can from their superiors. Jesus is our teacher and we want to learn everything we can from Him and His Word. That is why we are to have a place where we can go and be alone with Him to let Him teach us what we need to know.

When we come to Jesus to learn we have to put the world aside and enter into the spiritual worship with Him. Jesus comes to teach us in our room, in the private time, alone with Him. He will reveal Himself to us as we withdraw from the noisy world and enter into His presence.

The secret of prayer is in the inner chamber, where we get alone with the Father. He wants to meet our needs if we will only take time to get alone with Him.

Look up to the Father. See His love, His tenderness, and His mercy. How He longs to satisfy our requests.

When we pray secretly alone, before the Father, He will reward us openly, by pouring His blessings out on us. Go to Him in secret and gain confidence as He bestows His blessings on you.

DAILY PRAISES	**DAILY PRAYER REQUESTS**
1.	1.
2.	2.
3.	3.
4.	4.
5.	5.

March 21
Read Deuteronomy 32:7-14

Deuteronomy 32:12
"The Lord alone led him; no foreign god was with him."

Jesus always knows just what we need. When we let Him teach and instruct us it is so precious.

When our daughter went to Europe for the first time with a group of students, I was having a hard time adjusting to her being that far away from home. I was accustomed to her being away at college, a few hour's drive from us. The distance seemed to overwhelm me. After two days, I committed her travel to the Lord and that very day the Lord gave me this scripture, Deuteronomy 32:12. God is so faithful to His children. He can and will lead and take care of our children, no matter where they are, if we commit them to the Lord.

God has promised us that He will never leave us or forsake us. He is true to His Word. We can know that He is our Lord. If we obey Him, He will lead us. He loves us so much and wants to do so much for us. We often prohibit God from doing things for us because we do not listen or obey. We stand back at arm length and look at Him. We need to come boldly to Him and embrace Him and desire His nearness. He longs to take us in His arms and meet our every need. He is on our side. He loves us more than we realize. He delights in leading us in His paths. Enjoy the goodness of the Lord. Let Him lead you. You will never go astray.

DAILY PRAISES   **DAILY PRAYER REQUESTS**
1.   1.

2.   2.

3.   3.

4.   4.

5.   5.

March 22
Read II Corinthians 1:3-11

II Corinthians 1:4

"Who comforts us in all our troubles, so that we can comfort those in any trouble with the comfort we ourselves have received from God."

How long has it been since you have been comforted or helped by God in some special way?

Have you shared God's comfort with someone who has a similar problem that you have faced?

When people experience problems like ours we can really say, "I understand how you feel and know what you are going through."

Unless you have experienced the death of a child, you cannot feel what the parents feel. You can sympathize and feel sorry for them, but you cannot experience the pain and grief which they feel. You must have the first-hand experience, to be able to put yourself in someone's place, who is hurting.

I can say to parents who have lost a child, "I know how much it hurts, but God can comfort you as He comforted me."

I thank God that I have been able to comfort others as God comforted me. Also, as He gave me family, friends, and church to help me, I can help others. Comforting is just being there to listen, to hug, or to say, "I do understand." Comfort someone today. Whatever you have experienced, there is someone who is going through the same problems. You have been commissioned to comfort others.

DAILY PRAISES	**DAILY PRAYER REQUESTS**
1.	1.
2.	2.
3.	3.
4.	4.
5.	5.

March 23
Read Psalm 3

Psalm 3:6

"I will not fear the tens of thousands drawn up against me on every side."

We are not to fear people. People cause lots of temporary problems, but God is in control. We are to remain steadfast and faithful to God and let Him take care of the people who cause conflict.

We must put God first and be willing to witness and glorify Him before others. He will take care of the situation.

God will be our judge, not people. We will answer to God, not humans. I praise the Lord because He is going to be my judge, as well as everyone else. So often we worry about what people think and try to please them, when it is contrary to the Bible. We must seek to please God and praise Him. He is our risen Savior in whom we trust for eternal life. People can give us a hard time in this life, but with God's help we can overcome every obstacle that is planted in our path. God made the way for us to win the battle before us. Praise Him for the deliverance from perils of people who would hinder our work for the Lord. Remember He has angels stationed to help us.

DAILY PRAISES	**DAILY PRAYER REQUESTS**
1.	1.
2.	2.
3.	3.
4.	4.
5.	5.

March 24
Read Luke 16:19-31

Luke 16:31

"He said to him, 'If they do not listen to Moses and the Prophets, they will not be convinced even if someone rises from the dead.' "

People are looking for signs to make them believe and commit to God. They are only using this as an excuse or cop-out. The signs have been given in the Bible. Everything is included, in the Bible, that anyone could ever seek for in the way of a sign. It tells us more than anyone from the dead could reveal.

It is true, we do not want our loved ones to go to Hell. They will go there if they do not accept Jesus Christ. The Bible gives a step by step procedure on how to ask God for forgiveness of sins and have faith and believe on Jesus for Salvation. After believing on Christ we are to walk anew with Him, witnessing, sharing, and loving, so that all the world can see Christ in us.

People say they would believe if they could see a miracle take place. Well, miracles are taking place every second of every day. Just look at the new born babies; what a miracle! Take a look at a flower in bloom, a leaf, the solar system, the stars, or the souls that have been changed by believing in God. Yes, we can see miracles if we only look for them. People look for an excuse not to give their life to Christ. As long as they want excuses, they can find them, but the excuses will not stand on judgment day. Those using excuses should be aware of the consequences of those decisions. Jesus wants you to believe in Him NOW!

DAILY PRAISES
1.
2.
3.
4.
5.

DAILY PRAYER REQUESTS
1.
2.
3.
4.
5.

March 25
Read Proverbs 11:10-16

Proverbs 11:13

"A gossip betrays a confidence, but a trustworthy man keeps a secret."

In the book of Leviticus, tale bearing was forbidden by the people. We are to be good neighbors and not repeat what we hear. We may reason that it is truth, but if it does not build up the kingdom of God or glorify Him, it is tearing down someone.

When we carry tales we are wounding someone. We should mind our own business and take care of ourselves. We need to block out those stories that we hear that do not uplift others.

If we cease from carrying tales, strife will cease. We are to work together in love and fellowship to build up one another and make the church a place of true worship.

Put aside all feelings that are unlike God. Jesus told us to follow His example. All our sins are covered by the blood of Jesus, so get rid of those feelings that do not follow the example of Jesus. The Lord will help us have peace with everyone. All we have to do is to allow Him to be Lord of our life.

DAILY PRAISES   **DAILY PRAYER REQUESTS**

1.   1.

2.   2.

3.   3.

4.   4.

5.   5.

March 26
Read Acts 21:8-16

Acts 21:13

"Then Paul answered, "Why are you weeping and breaking my heart? I am ready not only to be bound, but also to die in Jerusalem for the name of the Lord Jesus."

What does the name of the Lord Jesus mean to you? Are you willing to die for His name? are you hiding His name in a closet someplace, afraid people will find out that you claim to be a Christian?

We must be bold for Christ and ready to accept the responsibility of being a Christian. A Christian has to be willing to suffer with and for Christ, as well as to rejoice with and for Him. We need to be as Paul, prepared to die for Christ, if necessary. Do not be ashamed of Christ, for if you are, someday He will be ashamed of you and cast you into outer darkness.

God is powerful. He is able to deliver you in every situation. Do not be afraid to honor Him as Lord. Listen to Him. Turn loose and let the Holy Spirit lead you. Be a doer of the Word and for Christ. Be a protector of the Word of God. Stand up and be counted as a Christian. It has been too long that Christians have taken a back seat and refused to get involved. We have to get involved. We cannot let the evil of this world take over and control what God has given us. Speak up for the right thing. Write letters to oppose those things with which the Bible teaches against. God will bless you for standing up for Him.

DAILY PRAISES	**DAILY PRAYER REQUESTS**
1.	1.
2.	2.
3.	3.
4.	4.
5.	5.

March 27
Read Luke 10:1-16

Luke 10:2, 3

"He told them, "The harvest is plentiful, but the workers are few. Ask the Lord of the harvest, therefore to send out workers into the harvest field. 3. Go! I am sending you out like lambs among wolves."

How much people would grow in Christ if they would only get involved in the harvest! There are so many hungry souls that desire to hear about Jesus. We fail to witness of His love and goodness to those who are hungry or hurting. We are failing God, when we let an opportunity go by and do not tell someone about Christ and His love for them. Think of all the associates and people you come in contact with each day or week. Are they all Christians? What effect do you have on their lives? Do they even know you are a Christian? Have you ever shared something about the Lord with them?

People are hungry for something. What they desire is the Lord. Christians are reluctant to share God's love. They are afraid of being rejected by others. The Bible tells us God's Word will not return to us void, when shared in love. God is for all people, not just a select group. He wants everyone to be saved. You are to be a laborer in this harvest for Christ. The rewards will be great. Peace and satisfaction will be ours in this life. We have the promise of a home in Heaven forever. Praise the Lord and share Him with others.

DAILY PRAISES	**DAILY PRAYER REQUESTS**
1.	1.
2.	2.
3.	3.
4.	4.
5.	5.

March 28
Read I Corinthians 13

I Corinthians 13:8

"Love never fails. But where there are prophecies, they will cease; where there are tongues, they will be stilled; where there is knowledge, it will pass away."

What a peace to know that love or charity or God will never fail. Prophecy will fail, because the rapture will take place and the Christians will leave the world. When the Christians have gone there will be no one to prophesy or speak in tongues or speak knowledge of God.

God never fails, because He loves us and gave His Son to redeem us. His Word is true. His love is real. We can depend on Him. He does not leave us or fail us. We are the ones who leave Him or fail Him. We must not keep guilty feelings about failings and errors that we have made, but ask for forgiveness. Remember His love covers all. He loves us so much that He keeps forgiving us for those failures. Let Him love you. Let Him forgive you and cover you with His love.

Jesus desires that everyone love and serve Him. Is that too much to ask? Just think of what He has done for us. He gave His all, in love, and did not complain that it was too hard or too much to be expected of Him. Let us practice loving as Jesus did. Make an effort to let your love show.

DAILY PRAISES	**DAILY PRAYER REQUESTS**
1.	1.
2.	2.
3.	3.
4.	4.
5.	5.

March 29
Read I Corinthians 10:1-13

I Corinthians 10:6

"Now these things occurred as examples to keep us from setting our hearts on evil things, as they did."

This Scripture is referring to the children of Israel as Moses was leading them out of bondage and into the Promised Land. They began to complain and lust for other things. God was providing for them so marvelously, yet they could not be content and enjoy the great things of the Lord. Let us not complain about what God is doing for us. Let us be content with the gifts and more of all things from the Lord. We need to pray and seek Him for what we need instead of complaining about the way things are. If we are willing to use what God has entrusted us with He will give us more to use for Him.

It is a dangerous thing to lust after things someone else has or things that are evil. We should praise God for what we have and ask Him to lead us toward more rewarding things.

Many people have lost their salvation by grumbling and complaining that others have a better life than they. We have just as much of the Lord as we want. We are as close to Him as we want to be. If you are dissatisfied with the way things are, do not complain or lust, but go directly to the Father. Tell Him your concerns. He cares for you and will listen and meet your needs if you are serious and faithful.

DAILY PRAISES	**DAILY PRAYER REQUESTS**
1.	1.
2.	2.
3.	3.
4.	4.
5.	5.

March 30
Read Isaiah 40:25-31

Isaiah 40:31

"But those who hope in the Lord will renew their strength. They will soar on wings like eagles, they will run and not grow weary, they will walk and not be faint."

By nature and personality, I have always been a very impatient person. In more recent years, I have come to the knowledge of learning to wait upon the Lord. I have to stop myself from running on ahead of the Lord. He has been teaching me about waiting. He truly is my strength, my expectation, my salvation, my defense, and my rock. I will learn by His grace and mercy to wait on Him.

For almost twenty years I prayed for my husband to be saved. I even began praying for him to be saved before we were married. So often I would become discouraged and give up. Many prayers were offered out of responsibility instead of sincerity. But once I made up my mind and got serious with God, about saving my husband, it was done. It came about by prayer, fasting, reading, and claiming the promises in the Bible. The night our daughter was killed, my husband gave his heart to God.

God always comes on time. His time of waiting is perfect. We only need to wait and trust as we stand on His promises. He will do the rest. We do not understand the working of the Lord. We might think it was a great price to pay for my husband's salvation. The devil thought he was taking away from our family, but by my husband being saved that night, meant one more will be in Heaven when we meet our daughter.

DAILY PRAISES   **DAILY PRAYER REQUESTS**
1.   1.

2.   2.

3.   3.

4.   4.

5.   5.

March 31
Read Romans 8:28-39

Romans 8:31, 32

"What, then, shall we say in response to this? If God is for us, who can be against us? He who did not spare his own Son, but gave him up for us all--how will he not also, along with him, graciously give us all things?"

We, who were without hope, have been given the hope and promise for eternal life. God gave His Son as a sacrifice for us. He was resurrected from the grave so that we might have life everlasting.

If we serve God, He will not withhold His blessings from us. We may not have earthly riches, as some do, but the riches we have are the joy, peace, strength, and comfort in serving the Lord. If He loved us enough to give His Son for us, He loves us enough to take care of us and meet our needs.

There is something for us to do. We must have faith, first of all, being confident of His promises. We must also keep His commandments and live according to the Bible. We have been told that there is a burden to bear as we serve the Lord. Do not expect to never encounter adversity. We are told to love our neighbors and do good to those who do not love us. If we love God and people and love good instead of evil, He will deliver us. He will meet every need. He will preserve us and give us eternal life. Praise the Lord.

DAILY PRAISES **DAILY PRAYER REQUESTS**
1. 1.
2. 2.
3. 3.
4. 4.
5. 5.

APRIL

April 1
Read Philippians 4:4-9

Philippians 4:8

"Finally, brothers, whatever is true, whatever is noble, whatever is right, whatever is pure, whatever is lovely, whatever is admirable--if anything is excellent or praiseworthy--think about such things."

I think every Christian should know this verse by memory. When Satan comes to us, all we have to do is quote Philippians 4:8 and he will flee.

We need to really concentrate on things that are good and worthwhile. As long as we have our minds on the lovely, true, and pure things. Sin cannot enter our minds and Satan cannot penetrate our thoughts that are excellent.

When we were born again we began to depart from the evil thoughts and deeds which originally had us bound. Let us meditate upon the wonderful things of God. If you just say, "Jesus, Jesus," or offer a praise or thanksgiving, you will be able to overcome and defeat the devil.

Oh, how wonderful it is to concentrate on the good things! Keep your mind on the beautiful and do not give room for the devil to dwell or make you think about unpleasant things.

DAILY PRAISES	**DAILY PRAYER REQUESTS**
1.	1.
2.	2.
3.	3.
4.	4.
5.	5.

April 2
Read Proverbs 3:1-20

Proverbs 3:9, 10

"Honor the Lord with your wealth, with the first fruits of all your crops; then your barns will be filled to overflowing, and your vats will brim over new wine."

God is the owner of all material resources. Everything we have or acquire are gifts from God. We have the power to choose whether we will develop our talents or hoard them. We have each been given marvelous gifts and resources. It is up to us, as individuals, to develop those gifts and let them profit us and the Lord.

Our stay on earth is temporary, therefore we should be rich toward God and lay up treasures in Heaven. God knows our hearts. He knows what place money, possessions, talents, love, and pride have in our hearts. He knows our priorities and our attitudes. You cannot hide anything from God.

We should not make getting earthly possessions the chief goal of our life. We need a greater emphasis on living for the Lord. We are to know Jesus as our personal Savior, first of all. Then if we are rich in this world's goods, it is a blessing from God. We cannot put our riches ahead of God. Rich people can live for the Lord. They have the means to bless many people and build up the kingdom of God. People sin when money is the love of their life rather than Jesus.

Christians are to pray, read the Bible, and follow the instructions therein. If we expect a blessing, we must obey His laws regarding the returning to the Lord a portion of that with which He has blessed us. We cannot out give God. The more we give, the more He gives us. If we are selfish with the Lord, we will suffer for it in some way. Let us be liberal when giving to the Lord. Give in the Name of Jesus.

DAILY PRAISES	**DAILY PRAYER REQUESTS**
1.	1.
2.	2.
3.	3.
4.	4.
5.	5.

April 3
Read Isaiah 12

Isaiah 12:3

"Sing to the Lord, for he has done glorious things; let this be known to all the world."

The Lord has done so much for me, there is a continuous praise to Him in my heart. I am so thankful He let me see and keeps me ever knowing that He is the one who has done so much for me. I know I can never praise Him enough for what He has done. I will continue to praise Him anyway.

The Lord is desirous and deserving of all praise. We should give Him thanks and let people know what He means to us.

We should sing His praises and make His presence known to all. Let them know that Jesus lives within in our hearts and we have a reason to sing.

When we have Christ we have everything to be thankful for in this life. He has won the victory and we are on His side. Because we are on His side we also have the victory.

Praise the Lord because you are saved. Praise Him always.

I praise the Lord because my parents taught me to love and serve God. I am thankful that I have taught my children to love God and serve Him. Above everything, I desire for my children to praise and serve the Lord with all of their hearts.

One of the most important things we can do is to let people see Christ in our lives. Let them see the marvelous things He has done for us and He will do the same for them. Continue to sing to the Lord. He is worthy of all praise.

DAILY PRAISES	**DAILY PRAYER REQUESTS**
1.	1.
2.	2.
3.	3.
4.	4.
5.	5.

April 4
Read Romans 8:28-39

Romans 8:28

"And we know that in all things God works for the good of those who love him, who have been called according to his purpose."

God is in charge of the universe, earth, country, and each individual. He is so immense, yet He is so intimate, that He knows each of us personally.

The grace of our Lord Jesus is sufficient to help us battle each trial that comes our way. With faith in Jesus, we can become what He has called us to be. We may not see the immediate results. Later on, however, we usually see why we were allowed a challenge.

God is the answer. Do not wait until troubles come to contact God. Keep a daily conversation going with Him. By praying and reading the Bible we will conform to be more like Him in a positive way. We can continue in love, faith, and holiness. ". . . . . .if God is for us, who can be against us" (Romans 8:31)

We have nothing to lose by putting our trust in Jesus. We have everything to gain. He is working all things out for our good and our glory. One of these days, maybe not until we get to Heaven, we will see and understand just where all of life's struggles fit into our life.

DAILY PRAISES	**DAILY PRAYER REQUESTS**
1.	1.
2.	2.
3.	3.
4.	4.
5.	5.

April 5
Read Ecclesiastes 7:1-14

Ecclesiastes 7:3

"Sorrow is better than laughter, because a sad face is good for the heart."

Godly sorrow causes us to repent and draw closer to God. It is sometimes necessary to feel the sorrow that Jesus felt. When we have unconfessed sin in our lives, we feel sad. We need to take care of the problem right then.

Peter wept bitterly with sorrow after denying Christ three times. (Matthew 26:75)

When we have repented through our sorrow, we begin to grow and use our mistakes as an aid to learn more about Christ and His will for our lives.

It is necessary to remove sorrow from our hearts, just as it is to remove evil from our physical being. We do this by calling out to God, asking for repentance. He will forgive and renew our spirit. We will be able to rejoice with our hearts lighter and better.

We cannot live with a sad heart continually. We must come back to reality after our sadness and enjoy life through Jesus.

DAILY PRAISES	DAILY PRAYER REQUESTS
1.	1.
2.	2.
3.	3.
4.	4.
5.	5.

April 6
Read Ephesians 4:17-32

Ephesians 4:30

"And do not grieve the Holy Spirit of God, with whom you were sealed for the day of redemption."

The Holy spirit is given to us as a helper and a comforter. He helps us to grow and mature. God allows us to grow in Christ a natural experience. If we stop growing, we are grieving the Holy Spirit by not allowing the complete will of God in our lives. We are responsible for the way we live. We will give an account to God of all unwholesome deeds, bitterness, and malice done in our lives. These things grieve the Holy Spirit. The

Holy Spirit is a person, for only a person can be grieved.

The work of the Holy Spirit brings changes to our lives. We have more faith and freedom. We have more power for prayer. We have more reasons for praising God. We are more aware of His working in our lives.

Let us continue to obey the Holy spirit until Christ returns to gather us to Heaven. Be careful that you do not do anything to grieve the precious Holy Spirit.

DAILY PRAISES	**DAILY PRAYER REQUESTS**
1.	1.
2.	2.
3.	3.
4.	4.
5.	5.

April 7
Read Hebrews 12:1-13

Hebrews 12:6

"Because the Lord disciplines those he loves, and he punishes everyone he accepts as a son."

The Lord corrects those He loves, just as a father or mother correct their natural children. If we are listening and regard the corrections of Jesus, He can deal with us as children.

We know that a reprimand is not a joyful thing, but painful and often embarrassing when administered. Afterwards, we can say that the reprimand taught us a lesson. We will grow and become faithful.

Just remember that we are rebuked because God loves us and desires that we walk in His will. He stands ready to accept our repentance. We have a tremendous promise if we endure. A home in Heaven is waiting. It will be worth much more than the reprimands or the rebukes we will receive on the way.

This life is so short and we are able to do so little for the Lord as we pass through. Let us be mindful of the love and care that Jesus has for us. Let us seek to serve Him in our fullest potential. When we fail or refuse to obey His will, God chastens us in order to correct our faults. Ask for forgiveness and go forward with new intentions and plans to do more for the Lord.

DAILY PRAISES	**DAILY PRAYER REQUESTS**
1.	1.
2.	2.
3.	3.
4.	4.
5.	5.

April 8
Read Philippians 2:12-18

Philippians 2:13

"For it is God who works in you to will and to act according to his good purpose."

God wants everyone to serve and praise Him, as they do His will. He gave each of us a mind of our own. He lets us make a choice as to whom we serve, as well as the various other choices of life we make daily. The choices we make without seeking God's will and guidance will prove to cause us a lot of pain and frustration. But the choices we make through prayer and after reading and seeking God's will and guidance are going to be satisfactory and prove smooth running.

God is working in each of our lives to perfect our imperfections. We are not sufficient in ourselves. Through Christ's guidance and knowledge, we can win the victory. We will be much happier knowing we are guided by the will of God. Our obedience cannot be separated from our faith in God. We will have peace if we trust Him as He directs us in major and minor decisions. He desires us to be happy and make the best choices possible. He is on our side.

DAILY PRAISES	**DAILY PRAYER REQUESTS**
1.	1.
2.	2.
3.	3.
4.	4.
5.	5.

April 9
Read I Peter 2:13-25

I Peter 2:21

"To this you were called, because Christ suffered for you, leaving an example, that you should follow in his steps."

Although Christ suffered for sinners, He arose again by the Spirit of God. We will suffer for Christ, but He will keep us by the spirit of the Holy Ghost.

We must deny ourselves and seek God's will for our lives. He is able to keep us in His will. God has promised us a home in Heaven, if we do His will and serve Him. However, He did not promise that we would be free from tribulation during our journey through this life. He promised to help us and give us victory on our road of life.

When tribulations come, remember we have the promise of God to deliver us and to help us reach Heaven. We must keep our eyes and our mind on Jesus. As we progress through these trials we look to Christ and plead the blood He shed for us on Calvary. Our sins are covered by His blood therefore we are under His care. He loves us. We can go to Him at any time.

DAILY PRAISES	**DAILY PRAYER REQUESTS**
1.	1.
2.	2.
3.	3.
4.	4.
5.	5.

April 10
Read Luke 6:27-36

Luke 6:32-33

"If you love those who love you, what credit is that to you? Even sinners love those who love them. And if you do good to those who are good to you, what credit is that to you? Even sinners do that."

Yes, it is easy to love and do good to the ones that love and do good things for you. Have you tried loving those who persecuted you or were mean to you? Have you done something good for the one who hates you? What about the one who tells lies about you? It is a test of true Christianity, if you can do good deeds for those who do bad things to us. We must show Christ through loving and doing good for evil. We are not as sinners who love only the ones that love them and can help them along in this world. We have to love everyone because Christ loved us as well as everyone else. We, as Christians, are made in His image and are striving to be like Him.

Today do something special for someone who has mistreated you or spoken evil about you. Show the love of Christ by loving your enemy and acting in faith toward winning them to Christ.

DAILY PRAISES	**DAILY PRAYER REQUESTS**
1.	1.
2.	2.
3.	3.
4.	4.
5.	5.

April 11
Read II Corinthians 12:1-10

II Corinthians 12:9

"But He said to me, 'My grace is sufficient for you, for my power is made perfect in weakness.' Therefore, I will boast all the more gladly about my weakness, so that Christ's power may rest on me."

When we have good health, use earthly wisdom, and are without trials or worries, we tend to depend upon ourselves. But when troubles come, we begin to call upon the Master for deliverance. His grace is sufficient in our strength or weaknesses. We must let Him be Lord of our lives when we are in the valley, as well as when we are on the mountain top.

Look for something good to come out of every trying time. Every trial helps us to grow in Christ. Each disappointment is a learning experience.

Let us give God the praise and glory for each trial as well as each mountain top experience. He is God in every experience of our life. So remember that He is God and desires us to allow Him to work in times of happiness and sadness. Put Him first in your life and let Him lead.

DAILY PRAISES	**DAILY PRAYER REQUESTS**
1.	1.
2.	2.
3.	3.
4.	4.
5.	5.

April 12
Read Job 13:13-25

Job 13:15

"Though He slay me, yet will I hope in Him; I will surely defend my ways to His face."

We will probably not have to suffer the many things that Job suffered, but we must be willing to suffer for Christ's sake.

We must be ready and able to take a stand for Christ. Even if it means our life or the life of a loved one. We must not give in to Satan.

God will be with us until the end. We should put our trust in Him. He will lead and guide us through all trials and troubles a He was with Job.

(Psalm 23:4) "Even though I walk through the valley of the shadow of death, I will fear no evil for you are with me; your rod and your staff, they comfort me."

Jesus has promised, He will never leave us or forsake us. Let us not leave Him out or forget about Him. His Word has promised He will always be there. His promises are true. Believe Him!

Call on Him for any reason. He cares about you. He will listen and help you.

DAILY PRAISES
1.
2.
3.
4.
5.

DAILY PRAYER REQUESTS
1.
2.
3.
4.
5.

April 13
Read II Corinthians 4:7-18

II Corinthians 4:16

"Therefore we do not lose heart. Though outwardly we are wasting away, yet inwardly we are being renewed day by day."

Sometimes we tend to give up when we have illness, trouble, or problems. That may be our human nature. The Spirit of God renews us if we will call on Him. He is ready and waiting to aid us in every situation. He wants us to come to Him in faith, believing that He is the answer.

The conditions around us may be hopeless, but we can have the peace of God inside and rest assured that He is renewing and refreshing us for our daily walk with Him.

When our eighteen-year-old daughter was killed, I was hurting and heartbroken, but I had the peace of God in my heart. I knew He was with me, helping me deal with our loss. I knew she was in Heaven, but I wasn't ready for her to be taken away. God knows best and knows what we can handle. He is always with us. We have to trust in Jesus.

DAILY PRAISES	**DAILY PRAYER REQUESTS**
1.	1.
2.	2.
3.	3.
4.	4.
5.	5.

April 14
Read Ephesians 3:7-13

Ephesians 3:10-11

"His intent was that now, through the church, the manifold wisdom of God should be made known to the rulers and authorities in the heavenly realm, according to his eternal purpose which he accomplished in Christ Jesus our Lord."

God has done the impossible by reconciling all humans to Him, if they will accept His grace. The church is observed by Christ and His angels. We are the church, if we have accepted Christ as our Savior.

God has given us such an opportunity to witness for Him. He prepared this beautiful earth and filled it with people, giving them wisdom and knowledge. God is the giver of all things. He allows us to do and have everything we claim as ours. He is the creator of all things. He gives the knowledge and lets people learn and invent.

God loves us so much that HE will not leave us or forsake us. He will not permit principalities or powers to separate us from Christ. We are the only one that can withdraw from God. But He will love us still. He is the kind of God that loves us with a love that is beyond all love. He is the only true God.

Let us take every opportunity to appreciate this earth and the inhabitants with whom we come in contact. Let us give people love so they will know we care, as we know the Heavenly Father cares, also.

DAILY PRAISES	**DAILY PRAYER REQUESTS**
1.	1.
2.	2.
3.	3.
4.	4.
5.	5.

April 15
Luke 15:1-10

Luke 15:10

"In the same way, I tell you, there is rejoicing in the presence of the angels of God over one sinner who repents."

Just imagine the rejoicing of the angels in Heaven when one soul is reborn! We should also be rejoicing when sinners repent. We should make every effort possible to speak positive words to new Christians and help them as they begin their walk with Christ. If they err or make mistakes we should help them get on the right track with love and teaching.

We have a responsibility to help others by encouraging and befriending them. This is especially important when troubles or sickness come. Troubles will come, as they do to each of us. Satan is not wanting to let go of his followers, so he will be after the new Christians. Let us lift up the new believers, just as we lift up those who are walking in faith.

Is there someone you can rejoice about today? Tell that new convert how happy you are that they have found the Lord. Tell Jesus how happy you are that another soul has been saved from hell.

Listen, strengthen, encourage, and praise those who are new to the faith and new to the church. You can be a leader and a light to them.

DAILY PRAISES	**DAILY PRAYER REQUESTS**
1.	1.
2.	2.
3.	3.
4.	4.
5.	5.

April 16
Read Revelation 21:1-14

Revelation 21:4

"He will wipe every tear from their eyes. There will be no more death or mourning or crying or pain, for the old order of things has passed away."

Praise the Lord for promises like this! How many times each day do you have disappointments or pain or sorrow? Can you imagine being without pain, sorrow, or disappointment? We have this promise from God, that there is a place prepared for those who love the Lord and who have accepted His plan for salvation. After we have passed from this life to Heaven, we will be free of sickness, hunger, troubles, tears, sins, pain, death or strife.

In Heaven we will be able to eat of the Tree of Life, drink of the Water of Life, praise God, reign with Christ, have peace, have perfect rest, sing a new song and be filled with the glory of God. Heaven is so much more than we, humans, can imagine or comprehend. But I know and understand enough, that I have a desire to go there. I long to see my Savior, who gave His life to save me. I want to meet my loved ones again. I want everyone to go to Heaven. Are you curious about Heaven? Are you ready to go there? I pray that the Lord will open your eyes and give you a desire to serve Him and ultimately reach Heaven when this life is over.

DAILY PRAISES	**DAILY PRAYER REQUESTS**
1.	1.
2.	2.
3.	3.
4.	4.
5.	5.

April 17
Read I Peter 1:3-12

I Peter 1:4

"and into an inheritance that can never perish, spoil, or fade--kept in heaven for you,"

Is your inheritance reserved in Heaven? Being saved is the down payment on your reservation in heaven. Believers are born again, not only to a hope, but also to the inheritance that is eternal.

No sin can enter Heaven, because Heaven is undefiled. It is a pure and holy place. It will be faultless. Oh, what a wonderful picture of Heaven we paint in our minds as we think of the streets of gold and the gates of pearls and all the gemstones there. But Heaven will be more that we can imagine.

It is the heritage for all who will come. Christ died for all people. All people are invited to Heaven. Let those desiring to inherit an incorruptible and undefiled land, ask for their sins to be forgiven and begin to serve God today. Salvation is for everyone who is willing to serve Christ. We will have Christ with us in this life to help us, but we will also have Him with us in our home in Heaven after this life.

Don't you want to go?

DAILY PRAISES	**DAILY PRAYER REQUESTS**
1.	1.
2.	2.
3.	3.
4.	4.
5.	5.

April 18
Read Matthew 18:10-14

Matthew 18:11

"For the Son of Man came to save that which was lost."

God's purpose in sending His Son to the earth was that souls may be saved. There was no other purpose for the life and death and resurrection of Jesus except to show the love of God. God wanted everyone to be saved. He wants all of us to fellowship with Him.

I cannot imagine anyone loving me enough to die for me; but Jesus did. He loves us so much. He wants us to spend eternity with Him. He doesn't want anyone to go to Hell with the devil. Hell was prepared for Satan and his angels after they rebelled against God.

All Jesus wants is for you to give your heart to Him and serve Him. Serve means to put Him first in your life and honor and obey His word. You can be His child by asking Him into your heart and walking with Him as He leads. He wants your praise, your honor, and your glory. Will you serve the Lord today? Will you let Him be the leader of your life?

DAILY PRAISES	**DAILY PRAYER REQUESTS**
1.	1.
2.	2.
3.	3.
4.	4.
5.	5.

April 19
Luke 17:1-10

Luke 17:4

"If he sins against you seven times in a day, and seven times comes back to you and says, 'I repent,' forgive him."

We must exercise forgiveness in small things as well s large things. Forgiveness is to be extended as long as it is needed and sought. There is never a point at which the believer should refuse to forgive. It is so much better to forgive and have the peace that comes from putting all things behind us rather than carry a grudge and an attitude of forgiveness.

In Matthew 18:22 Jesus took the two perfect numbers, ten and seven, and multiplied them by seven more (seventy times seven). The sum is not intended to be four hundred ninety, but it signifies an endlessness number of times to forgive. Forgiveness is forever and always available. Forgiveness is unlimited.

We must never take advantage of the mercy of God. Every individual needs to understand that he will answer to God for his conduct. He will be judged on the merits of his own deeds. That is why we need to walk close to the Lord and maintain a right relationship in dealing with others as well as our relationship with Jesus. Helping and forgiving others ought to be a way of life for every believer.

If we fail to forgive, it will alter our relationship with the Lord. An unforgiving attitude closes God out of our lives. We must be willing to sincerely forgive. Do you readily forgive others? According to the Bible we must be willing and eager to forgive.

DAILY PRAISES	**DAILY PRAYER REQUESTS**
1.	1.
2.	2.
3.	3.
4.	4.
5.	5.

April 20
Read Matthew 5:1-12

Matthew 5:10

"Blessed are those who are persecuted because of righteousness, for theirs is the kingdom of heaven."

Christ never knew sin, yet He was persecuted and suffered for our sins. Man is not perfect; therefore, we will also suffer persecution of some kind for the sake of Christ.

We are to be courageous Christians and not be afraid to suffer. Christ is sufficient and will supply every need. He will make a way for our deliverance, if we are faithful and trust in Him with unerring faith.

People suffer through fear, affliction, persecution, rejection, and defeat. But God is greater than evil. We only need to look to Christ and ask Him for His will in our lives. We need to commit our suffering to Christ. Faith in Christ will help us overcome our problems. Jesus will carry us through every difficult circumstance.

Resist the devil and he will flee from you. Do not be intimidated by Satan. He has already been defeated at Calvary. Look to Jesus Christ and do not fear.

We defeat Satan by using the Word of God on him when he comes to tempt us. Jesus used the Word to defeat the devil. We must be sure that we can also use Scripture to gain the victory. We belong to Christ. He paid the price for us. Let us realize who we are and that we do have authority over the enemy. Use the Word in the Name of Jesus.

DAILY PRAISES
1.
2.
3.
4.
5.

DAILY PRAYER REQUESTS
1.
2.
3.
4.
5.

April 21
Read Psalm 119:9-16

Psalm 119:11

"I have hidden your word in my heart, that I might not sin against you."

By prayerful meditation on God's Word we can obtain purity and perfection. Obedience of the Word will bring cleansing from sin. The Word of God brings us into conformity with God's will. God gives us the strength and grace to obey His Word when we have the desire to do so.

Young people may be especially vulnerable to sin because of a lack of knowledge and experience. They need to read the Bible to be cleansed and kept from going astray. It is best to teach our children to obey God's Word while they are young. When they grow older they will know about living a Christian life for the Lord.

Those of us who are more mature should teach the cleansing power of the Bible by our example of holy living in obedience to God's Word.

There is protection against sin if we seek God with a sincere heart. Pray that God will keep and preserve us from wandering away from God's commandments. Seek God's will in your life.

We never graduate from God's Word. As long as we live we need to receive more and more of the Word of God. We need to write it on our hearts and hide it there like a precious jewel. Because it truly is a special treasure.

Determine to spend more time reading and studying God's Word. It will cause you to grow and mature.

DAILY PRAISES **DAILY PRAYER REQUESTS**

1. 1.

2. 2.

3. 3.

4. 4.

5. 5.

April 22
Read John 3:1-21

John 3:16

"For God so loved the world that he gave his one and only Son, that whoever believes in him shall not perish but have eternal life."

Much emphasis is given in the Bible about personal relationships between our Lord and others. In John four, the woman at the well; in John three, there is Nicodemus; and in Luke nineteen, Zacchaeus underscores three basic needs of humans recognized by Jesus. These needs are:

1. The need for recognition and identity.
   A. Jesus used the person's name.
   B. He perceived a special skill or talent.
2. The need to be wanted.
3. The need to be needed.

The magic of Jesus' love is that He recognized each of us as an individual by knowing our names and our talents. He said even the hairs of our heads are numbered. He makes us feel like we are somebody special. We really are special to Jesus. We are wanted and needed in God's Kingdom. We are unique and precious individuals in His sight. He loves us all so much that He personally calls us to come unto Him. He loves us in spite of our weaknesses. We are called to love Jesus as Jesus loves us. Let us show our love to the world as Jesus has shown His love to us and as we have accepted His love.

DAILY PRAISES	**DAILY PRAYER REQUESTS**
1.	1.
2.	2.
3.	3.
4.	4.
5.	5.

April 23
Read John 13:1-14

John 14:1

"Do not let your heart be troubled. Trust in God, trust also in me."

What security we have by believing in God and His Son, Jesus Christ! Because we believe in Him, He will deliver us and save us when trouble comes, as well as from temptations.

Because we believe and have been cleansed by the blood of Jesus, we are looking for His return to transfer the Christians from this earth to Heaven. God gave His Son that we might have eternal life. It is for as many as will accept it. If we have Jesus living in us, we have eternal life.

We have to live in the world until Christ returns, but we do not have to be part of the world. As we see morals sinking to a lower level than ever before, it must not overwhelm us. The Bible tells us the last days will be as they were in the days of Noah and of Lot.

We must hurry and become more like Jesus. The time to prepare is short. We need to keep our eyes on Jesus and look for His soon return to Rapture the church away.

Are you ready to go in the Rapture if it takes place today? You do not have to worry or fret. You can be secure about your future.

Jesus is not a crutch but a valid way of life. There is peace and joy in living for Christ.

DAILY PRAISES					**DAILY PRAYER REQUESTS**
1.							1.
2.							2.
3.							3.
4.							4.
5.							5.

April 24
Read Proverbs 20: 3-10

Proverbs 20:5

"the purposes of a man's heart are deep waters, but a man of understanding draws them out."

We should always seek counsel from our Savior and keep our hearts full of guidance. Many times I get so excited about something that I go ahead of my Lord. I do not take the time to seek His counsel and find out if it is what He wants me to do at the time. I have to go back and ask for forgiveness and ask the Lord to lead, guide, and direct my path in all that He would have me to do.

Lord, help me to stay in your will, by seeking your counsel first and having it in my heart to draw out. Help me to seek your guidance before I begin my direction. I earnestly desire to be led by you. I often let self get in the way and motivate me. Help me to follow your direction instead of my own. You are a well of living water to which I can go and get the help I need.

Lord, keep me humble, realizing all things come from you and you are in control. Help me to know that I can draw from your counsel and you will give me understanding.

Thank you, Lord, for counsel, understanding, and guidance.

DAILY PRAISES	**DAILY PRAYER REQUESTS**
1.	1.
2.	2.
3.	3.
4.	4.
5.	5.

April 25
Read Psalm 66

Psalm 66:18-19

"If I had cherished sin in my heart, the Lord would not have listened; but God has surely listened and heard my voice in prayer."

It is important that we ask for forgiveness every day. Jesus wants us to serve Him and we must serve Him with all our heart, which means being renewed daily. Our prayers should be from our heart that has been forgiven and free from known sin, if we expect to get our prayers answered. God wants us to be dedicated to Him.

Do not be ashamed to confess your unknown sins as well as those you know. The Lord is waiting to hear from you and forgive you.

Ask others for forgiveness, as well as Christ. It is a peaceful feeling to be forgiven and have nothing to hide. We must not have wrong attitudes, bad thoughts, not be filled with pride, not have wrong priorities, or reactions that are unlike our Lord. We just cannot keep those thing in our mind and please God.

God is waiting for us to ask for forgiveness for our sins which are so easily hidden. He is just. He only wants to forgive. He wants us to ask Him in communication with Him. When we forgive people and are forgiven, our prayers will reach the Lord and be answered.

DAILY PRAISES	**DAILY PRAYER REQUESTS**
1.	1.
2.	2.
3.	3.
4.	4.
5.	5.

April 26
Read Luke 17:1-10

Luke 17:6

"He replied, 'If you have faith as small as a mustard seed, you can say to this mulberry tree, 'Be uprooted and planted in the sea,' and it will obey you.'"

How is your faith? How much faith do you have? In order for our faith to work, we must commit to God, our hearts and minds. Our total person must be led by His Spirit. We must walk and talk in faith. Exercise faith in small things as well as large things. Faith grows in a climate of love.

Ask in faith according to the Word of God. Be obedient to God and abide in Him. Faith is also a gift to be received for certain needs. Anyone can have the gift of faith operating in them by being obedient and believing God.

Pray, hold fast, and make progress in building up your faith. Unbelief limits God. How sad to think that we would limit the working of God. The more we are filled with the Spirit of God, the more faith is active in our lives. Continue in faith. Build and act on it. Faith is available to all who will receive and believe.

Faith that is bathed in prayer, will have much success. Faith can remove the problems that hinder us from our work in the Kingdom of God.

DAILY PRAISES   **DAILY PRAYER REQUESTS**
1.   1.

2.   2.

3.   3.

4.   4.

5.   5.

April 27
Read Luke 17:10-37

Luke 17:33

"Whoever tries to keep his life will lose it, and whoever loses his life will preserve it."

We must deny our selfish nature to walk with Jesus. We should seek to satisfy Jesus as He tells us instead of our earthly desires. This fleshly body will die and return to dust, but the spiritual soul will live forever. If we deny self and take the cross of Jesus and follow Him we are preserving our life forever.

If we seek to satisfy self, we will die and not have eternal life. This life is so short and eternity is forever. This is an alarming thought! Just think of FOREVER! It is such a small thing to give your life to Jesus and live forever with Him in eternity. Just think of the consequences involved in satisfying yourself rather than making Jesus your Lord. Is the other choice, being away from Jesus love forever, worth it?

You can lose your life in this world for a home in Heaven, throughout all eternity. That is a marvelous thought. Come to Christ today, let Him forgive you of all your sins and live in your heart as you serve Him. Deny yourself of those selfish things and satisfy your Savior by living a life filled with the Spirit and following the teachings of Jesus. It is a good life, living with Jesus in your heart. We will not be denied those things that are best for us when we serve Christ. He meets our needs. He is a loving, caring Father.

DAILY PRAISES	**DAILY PRAYER REQUESTS**
1.	1.
2.	2.
3.	3.
4.	4.
5.	5.

April 28
Read Romans 2:1-16

Romans 2:4

"Or do you show contempt for the riches of his kingdom, tolerance and patience, not realizing that God's kindness leads you toward repentance."

Oh, how good God is! Just think of all the sins He has forgiven. He will never remind us or accuse us of those sins again. He has cast them far away from us, as far as the East is from the West. That is a wonderful feeling, to know all is forgiven and you will not be punished for those sins.

God is so merciful and longsuffering toward us. I prayed for my husband to be saved for twenty years. I was not always as close to God as I should have been, but God was merciful and compassionate. I praise Him for answering prayers, because today my husband is a wonderful Christian and witness for the Lord.

Yes, God in His love will suffer with us. He will help us fight. Together we will share the joy and victory of our merciful God. His purpose in kindness is to give us an opportunity to repent.

DAILY PRAISES	**DAILY PRAYER REQUESTS**
1.	1.
2.	2.
3.	3.
4.	4.
5.	5.

April 29
Read Matthew 4:18-25

Matthew 4:23

"Jesus went throughout Galilee, teaching in their synagogues, preaching the good news of the kingdom, and healing every disease and sickness among the people."

There is a great difference in having fun and being happy. Pleasure is merely external. Happiness is an internal feeling and satisfaction. Money and position do not guarantee happiness. Real happiness comes when we accept Jesus Christ and let Him be the Lord of our life.

Jesus found many people eager to hear His message and receive His blessings. The message of Jesus was three fold:

1. Preaching
2. Teaching
3. Healing.

His message was the truth about God. He spoke of absolutes and uncertainties. He sought to correct any misunderstandings, misinterpretations, or wrong conclusions about truth. He told the people the truth, then turned the truth into deeds by healing and meeting the needs of the people. No other person has ever offered so much to humanity as Jesus offers. He is the ultimate fulfillment of humanity's needs. Jesus offers life on the highest plane. Let Him give you that life today.

DAILY PRAISES	**DAILY PRAYER REQUESTS**
1.	1.
2.	2.
3.	3.
4.	4.
5.	5.

April 30
Read I Corinthians 14:1-17

I Corinthians 14:1

"Follow the way of love and eagerly desire spiritual gifts, especially the gift of prophecy."

It is so important to love one another. It is easier to love some people more than others. We often find conflicts with our ideas and goals. We can love in spite of those differences.

God made each of us unique. No two are alike. We can find a common ground of love. Because Jesus loved us all enough to give His life for each one, we are obligated to love each other.

For the good of the church, we are to show love. How can a church prosper if there is hate and backbiting in the congregation? We are to build up the church. Love is the way to build for Jesus. When we love as Jesus directed us, we will have spiritual gifts and be able to grow the church.

The gift of prophecy comes by loving God, others, and the church. If the gift of prophecy is received it will edify the church and the people of the church.

God is love and He communicated His love to us and commands us to love one another. Love supersedes all the other gifts because it will outlast them all. Love will be the governing principle that controls all that God and His redeemed people are and what they do.

DAILY PRAISES	**DAILY PRAYER REQUESTS**
1.	1.
2.	2.
3.	3.
4.	4.
5.	5.

MAY

May 1
Read Romans 12:9-21

Romans 12:12

"Be joyful in hope, patient in affliction, faithful in prayer."

Are you waiting for a prayer to be answered? Do not give up. Keep holding on in faith. We are to be patient, as God is patient with us, His children. If we have prayed according to His will and are living by His Word, we have the promise, if we are patient and persevere. The answer may not be what we wish, but it will be God's will. He knows what is best for us.

God's timing is perfect. He knows exactly the moment to work. We are to watch and pray, waiting for the Lord to answer our prayers. If we give up, what hope have we? Let us endure with patience because our very soul depends upon it.

Let us strive to have patience as God has. Just think of the patience God had when dealing with the Israelites, as well as the people of today. He deals with sinners patiently, as He waits for them to come to Him. Possibly He is delaying His second coming, because of His patience with people. God will give us Christ like patience if we ask in faith. He will give us patience to endure trials and temptations in this present life.

Seek patience from God. In learning patience, we will grow and mature beyond our greatest expectations. We may encounter many trials, but we have the Holy Spirit to help us overcome those trials.

DAILY PRAISES　　　　　　**DAILY PRAYER REQUESTS**

1.　　　　　　　　　　　　1.

2.　　　　　　　　　　　　2.

3.　　　　　　　　　　　　3.

4.　　　　　　　　　　　　4.

5.　　　　　　　　　　　　5.

May 2
Read Luke 9:57-62

Luke 9:58

"Jesus replied, "Foxes have holes and birds of the air have nests, but the Son of Man has no place to lay his head."

Jesus was hated and persecuted when He walked on earth. Some people are still treating Him with the same hate today. Is He King and Lord of your life or are you persecuting and Hating Him by not allowing Him into your heart?

If you have not committed your life to Christ, you are persecuting Him. Why do you neglect Jesus, who gave His life for you? Is it because you are stubborn? Are you strong willed and want your will and your way rather than Jesus' way? Are you just slacking, concerning your future? Do you just not care about Jesus? Maybe you are too sensually oriented to give your life to Jesus. Are you just seeking to satisfy yourself for the time being and have made no future plans for eternity?

Why not make a home for Jesus in your heart today? It will be filled with rewards on this earth as well as the rewards which are to come in Heaven.

Jesus has prepared a Heavenly Home for us, if we will accept Him. We will be with Him in that new Home. Please, come and go along to that Mansion in Heaven. Follow Him regardless of the price. It will be well worth everything you give up for Jesus.

DAILY PRAISES	**DAILY PRAYER REQUESTS**
1.	1.
2.	2.
3.	3.
4.	4.
5.	5.

May 3
Read II Corinthians 4:1-18

II Corinthians 4:8-9

"We are hard pressed on every side, but not crushed; perplexed, but not in despair; persecuted, but not abandoned; struck down, but not destroyed."

There are times when our human bodies and spirits are filled with pain and persecution. We feel like we have reached our limit and can't go on, but God is always there to comfort and help us recover. What a wonderful God He is! Although we would fall and fail on our own, He is there to catch us and lift us up above our troubles.

When burdens seem unbearable, God is always there. We only have to cast our cares on Him and let Him carry those burdens. He is everywhere. He is Lord over all. He is ready to refresh and renew us when we are closed in with trouble. He speaks to us in the midst of despair, like a wave of fresh air. He will help us to be victorious in times when we feel forsaken.

We have chosen to be on God's side and He will fight for us and help us win the battle. There is no need to be depressed or to feel forsaken, because God is with us. He will help us. He will fight for us. He has given us the Holy Spirit to accompany us in all our troubles. We do not have to be destroyed or put down by the enemy. We are owners of VICTORY through Jesus!

DAILY PRAISES	**DAILY PRAYER REQUESTS**
1.	1.
2.	2.
3.	3.
4.	4.
5.	5.

May 4
Read II Timothy 1:3-14

II Timothy 1:12

"That is why I am suffering as I am. Yet I am not ashamed, because I know whom I have believed, and am convinced that he is able to guard what I have entrusted to him for that day."

I am not ashamed of Christ. Even if it means suffering for Him, I will not be ashamed because He is with me through every persecution. I do not understand the reason for all suffering, trials, or temptations, but it is not for me to reason why. It is for me to KNOW that God is able to deliver and bring me through every adversity. He is able to guide and lead me and my family, if we let Him. We must have faith that God will keep us and help us to be over comers.

Commit all your burdens and problems to the Lord. He is able to bear you up through them all. He wants you to leave your cares with Him. He is our answer in times of trouble as well as all the time. Let god have your problems. He will work through them with you. Just live for Him and be willing to trust Him to lead you.

From the beginning of time God had a plan for saving people. That plan was Salvation through Jesus Christ His Son who died on an old rugged cross to redeem everyone from their sins. That plan is still in effect today. It is through the blood of Christ that we can have Salvation and be healed as well as all other needs met.

DAILY PRAISES
1.
2.
3.
4.
5.

DAILY PRAYER REQUESTS
1.
2.
3.
4.
5.

May 5
Read Matthew 16:21-28

Matthew 16:24-25

Jesus said to his disciples, "If anyone would come after me, he must deny himself and take up his cross and follow me. For whoever wants to save his life will lose it, but whoever loses his life for me will find it."

We must be dedicated to serving the Lord. We must love with our entire hearts, souls, and minds. It is important to deny ourselves daily and praise and glorify God. We are to be a witness to the unsaved of the world.

We are to have a determined mind and not be tossed to and fro as a wave upon the sea. We are to sail steadily on life's sea, if it is rough or smooth. We are to be the same, relying on Jesus as we carry His cross. Regardless of the circumstances, we are to follow Him, as He leads us.

Every Christian should read the Bible and study to learn more about God and His plan for their lives. It is a powerful tool in guiding us as we follow Christ.

Our obligation is to take care of ourselves and not be a busybody and interfere in other people's business. We must maintain self-control in our lives. In doing these things we will be denying our wishes and fulfilling the wishes of Jesus.

Our material possessions must be dedicated to the Lord. Everything that we possess comes from God. We are to share with others as well as give a tenth to the Lord.

DAILY PRAISES   **DAILY PRAYER REQUESTS**
1.   1.

2.   2.

3.   3.

4.   4.

5.   5.

May 6
Read II Timothy 2:1-13

II Timothy 2:10

"Therefore, I endure everything for the sake of the elect, that they too may obtain the salvation that is in Christ Jesus, with eternal glory."

We must identify with Christ. If we identify with Him in life, we will be assured of identification with Him through death. We must choose Christ and continue with Him through suffering and rejoicing.

Make a choice to serve God and continue to walk with Him. If we share His cross and suffering, someday we will share His crown and glory. We will be united in Heaven and live with Him. Oh, what a glorious thought!

By confessing Christ before the people of this world, He will confess us before God and His angels in Heaven. How exciting, to be claimed as Heaven's own.

There is no suffering too great to bring about the salvation of God's people. There are those who will yet believe and come to God because of the light you shine in this dark world.

Let us love one another and encourage each other. Let us serve Christ together, through determination, working, suffering, praising and honoring Him above everything. It is worth it all to live a Christian life. God can supply all our needs if we stay in tune with Him as the Bible directs.

DAILY PRAISES	**DAILY PRAYER REQUESTS**
1.	1.
2.	2.
3.	3.
4.	4.
5.	5.

May 7
Read Proverbs 10:11-24

Proverbs 10:12

"Hatred stirs up dissension, but love covers all wrongs."

We are new creatures in Christ. We are for Christ and walk like He taught us. We are royal, holy, and special because we are His children. He loved us so much He gave His life for us. He came in love and love covers all sins. He took our sins on the cross at Calvary, so we could confess them and be saved.

We are continuously commanded, in the Bible, to love one another. We are to love our neighbors as ourselves. Through our showing love, we are to be the light of the lost world.

To know Jesus is to have life. Eternal Life! Allow Jesus to love you. Begin to grow and bloom through love. All things are possible through love. Let love show through you. Love will cover all wrongs and promotes forgiveness.

DAILY PRAISES	**DAILY PRAYER REQUESTS**
1.	1.
2.	2.
3.	3.
4.	4.
5.	5.

May 8
Read Philippians 1:12-26

Philippians 1:20

"I eagerly expect and hope that I will in no way be ashamed, but will have sufficient courage so that now as always Christ will be exalted in my body, whether by life or by death."

We should be proud to be Christians. We need to stand for God. If we do not have boldness, pray for God to give you that boldness to witness for Him. We may not be in prison, as Paul was when he wrote about not being ashamed to be a Christian. Where ever we are we are to stand boldly for Christ.

We need to make Christ larger in our lives. We belong to God. We have a responsibility to pray for one another as we serve Christ together. We should strive to keep every promise that we have been given by the Lord. We should be willing to do the will of God unequivocally. When we follow Jesus Christ we will not be lead astray by false doctrines. Let us keep our eyes on Christ and not on ourselves or others.

Be holy and trust Jesus. Heaven is going to be wonderful. We will have more of Christ after death than we have now. Let us concentrate on the good that is yet to come. Let us relax and enjoy what we now have in this life. We are the product of the Lord. Let us praise Him and rejoice.

DAILY PRAISES	**DAILY PRAYER REQUESTS**
1.	1.
2.	2.
3.	3.
4.	4.
5.	5.

May 9
Read Acts 2:1-13

Acts 2:4

"All of them were filled with the Holy Spirit and began to speak in other tongues as the Spirit enabled them."

The tongue is the hardest part of the body to tame and control. When we allow God to come into our lives and fill us with the Holy Spirit, He takes control of our tongue and speaks through it, as a symbol that we have submitted our will to god and are willing to let Him lead and guide us.

We cannot buy the Holy Spirit. Neither can we bargain with Gods for Him. Those who love God and accept Him and keep His commandments are filled with the Holy Spirit. He is a Comforter, sent to us as Jesus promised.

We are speaking directly to God when we are praying in the Holy Spirit. The devil cannot interfere with our prayers in the Spirit. The devil cannot delay our prayers to our Heavenly Father.

Praise God for the joy of the Holy Spirit! Accept Him as you accept Jesus. Let the Holy Spirit lead you in faith. Believe that God will reward those who diligently seek Him. Yield your body and soul to Jesus along with your mind and tongue. Just keep praising God for sending Jesus and the Holy Spirit.

DAILY PRAISES	**DAILY PRAYER REQUESTS**
1.	1.
2.	2.
3.	3.
4.	4.
5.	5.

May 10
Read Luke 6:27-36

Luke 6:27

"But I tell you who hear me: Love your enemies, do good to those who hate you."

When we have Jesus in our lives we can pray for those who do us wrong. We are told repeatedly in the Bible to do good for evil. As we do good for evil we are winning souls to Christ for they will not be able to withstand the good we do in return for their evil deeds.

Non-Christians often persecute Christians out of ignorance. They have not learned the Word of God and it is our duty to minister to them. We must forgive them and ask God to help in their ignorance.

Each time we do good for evil we will be blessed by the Lord. For we are His children and we are following His commandments. As long as we are doing His will, we are living by His promises.

All things are possible through Christ. He will answer prayer. Speak to Him and wait upon Him for the answer. That boss or those fellow workers or neighbors who have been giving you a hard time, because of Christ, can be won to Him through love. Give them words of love at every opportunity. Give them some small token of love. Take them to lunch or for a coffee break. Get to know them better. Learn why they are persecuting Christ through you. As you minister to those people and continue asking God to give them to you as souls in the Kingdom of God, He will answer the prayer. He will meet the need. Praise Him for answering.

DAILY PRAISES	**DAILY PRAYER REQUESTS**
1.	1.
2.	2.
3.	3.
4.	4.
5.	5.

May 11
Read Hebrews 11:11-28

Hebrews 11:25

"He chose to be mistreated along with the people of God rather to enjoy the pleasures of sin for a short time."

Moses chose to suffer with the Israelites rather than enjoy the lustful pleasures of this earth. We, like Moses, must choose whom we will serve. We can only serve one master. We either serve God or Satan. When we serve Satan we know it will only last for a little while and we will have eternal punishment as a consequence if we do not repent.

When we serve God, we know that we have a life of eternal bliss in Heaven with Jesus Christ. We will have happiness and joy forever. We may have to suffer on this earth for God's cause, but it will be worth everything to gain a home in Heaven.

When we do suffer for the Lord, He is right there with us. With our hand holding onto His we will make it by following His leading. He is the best companion we could ever hope to have.

DAILY PRAISES	**DAILY PRAYER REQUESTS**
1.	1.
2.	2.
3.	3.
4.	4.
5.	5.

May 12
Read Romans 5:1-11

Romans 5:3-4

"Not only so, but we also rejoice in our sufferings, because we know that suffering produces perseverance; perseverance, character; and character, hope."

How much better we perform when we have gained experience! Sometimes experience is earned the hard way. We gain experience through trial and error. Often we make incorrect decisions and suffer the consequences. All of this is gaining experience for the future.

We are to be happy as we walk through this life of tribulations and trials, because we are experiencing growth and maturity. To grow and mature we will suffer somewhat. We know that Jesus suffered while He walked on this earth and if we walk with Him we will also suffer. Let the Holy Spirit be your comforter during suffering. The Holy Spirit was given to us as a comforter and guide. We can have grace and peace as we experience trials and tribulations because we are filled with the Holy Spirit. Through faith in God we will be able to stand against all the troubles and pain that come our way.

DAILY PRAISES	**DAILY PRAYER REQUESTS**
1.	1.
2.	2.
3.	3.
4.	4.
5.	5.

May 13
Read Ephesians 3:14-21

Ephesians 3:19

"And to know this love that surpasses knowledge-that you may be filled to the measure of all the fullness of God."

Do you personally know the love of God? God loves us so much; He gave His Son to die for our sins. He died so that we could live forever with Him, when we repent of sins and accept Jesus, we have life eternally with Him.

There is so much God desires to do for us, if we only turn our lives over to Him. Our strong wills have to be turned over to God to let Him lead and guide us. He desires to give us love, peace, truth, joy, grace, forgiveness, knowledge, a host of other things as well as a Home in Heaven.

We can be filled with His goodness and fullness if we will meditate and read His Word as we pray daily. We can be a witness for Him wherever we are. Let the love of God shine through you.

We are living beneath our privilege in God. He wants so much for us and we do not reach our potential through Him. Let us love the world through Him. God loves everyone and He needs us to show His love wherever we are.

DAILY PRAISES	**DAILY PRAYER REQUESTS**
1.	1.
2.	2.
3.	3.
4.	4.
5.	5.

May 14
Read Matthew 17:14-23

Matthew 17:20-21

"He replied, 'Because you have so little faith, I tell you the truth, if you have faith as small as a mustard seed, you can say to this mountain, 'move from here to there' and it will move. Nothing will be impossible for you."

The disciples were unable to cast a demon out of a young man and Jesus did it. Jesus instructed the disciples on their faith. They failed to work a miracle because of unbelief.

There is no reason for unbelief. Jesus came to die for us. He paid the price, we believe Him. We can have faith through trusting Him. He is there to increase our faith. What is holding our faith back? We need to step out in faith. Faith will work a miracle for us.

A faith that is bathed in prayer will be able to remove great difficulties from our lives. All things are possible if we only believe in faith through Jesus Christ.

We will be able to do so much if we will only believe God's word and pray as we believe. The things which we are praying for can be a reality through faith. Believe when you pray.

DAILY PRAISES   **DAILY PRAYER REQUESTS**
1.   1.

2.   2.

3.   3.

4.   4.

5.   5.

May 15
Read Matthew 16:21-28

Matthew 16:27

"For the Son of Man is going to come in his Father's glory with his angels, and then he will reward each person according to what he has done."

We are looking for the soon return of Jesus to gather His children Home. It will be a glorious day for all those who have accepted Jesus and have Him in their hearts, minds, and souls. When we give ourselves to the Lord completely, He will add all the things we need to live a contented life. It is important to put Jesus first.

One day we will stand before Him at the judgment of God. He will reward us according to what we have done for the glory of God. If we have accepted Jesus, the blood of Jesus has covered our sins. We are pardoned and will get our reward for the work toward the Kingdom of Heaven.

This is the time to glorify god by helping to win souls. We can win souls by ministering to the sick, the aged, the heartbroken, and the less fortunate.

For those unsaved, everything is lost at death. That is everything that was or is good. What a wasted life to spend it serving self or Satan. Life is not the end. There will be life for all eternity somewhere. Why not prepare for Heaven while there is time?

DAILY PRAISES
1.
2.
3.
4.
5.

DAILY PRAYER REQUESTS
1.
2.
3.
4.
5.

May 16
Read Matthew 18:1-9

Matthew 18:3

"And he said, "I tell you the truth, unless you change and become like little children, you will never enter the kingdom of heaven."

We have all watched children play together. Sometimes they get mad, but in a few minutes it is over. They have forgotten and forgiven each other. They are ready to resume play. They refuse to remember what each other said or what they did. They are so trusting and unpretentious. Jesus tells us to be like these little children, by forgiving and forgetting those who have sinned against us. As bad as it hurts, we have to do what the Bible says.

It is not wise to glory in our own accomplishments, but glorify the Lord for the accomplishments that come through Him. God gives grace to the humble, but He resists the proud, according to James 4:6. If we are like the children we will not have an attitude of, 'I'm better than you'.

We can't do things through strife or vain glory, but in love and caring. In due time, we will receive our reward for humbling ourselves, like children, before God. We should be willing to allow Jesus to lead and guide us as little children. We are just like His little children. We are ever growing and learning from Him. He is our Father and we can trust Him to lead us in the right path. Just trust Him.

DAILY PRAISES
1.
2.
3.
4.
5.

DAILY PRAYER REQUESTS
1.
2.
3.
4.
5.

May 17
Read Luke 16:1-15

Luke 16:13

"No servant can serve two masters. Either he will hate the one and love the other, or he will be devoted to the one and despise the other. You cannot serve both God and Money."

We all have a master. Who is your master? Whom do you serve today?

Take an inventory of your life. Do you spend your time pleasing other people, yourself, or pleasing God? If you please others or yourself, you probably aren't pleasing God as your Master. If you love the world and the things in the world more than God or desire the things in the world more than you desire to go to church or serve God, you are missing the mark. According to the Bible we are to love God and desire to do His will. We are to assemble together with others who believe and be filled with refreshing so we can go forward and encourage others to be refreshed.

We were created to serve God. We are to let Him be our Master. If we serve Him we will not be disappointed in the end. This world and the things which seem so important will eventually pass away. But we will have life eternal, by serving God.

Be rewarded with Christ today. Let Him be your Master. He will take care of you and your every need. He will give peace and comfort that the world cannot provide.

DAILY PRAISES	**DAILY PRAYER REQUESTS**
1.	1.
2.	2.
3.	3.
4.	4.
5.	5.

May 18
Read Luke 15:11-32

Luke 15:20

"So he got up and went to his father. But while he was still a long way off, his father saw him and was filled with compassion for him; he ran to his own son, threw his arms around him and kissed him."

This parable is such a good example to apply to parents and children as well as to God and humans.

We love our children so much, but God loves them more. We will always have a home for our children to dome and go and stay with us. God has prepared a way for us to come to Him. He has prepared a Heaven for all who will come and stay with Him forever.

We want to hear from our children when they are away from home. God wants to hear from us. He is waiting for us to call Him and talk about our concerns.

We love to give our children gifts. God loves to give His children the best He has. He gave His Son, Jesus for us. Therefore, we can have our sins forgiven through the blood of Jesus. God blesses us with material wealth as well as spiritual blessings. He continues to give us gifts. The best gift is waiting for us in Heaven when we shall see the Lord.

We are thrilled when our children return home from distant place. God is so happy and rejoices when sinners repent and come home to Him. He is calling for everyone to come to Him. He has so much love to give each of us. Each person is special to Him. He has something special for each one. Each of us has so much to gain by coming to Jesus. He is waiting for you right now. Why not call on Him and return Home?

DAILY PRAISES	**DAILY PRAYER REQUESTS**
1.	1.
2.	2.
3.	3.
4.	4.
5.	5.

May 19
Read Luke 12:35-48

Luke 12:40

"You also must be ready, because the Son of Man will come at an hour when you do not expect him."

I look for the return of Christ any day now. When He returns He will gather the Saints, living and dead. God does not want anyone to be lost. He wants everyone to be saved and go with; Him to Heaven when He returns. He is a God of love and patience. He is not wanting to catch you doing something wrong, so He can ZAP you and send you to Hell. He waits patiently for you to come to Him and serve Him.

The hour of His return is so near. He tells us in His Word that He will return (John 14:1-3). Prophets in the Old Testament prophesied that He would return.

We see signs of Christ's coming as mentioned in the Bible; people are disregarding God, we have lawlessness, drugs, alcohol, x-rated movies, self-glorification, homosexuality, population explosion, an attitude of 'if it makes you happy. Do it', people are living to older ages, the church is mingling with the world, starvation is widespread, luxuries are plentiful, people are committing suicide, and many, many other signs.

Read and pray. Be ready for we will be moved with force and speed to Heaven We know for sure that Christ is going to return for us, but the time is not certain. No one knows the day or hour of His return. There will not be time to get ready when we see Him in the air. It is a blessed hope for we shall see Him as He is and be with Him. It is a fearful thing for sinners. Get ready to go with Him when He returns. His return is a wonderful promise for those who have accepted Jesus as their Savior.

DAILY PRAISES	**DAILY PRAYER REQUESTS**
1.	1.
2.	2.
3.	3.
4.	4.
5.	5.

May 20
Read Luke 15:1-7

Luke 15:7

"I tell you that in the same way there will be more rejoicing in heaven over one sinner who repents than over ninety-nine righteous persons who do not need to repent."

When you become a Christian you are a witness for Christ. You have a mission to be a light to sinners. Christ came to save sinners and after we become servers of Christ we should seek and pray to be led, so we can help people receive Christ.

It is a wonderful experience to become a Christian, but we must be concerned about the unsaved. Christ died for all and He wants everyone to seek repentance from sin.

Jesus changes others just as He changed us when we accepted Him. Do not be satisfied with your Christianity and sit idly by while precious souls are yet to be saved. There are people lost and dying without Jesus. They need the message of the cross.

Have you witnessed to friends and relatives that need to know Jesus? Can they point their finger at you in the judgment and say that you did not tell them about Christ and His saving grace? You were saved for a purpose. One purpose was to win others to Christ. Are you winning others for the Lord?

DAILY PRAISES	**DAILY PRAYER REQUESTS**
1.	1.
2.	2.
3.	3.
4.	4.
5.	5.

May 21
Read Luke 12:22-34

Luke 12:31

"But seek his kingdom, and these things will be given to you as well."

Is God first in your life? People who put God first are happy people. The blessings of the Lord are their riches. They have a happy life on earth and the promise of an Eternal Home in Heaven. God supplies every need, makes a way, when tempted or tried. He comforts the heartbroken and weary. If we continue in His love and commandments no one can separate us from God. Today is the day to put God first and keep Him there. The rewards will be tremendous. They will be temporal as well as Eternal. We can have happiness and satisfaction in this world as well as the world to come. We shall reap our crown of glory eventually by remaining true and letting God be number one.

God will supply us with things to make us satisfied if we keep Him first. He wants us to seek the Spiritual benefits of the kingdom of God rather than the material possessions of this world. Let this be the day that you put God first. He will make you much happier as well as adding all the things you need. You will grow and reap rich rewards. You will look forward to the return of Christ with anticipation.

DAILY PRAISES	**DAILY PRAYER REQUESTS**
1.	1.
2.	2.
3.	3.
4.	4.
5.	5.

May 22
Read Acts 20:22-38

Acts 20:24

"However I consider my life worth nothing to me, if only I may finish the race and complete the task the Lord Jesus has given me- the task of testifying to the gospel of God's grace."

Today is the date of my dad's birth. He was the most wonderful dad. He loved Jesus and served Him with a zeal and a love for life. He was not a preacher but he could conduct a church service. He had a big bass voice and loved to sing. Many people preferred to hear him rather than the minister. He never failed to offer people a chance to accept Jesus Christ in a church service. He was a witness to all the neighbors, family, and strangers who came into his store and Post Office. He gave generously to those in need. He is now in Heaven awaiting the rest of his family to join him. He often talked about finishing the race. He finished it gallantly.

The Lord has given us life and saved us from death and Hell. Everything we are we owe to the Lord. He has given us health, strength, and victory to witness for Him. No matter the trials we encounter, we should not let them separate us from Christ. He is able to deliver us as He delivered the prophets in the Bible. He will never leave us or forsake us. We must not leave or forsake Him.

Let us serve God with joy and strive to endure regardless of the cost. Our reward is at the end of the race, if we finish and do not faint. We will have a new body and a new life if we continue in Christ.

This life is worth living. It can be happy and productive is we are willing to let the Lord lead and guide us. If the occasion arises and we are given the choice of denying Christ or lose our life, we better be ready to lose our physical body for Christ. Our soul and our spirit will live forever. Be willing to witness for Christ in spite of the cost in this world. Look to the world that is to come.

DAILY PRAISES	**DAILY PRAYER REQUESTS**
1.	1.
2.	2.
3.	3.
4.	4.
5.	5.

May 23
Read 9:57-62

Luke 9:60

"Jesus said to him, 'Let the dead bury their own dead, but you go and proclaim the kingdom of God.'"

We, as Christians, have been called by God to be a witness for Him. I think of all the flimsy excuses people use, as to why they cannot take a job in the church or sing in the choir or attend services.

God gave His Only Son for us. Then surely we can give our all for Christ and His service. We are to leave all for Him. This means dedication of ourselves to God. Loving Him with all our souls, minds, and strengths is required. We are to live daily through prayer, faith, and bible reading. We are to daily deny ourselves and control ourselves. We should be aware of the needs of others, but not nosey.

Material possessions should be dedicated to the Lord. He gave us those possessions and we should put them in His care. Our children should be committed to God and taught His Word. He gave us those children and He can take care of them much more accurately than we can.

We have a great responsibility to fill if we are to do the word, 'Christian' justice. Pray and seek guidance of the Lord to be a witness where you are in Christ.

The man in our reading today could have wanted to wait for years until his father died, before preaching for the Lord. Our job is to do the Lord's work now, while we still have time.

DAILY PRAISES	**DAILY PRAYER REQUESTS**
1.	1.
2.	2.
3.	3.
4.	4.
5.	5.

May 24
Read John 14:15-31

John 14:27

"Peace I leave with you; my peace I give you. I do not give to you as the world gives. Do not let your hearts be troubled and do not be afraid."

I consider peace one of the greatest promises to Christians. Although the world may be in turmoil and strife, we, as Christians, can have peace in our hearts.

I felt peace deep within my soul during the tragic death of our daughter. Far beneath the pain and sorrow and grief I had peace the world knows nothing about. That peace is only possible through Christ.

We have assurance through Jesus that we will have peace as we press toward the mark that is ahead of us. We do not know what tomorrow will bring but we know that we have Jesus and He will supply our peace and comfort.

We must walk daily with Jesus and commune with Him because we have hope in an Eternal life. Be not afraid or troubled, but let Christ give you peace and contentment.

DAILY PRAISES　　　　　**DAILY PRAYER REQUESTS**

1.　　　　　　　　　　　　1.

2.　　　　　　　　　　　　2.

3.　　　　　　　　　　　　3.

4.　　　　　　　　　　　　4.

5.　　　　　　　　　　　　5.

May 25
Read Daniel 6:13-24

Daniel 6:20

"When he came near the den, he called to Daniel in an anguished voice, "Daniel, servant of the living God, has your God, whom you serve continually, been able to rescue you from the lions?"

I love this example of God's protection power. I think of the days when my four brother were in the service and how my parents would pray for the Lord to protect them and bring them home safely. My oldest brother was wounded three times but each time the Lord delivered him home safely.

This is the date of my Mother's birthday. I remember her continued faith in God for the safety of her family. Every morning I awoke to hear my Dad and Mother pray. It was the last thing I heard at night as they prayed aloud. Those prayers always contained prayers for the angels to protect and guard their children. The Lord kept His hand on each of us until we all accepted Jesus as our Savior. My Mom was a prayer warrior.

God is able to deliver you today, just as He delivered Daniel from the lions. He is still the same God. He has not changed. He wants people to serve Him continually. People who will not worship anything but Him, will be rescued and blessed. He wants people to take a stand for Him. They will be much stronger, once they have made that commitment to serve God regardless of the cost. He will deliver you in time of distress. So be faithful and true to the Holy God. You will be like Daniel and able to say that God has been with you and has delivered you through the trials and troubles that come your way.

DAILY PRAISES	**DAILY PRAYER REQUESTS**
1.	1.
2.	2.
3.	3.
4.	4.
5.	5.

May 26
Read James 1:2-18

James 1:1-2

"Consider it pure joy, my brothers, whenever you face trials of many kinds, because you know that the testing of your faith develops perseverance."

All my life I have been an impatient person. I want things done right away. I want prayers answered now or immediately.

In 1977 I had a terrible burden to pray for my husband to be saved. I was also asking for patience, as I realized my shortcoming in this area. In May of that year, our beautiful, eighteen-year-old, Christian daughter was suddenly killed. That very night my husband accepted the Lord. I did not question God as to why our daughter died. I saw immediate results. It did not make the pain of her death easier, but we could share our pain together and confide our hurts with each other and in the Lord.

It is unlikely that your faith will be tried as mine has been. Or that you will have to suffer the pain that I have suffered. God has a unique plan for each of our lives. Some people let God work His plan in their lives easier than others. Let us patiently endure and be willing to follow God's plan. There is a promise to obtain if we will endure with patience.

I can look back and see that there were times I failed to obey the calling that God had for me. I fell short of my duty to God. Sometimes our heart has to be broken to bring us around to doing what we were meant to do. Follow the call that God has on your life.

DAILY PRAISES	**DAILY PRAYER REQUESTS**
1.	1.
2.	2.
3.	3.
4.	4.
5.	5.

May 27
Read Luke 10:25-37

Luke 10:37

"The expert in the law replied, "The one who had mercy on him." Jesus told him, "Go and do likewise."

The Bible tells believers to show mercy and love to others. How long has it been since you seriously showed mercy to someone with a problem?

Humans seem to be losing their natural affection for others. We need to be stirred by God. We need to pray for God to place souls in our path that have needs of Salvation, comfort, or a friend. We are not alone in this world; therefore, we should be concerned about others.

We need to have compassion as Jesus did and let that compassion live within us. When we see hurting individuals we need to help them by just being there to offer empathy, if nothing else. We need to ask God to give us these feelings to help others. We need to show that we care for those hurting.

Our concern should be to help the lost come to Christ. It seems that we have let television, social life, telephone, computers and a fast way of living replace the altar or our prayer time. God help us to be concerned about this human race. Let us be especially concerned about those that have not accepted Jesus Christ.

DAILY PRAISES   **DAILY PRAYER REQUESTS**
1.   1.

2.   2.

3.   3.

4.   4.

5.   5.

May 28
Read Luke 11:1-13

Luke 11:10

"For everyone who asks receives; he who seeks finds; and to him who knocks; the door will be opened."

God has promised to hear our prayers. He hears the prayers of the repenting sinners. He forgives sin and receives each one that calls on Him. I am so thankful I was raised in a Christian home and taught our children to go to church and accept Jesus as their Savior.

This date is very difficult for me because it is the date our daughter was killed. I am thankful she had given her heart to Jesus and lived for Him. Her death was a shock, but she was ushered into the presence of Heaven that night, where she is safe forever more. We can go to see her and spend eternity with her when our lives on this earth has ended.

As Christians we know that our prayer will be answered because God has promised to hear and be aware of our circumstances. Our prayers may not be answered according to our will, but they will be answered according to God's will and on God's time schedule.

God hears us and delivers us in time of trouble and trials or He will make a way for our escape. We must glorify God for this deliverance and answered prayer. Yes, He provides. We have to wait for the answers to our prayers. Sometimes God delays in answering prayers to let love develop and faith deepen. This waiting teaches us patience as well as maturing in Christ. Let your faith go and grow. Let your prayers be answered. Let your faith soar. We are winners regardless of the pain it took to get us to where we are now.

DAILY PRAISES
1.
2.
3.
4.
5.

DAILY PRAYER REQUESTS
1.
2.
3.
4.
5.

May 29
Read Matthew 6:5-15

Matthew 6:6

"But when you pray, go into your room, close the door and pray to your Father, who is unseen. Then your Father, who sees what is done in secret, will reward you."

Prayer is such an important part of our lives. When we pray we communicate with the Father. When we pray we display our attitude of the human spirit. We should not glory in ourselves, but glory in God. We should be persistent in prayer, using our rooms to talk and listen to God. We should be humble and penitent in prayer. Our prayers should be in love, seriousness, simplicity, and a forgiving spirit.

Prayer is to be offered to the Lord, in the Name of Christ, as we let the Holy Spirit lead us and help us pray. We should pray regardless of our mood. There is no substitute for prayer.

Prayer is thanksgiving, praise, petitions, and intercessions for others. As my parents prayed aloud every morning and night in their room, I heard their prayers. I felt secure that I was included in those prayers. The Lord answered their prayers by keeping their children safe and leading them and directing them. Today is the anniversary of my parents. They had a wonderful marriage and raised nine children. They died within seven (7) months of each other. They were attached to each other in love.

Pray in secret, in times of spiritual conflict, and every day to seek guidance from the Lord. The Lord will teach us to pray as we diligently seek Him.

DAILY PRAISES   **DAILY PRAYER REQUESTS**

1.   1.

2.   2.

3.   3.

4.   4.

5.   5.

May 30
Read Luke 11:9-13

Luke 11:10

"For everyone who asks receives; he who seeks finds; and to him who knocks' the door will be opened."

It is a peaceful and satisfying feeling to know your name is written in Heaven. Once our sins are forgiven and our name recorded in the Book of Life, we are responsible to continue walking with the Lord. Many people are daily watching us. They need to knock on the door and let Christ come into their hearts. We are the light to the world. how does your light shine? Are you helping people have their names recorded in the book of Life?

Everyone will stand before God. Our name must be recorded there for us to enter Heaven. Rejoice and be glad that you have let the Savior in when He knocked on the door of your heart. Don't just be satisfied that your name is written there but help others get their name recorded in Heaven.

If you are not sure you have received Christ, make sure right now. Ask God to forgive all your sins. Begin to serve Him daily by reading your Bible, praying, witnessing to someone, and praising him for saving you.

DAILY PRAISES　　　　　**DAILY PRAYER REQUESTS**

1.　　　　　　　　　　　　1.

2.　　　　　　　　　　　　2.

3.　　　　　　　　　　　　3.

4.　　　　　　　　　　　　4.

5.　　　　　　　　　　　　5.

May 31
Read Ephesians 3:14-21

Ephesians 4:31-32

"Get rid of all bitterness, rage, and anger, brawling and slander, along with every form of malice. But be kind and compassionate to one another, forgiving each other, just as in Christ, God forgave you."

We, as Christians, have a responsibility in view of Christ's coming again. We are to watch and pray for we do not know the day or the hour He will return.

We are to be kind and loving toward others so that they may see that we have the love of Christ in our hearts. By showing love we will be ready for the return of Jesus.

We are new people, like Christ, being kind and caring for others. Our mind should be filled with the Word of God as we meditate on Christ daily. We should attend church to refuel our hearts to encourage others.

We need to give time to the Lord. We can praise Him each day for the blessings He gives us. We can give our time to help others and doing what they aren't able to do. There is a great blessing in doing for those who need our help.

Expect the return of Christ today and stay "Rapture Ready".

DAILY PRAISES	**DAILY PRAYER REQUESTS**
1.	1.
2.	2.
3.	3.
4.	4.
5.	5.

JUNE

June 1
Read Acts 14:21-28

Acts 14:22

"Strengthening the disciples and encouraging them to remain true to the faith, 'We must go through many hardships to enter the kingdom of God, they said.'"

Being a Christian is a wonderful experience. We continually have Jesus walking with us. We are never alone. We have the promise, that if we live according to the Bible, He will never leave us or forsake us.

Life may be filled with disappointments, troubles, and strife, but Jesus will be with us through each confrontation. He will give us words, thoughts and deeds if we really rely on Him.

Our Christian walk is not without trials. But again, we have the promise that we can overcome every obstacle by keeping our faith in Christ. Regardless of the situation facing you today, you can be an overcomer. Give Jesus your problems. He will help you get through each trial as a victorious believer. You will learn from each trial. Praise God for victory

DAILY PRAISES	**DAILY PRAYER REQUESTS**
1.	1.
2.	2.
3.	3.
4.	4.
5.	5.

June 2
Read Luke 12:22-34

Luke 12:28

"If that is how God clothes the grass of the field, which is here today, and tomorrow is thrown into the fire, how much more will he clothe you, O you of little faith."

God is in charge of the universe, as well as our individual lives. Consider the things you have power to change. Think about God and how He is in charge and has command and can work when none can hinder.

Our Heavenly Father knows our needs before we tell Him in prayer. He is capable and willing to provide. He cares so much for us and wants us to be provided for in a way that will lead us to a path of righteousness.

Our hope is in God. He will not forget or fail us. Our faith has saved us and given us peace according to God's plan. Our faith will lead us and help us to follow the will of God.

Do not worry or fret for God will take care of you. Oh how He loves you and me. His love is measureless. He will provide our needs. It may not be what we want, but it will be sufficient. Look up and let your faith take hold to believe for what you need.

You may not understand all the things that are going on around you, but rest assured God is in control and all will be worked out to His glory and good. We may not understand why things happen or do not happen, but trust God, He is in charge.

DAILY PRAISES
1.
2.
3.
4.
5.

DAILY PRAYER REQUESTS
1.
2.
3.
4.
5.

June 3
Read Luke 12:13-21

Luke 12:15

"Then He said to them, 'Watch out! Be on your guard against all kinds of greed; a man's life does not consist in the abundance of possessions'."

Are you happy? Why or why not? Do you desire things you do not possess? Do you skip church or daily Bible reading to work for things of this earth? Are you trying to keep up with friends or relatives in obtaining possessions?

Consider your health and the health of your family, as you think of happiness. Be thankful to have good health, enough food and sufficient clothing. God will provide the necessities of life, for He takes care of the birds, animals, and plants. We are of much more importance to Jesus than these. He will take care of us, if we put our trust in Him.

Our abundance is in what we do for God in this life. Let us show love, righteousness, and godliness to the world. Let us do some good for widows, orphans, or other deprived people. We will not be able to carry anything out of this life except our faith in God.

Now there is nothing wrong with having lots of things and money. The wrong is putting the things and money ahead of God in your life. God must be first. We must put Him first and He will supply the other things, as well as money, as we serve Christ. He will cause us to be happy and content in this world as we worship and serve Him.

DAILY PRAISES	**DAILY PRAYER REQUESTS**
1.	1.
2.	2.
3.	3.
4.	4.
5.	5.

June 4
Read Luke 12:1-12

Luke 12:8

"I tell you, whoever acknowledges me before men, the Son of Man will also acknowledge him before the angels of God."

We have a marvelous promise to hold onto, if we stand for Christ and confess Him before this world. Jesus will recognize us as His children before the angels of God. Praise God!

How can we expect God to recognize us if we do not let our lights shine in this sinful world? We are the light of the world for sinners. When we are evil spoken of and rejected by humans, for our faith in Christ, we have the promise of reigning with Christ, if we continue to follow Him.

Do not be led away from steadfastness by this evil world. If we deny Christ, He will likewise, deny us.

Like the apostles, we may be persecuted. But God's grace is sufficient. The suffering we endure will not begin to compare to the glory we will share in Heaven.

Let us put our minds on Heaven, our ultimate goal, and look forward to the things that are to come. We cannot begin to imagine the glorious things to come.

DAILY PRAISES
1.
2.
3.
4.
5.

DAILY PRAYER REQUESTS
1.
2.
3.
4.
5.

June 5
Read I Thessalonians 1:2-10

I Thessalonians 1:9

"For they themselves report what kind of reception you gave us. They tell how you turned to God from idols."

Everybody is worshipping someone or something. Everybody is searching for the truth. We, as Christians, have a tremendous obligation to be a light to a lost and dying world. It is easily understood why people turn to drugs, alcohol or other substitutes during times of trouble or indecision. If people do not have God to comfort them and give them peace, they use other means to try and get that peace or relief from trouble.

Let us be a light to the lost world and help people open their eyes. Let us apply the Word of God in our lives to help others turn to a living God for refuge rather than some substitute that does not work. Jesus works. He has been proven over and over again. He is real. He is true. He can be trusted to provide whatever we need. Turn totally to Him today and rely on Him for complete deliverance. He is the only answer. Other substitutes are only temporary and cause more troubles. Jesus is forever.

DAILY PRAISES	**DAILY PRAYER REQUESTS**
1.	1.
2.	2.
3.	3.
4.	4.
5.	5.

June 6
Read Luke 8:22-39

Luke 8:35

"And the people went out to see what had happened. When they came to Jesus, they found the man from whom the demons had gone out, sitting at Jesus' feet, dressed and in his right mind; and they were afraid."

Someone is watching you. When you give your life to Jesus, people begin to look at your life. They want to know if you have really changed. When you have repented, at the feet of Jesus is the best place to be. It is the place to learn and grow spiritually. It is a place of comfort and rest. It is a place of thanksgiving and prayer.

There is room for all at the feet of Jesus. As long as we stay at the feet of Jesus we will follow His leading and He will guide us.

At the feet of Jesus, you will be a witness to others. I remember when my husband was saved. The men at work took bets on how long his "religion" would last. Praise the Lord, all of those "odds makers" were the losers. It is over thirty years now and he is still growing and serving the Lord in love. He is a witness to those who doubted his sincere conversion to the Lord. We can be used by Jesus if we stay in His will at his feet, looking up to Him.

DAILY PRAISES
1.
2.
3.
4.
5.

DAILY PRAYER REQUESTS
1.
2.
3.
4.
5.

June 7
Read Hebrews 3:1-19

Hebrews 3:13

"But encourage one another daily, so that none of you may be hardened by sin's deceitfulness."

Jesus desires us not to look back at sin, when we have placed our faith in Him. We should not desire the life we lead previously.

Satan desires us and keeps stalking us, trying to fill our hearts with lust for the world. He does not want to give up anyone. That is why we must be grounded in God's Word, praying, attending church, and comforting one another in Christ. Satan will continue to place evil thoughts in our minds, but we must choose courage and rebuke him through the blood of Jesus.

Seek wisdom and knowledge from God, because He is sufficient in all things and will make a way for deliverance. Be willing to be led by the Spirit of God for a life of peace and satisfaction.

Encourage someone today who is struggling with problems. Both of you will be blessed by your encouraging words and deeds. We, as believers, need one another to uplift and strengthen one another. We must stand together for Christ. By standing together we will be a light and help others. Speak words of encouragement, not words of defeat. The victory is ours. Let us lay hold of it and claim it in Jesus' Name.

DAILY PRAISES	**DAILY PRAYER REQUESTS**
1.	1.
2.	2.
3.	3.
4.	4.
5.	5.

June 8
Read II Corinthians 1:1-11

II Corinthians 1:9

"Indeed, in our hearts we felt the sentence of death. But this happened that we might not rely on ourselves but on God, who raises the dead."

God was yesterday—
God is today—
God will be tomorrow—
God is omnipresent—

Human strength cannot solve the problems of the world or escape the evil forces that surround us. The deliverance is through God. He gives us hope in a hopeless situation. He directs us through all our trials and troubles. He gives us blessings in abundance. He is not slack concerning His promises to us humans.

What has God done for you in the past?
What is He doing for you today?
What will you ask Him to do for you tomorrow?

Have you thanked Him and praised Him for all that He has done for you? Why not offer a special praise and thanks for all that He has done for you right now? He is greatly to be praised. Lots of needs are met during praise and rejoicing to the Lord. Do not hold back. Give Him the praise He so richly deserves.

DAILY PRAISES	**DAILY PRAYER REQUESTS**
1.	1.
2.	2.
3.	3.
4.	4.
5.	5.

June 9
Read Colossians 3:1-17

Colossians 3:2

"Set your mind on things above, not on earthly things."

God does not force us to change as we become Christians. We have a desire to put off the "old man" and become like Christ. God does not put the old ways aside; we must do that. The old things and ways are still there, but we must not look or long for the old way. We must look to the new things and the new way of walking in Christ. If we love the world and the things in it more than we love Christ, we do not have the true love of God within us.

This world and the things in it will pass away one day. Try not to get too attached to things in this life. Renew your mind through Christ and follow Him. We will live forever if we are Christians and serve God as His Word directs.

"Things" are nice, but you cannot take them with you when you leave this world through death or the return of Jesus. Do not lose your fingernails hanging onto "things" when your time comes to leave this world. Enjoy what God has given you, but be willing to let it go for God.

Let us desire to be like Christ and look for His appearing just any day now. Let us rejoice that He loves us and cares for each of us and calls us by our name. We have heard that Jesus will return soon, since we were born, but it will happen one day, when we least expect it. Be ready for His return any day.

DAILY PRAISES	**DAILY PRAYER REQUESTS**
1.	1.
2.	2.
3.	3.
4.	4.
5.	5.

June 10
Read Hebrews 11:11-28

Hebrews 11:16

"Instead, they were longing for a better country-a heavenly one. Therefore, God is not ashamed to be called their God, for he has prepared a city for them."

Heaven will be a perfect country. Everything was planned just right. God will be our light. We will have no need for a sun or moon. We will all share in the joy and victory in Heaven.

It is a blessed hope, looking for Christ's return. That will complete the process of our Salvation. Christ gives us a blessed hope of another life in a far better country than we have now. We will all sit together in the Kingdom of God.

Blessed is the hope we have as Christians. Be proud to be a Christian and look for Christ's soon return. He will come to those who are looking for His return. If you are ready and looking for Him, you will not be left behind, but will meet Him in the air when the trumpet sounds and be with Him forever in Heaven. We will rejoice and praise God forever together.

DAILY PRAISES	**DAILY PRAYER REQUESTS**
1.	1.
2.	2.
3.	3.
4.	4.
5.	5.

June 11
Read Matthew 6:19-24

Matthew 6:21

"For where your treasure is, there your heart will be also."

What is your most prized possession? Is it your home, your money, your children, your spouse, your automobile, fame or your soul?

Where are your treasures stored? Are you storing them in Heaven or on earth?

The earth and its contents will pass away one day. Heaven will last forever. It will never end.

When you are born into God's family you begin to store treasures in Heaven. Each act of kindness you do to glorify God is stored in your treasures in Heaven. Each trial and tribulation you endure will be found as a treasure in Heaven.

I have a daughter in Heaven. I also have a mother, father, two sisters and two brother there. I think of them as treasures in Heaven. I would not want to miss being reunited with my family again. My heart is in Heaven.

There is nothing wrong with having nice things in this world and enjoying living here, but don't let this world be your heaven. There is a better place. A place where there will be no sorrow, crying or pain.

Turn your heart's desire toward Heaven's treasures; they will never fade away. You will never be sorry. You cannot imagine the happiness, rejoicing, and joy in Heaven.

DAILY PRAISES   **DAILY PRAYER REQUESTS**
1.   1.

2.   2.

3.   3.

4.   4.

5.   5.

June 12
Read John 14:1-14

John 14:2 (King James)

"In my Father's house are many mansions: if it were no so I would have told you. I go to prepare a place for you."

Heaven is a house of many mansions. Our finite minds cannot imagine the extent, grandeur, or beauty of those mansions. We are told in the Bible that Paul and John saw Heaven and it was unspeakable and illegal for him to speak about. We do not have all the details about Heaven, but we know it will be a joyous place. There will be no pain, no tears, no sorrow, no frowns or dying in Heaven. We will have a new, glorified body. We will have fellowship with others as well as with Jesus. We will be happy, even elated. We will be busy, not just work but enjoyable busyness.

Jesus took our sins so we could be saved and live in a Heavenly Home eternally. There is such a small price for us to pay, accept Jesus today. That is not even a price for us, it is a free gift. We will be happy, as we serve the Lord. Commit your life to Him because He loves you and cares about you. He wants you in Heaven with Him some day. He has prepared Heaven for you. It is a place of joy for those who love Him.

DAILY PRAISES　　　　　**DAILY PRAYER REQUESTS**

1.　　　　　　　　　　　　1.

2.　　　　　　　　　　　　2.

3.　　　　　　　　　　　　3.

4.　　　　　　　　　　　　4.

5.　　　　　　　　　　　　5.

June 13
Read Hebrews 4:1-13

Hebrews 4:2

"For we also have had the gospel preached to us, just as they did; but the message they heard was of no value to them, because those who heard did not combine it with faith."

We, as Christians, must retain faith. For by faith we will enter Heaven, a place of rest, when our earthly life is finished.

We must work, pray, read the Word, and witness to others as we keep the hope of Jesus alive until He returns. The more we do for Him, the more we learn, and the more we learn, the more we will be able to grow as Christians.

Yes, it is a marvelous hope, of eternal life, which we have been promised if we endure faithfully. We will enter into a Heavenly land, which will be a place of rest, among so many other wonderful things.

Let us remember to keep our faith in Jesus and live as the Bible instructs. Salvation is evidenced by our continued faith in Jesus. We are to persevere through this world in order to enter into the rest, God has prepared for us. It is not our rest, but God's rest for us.

DAILY PRAISES	DAILY PRAYER REQUESTS
1.	1.
2.	2.
3.	3.
4.	4.
5.	5.

June 14
Read I Corinthians 15:35-58

I Corinthians 15:55

"Where, O death, is your victory? Where, O death, is your sting?"

Because of our human nature, we dread the thought of death. Maybe because it is a mystery and we will only experience it once which is final. Therefore, we tend to fear death.

We should live and work for Christ as long as He allows us to live on this earth. When He calls us home, we can be assured the sting will be removed from death. I believe the fear and dread will be gone. Our faith in Christ will assure us of an easy crossing to the Heavenly side. Oh, yes, we may be suffering physically or mentally in tremendous pain, but our spiritual warfare will be winning a glorious victory.

Since we haven't experienced death, we don't know what to expect, but we know that Jesus will be right by our side when we breathe our last breath on earth and enter the next moment into Heaven.

When Jesus raptures the Saints, the graves will open wide for Christians to meet Him in the air. The graves will give up their victory over death. Praise the Lord, because we have the hope of victory over death.

DAILY PRAISES
1.
2.
3.
4.
5.

DAILY PRAYER REQUESTS
1.
2.
3.
4.
5.

June 15
Read Isaiah 40:1-18

Isaiah 40:1
"Comfort, comfort my people."

Jesus came to die on the cross for everyone. All people are loved by God and urged to turn to Him for repentance. He loves those who have not yet given their lives to Him. He is constantly making a way to get His Word into their lives. We, as Christians, are living proof of Christ and His redemptive power. Wherever we go and whatever we do Christ is seen or not seen in our lives.

We have a responsibility to let our light shine forth to comfort Christians as well as sinners. It is our duty to be comforters.

Do you know someone in despair today? Have you shared Christ with them and tried to show them the way with love and comfort? For weeks I sat with a mother who lost her second son in an automobile accident. There was nothing I could do but be there. When she called, I knew she needed to be comforted. I made time to be there for her. I couldn't imagine two children dying. I had only the heartbreak of one child being killed.

Let us be a positive effect in this world by loving and comforting those who are hurting. The way to win people to the Kingdom of God is through love and comfort. Let the world know which side you are living for. Give comfort to those who need you.

DAILY PRAISES	**DAILY PRAYER REQUESTS**
1.	1.
2.	2.
3.	3.
4.	4.
5.	5.

June 16
Read Matthew 5:13-20

Matthew 5:14

"You are the light of the world. A city on a hill cannot be hidden."

Today there are more people seeking happiness than ever before. They try every "new thing" to find happiness. Happiness is not for sale. It is a reward for Kingdom dwellers. Kingdom living will help rid us of those impulsive actions. It will help us exercise discipline over our lives. Jesus commended the person whose ambition is to become righteous. We must take the robe of righteousness which Jesus Christ has wrought and allow Him to clothe us to find full satisfaction.

The world is in darkness. It is blinded to the spiritual light. We, as believers, shine for the dark world to see. We shine because we follow Jesus. Jesus frowns on us if we do things to be seen of men. He encourages us to shine that men might see us. All we have to do is live a Christian life and others will see God in us. People see God through our conduct and our words. Converts come when they see Christ in our lives. Oh, how we need to be fully illuminated by Christ. Our light comes from the Father. Let us let the light shine bright.

Do people see Christ in you? Is your light shining brightly? Could someone be led to Christ by your life? Are you following the footsteps of Jesus? Choose His light today.

DAILY PRAISES
1.
2.
3.
4.
5.

DAILY PRAYER REQUESTS
1.
2.
3.
4.
5.

June 17
Read Mark 12:28-34

Mark 12:33

"To love Him with all your heart, with all your understanding and with all your strength, and to love your neighbor as yourself is more important than all burnt offerings and sacrifices."

Love means adoration or devout affection humans have toward God. The heart is the seat of emotions, especially of love affection, as distinguished from the head. The head is the center of the intellect and reasoning. The inmost feelings or thoughts are produced in the heart.

Understanding means the sum of mental powers by which knowledge is acquired, retained, and extended.

The soul is the rational, emotional, and will power faculties in man. It is conceived of as forming an entity distinct from the body. The soul will survive death and live on in joy or misery.

Strength could be thought of as the capacity of the body to sustain the application of force without yielding or breaking.

So if we concentrate on loving God with all of our heart, understanding, soul, and strength we will not have a problem loving our neighbor or brothers and sisters. We will walk humbly and pleasingly before the Lord.

DAILY PRAISES	**DAILY PRAYER REQUESTS**
1.	1.
2.	2.
3.	3.
4.	4.
5.	5.

June 18
Read Luke 12:22-34

Luke 12:33

"Sell your possessions and give to the poor. Provide purses for yourselves that will not wear out, a treasure in Heaven that will not be exhausted, where no thief comes near and no moth destroys."

Have you ever had the opportunity to give to someone who did not have their needs met? It may have been as simple as a turkey for Thanksgiving dinner. What a pleasure to see the smiles on faces of those who have been filled with a need. I believe that type of giving, if given from the heart and not from show, is laying up treasures in Heaven. God bless those who give joyfully.

God allows us to have material possessions. All things that we possess are from God. We should not trust in riches or material possessions, but trust God, who gives us riches.

All material possessions will pass away. Only what we have sown for the Master will last.

If we have been blessed with material gain, we should praise God for it. We should be willing to give back to Him as He has blessed and given to us.

Do you know someone who could use a good meal or some new clothing or a heat bill paid? Is the spirit of God urging you to share with someone today? You are the only one that can answer the call God is giving you. You will be storing treasurers in Heaven when you give and share unselfishly in the Name of Jesus. Give out of your heart. Give for the glory of God, not for your glory.

DAILY PRAISES	**DAILY PRAYER REQUESTS**
1.	1.
2.	2.
3.	3.
4.	4.
5.	5.

June 19
Read Ephesians 4:17-32

Ephesians 4:32

"Be kind and compassionate to one another, forgiving each other, just as in Christ God forgave you."

God is merciful and forgiving by nature. He expects us to be the same. If we fail to forgive it can alter our relationship with the Lord. An unforgiving attitude closes the Lord out. He is always ready to forgive, but He cannot enter a heart that refuses to forgive. When we offer forgiveness to others it must be from the heart. We know that mere lip service will not be accepted by God.

What is the reason for being kind and tenderhearted? It is God's love to humans, by giving Jesus Christ. God loves people. Jesus is our example of kindness and tenderheartedness. He showed great kindness to the helpless. He had compassion on the sick and healed them. He was kind to those whose lives were out of control. It was those we would have written off as losers and worthless. Yes. Our Jesus loved those people and showed mercy on them. Jesus loved the little children and blessed them. He wept as He faced the reality of the death of Lazarus. He wept over the fate of Jerusalem. The love of God is shown in the many examples of Christ's interaction with mankind. This is to be the basis for direct kindness, tenderheartedness, and forgiveness in our relationship with one another.

Do you really love others in words and deeds? Do you show kindness, as Jesus did? Do you have compassion on those less fortunate or those going through trials? Today could be a good day to examine your life. You will be blessed when you love and forgive others.

DAILY PRAISES	DAILY PRAYER REQUESTS
1.	1.
2.	2.
3.	3.
4.	4.
5.	5.

June 20
Read Mark 12:18-27

Mark 12:24

"Jesus replied, 'Are you not in error because you did not know the Scriptures or the power of God?'"

We are victorious through Jesus Christ. He gives us answers through His Word. In the Name of Jesus, we have power to rebuke Satan and order him to remove his hands from our lives and the lives of our children and loved ones. Greater is He that is in us, than he that is in the world. There is a deep source of power through Jesus, by the Holy Spirit, which is ours to use against Satan. We can build on this source of power by spending time in prayer, earnestly before the Lord. By reading, meditating on the Bible, and learning the Word, we will be able to have wisdom and guidance to be confident in Jesus. If we keep our minds clean and on Christ we will be mentally alert, as Jesus was.

Christ knows our needs as He surveys our lives and ministers to us in a way that best fits us. We have the heritage of His care to sustain us through life's journey. It is a wonderful thing to know God's presence surrounds us and keeps us going.

We have the responsibility to learn the Word and write it in our hearts so we will be able to fight against the powers of evil. God is not limited as to what He desires to do for us. How much time do you give to the Lord each day? Do you give Him enough time to let Him speak to you? Are you too busy with selfish things to let the Lord speak to your heart? Take the time to listen to the voice of the Lord. Let Him speak to you through His Word and through His power.

DAILY PRAISES	**DAILY PRAYER REQUESTS**
1.	1.
2.	2.
3.	3.
4.	4.
5.	5.

June 21
Read Matthew 5:1-12

Matthew 5:3-4

"Blessed are the poor in spirit, for theirs is the kingdom of heaven. Blessed are those who mourn for they will be comforted."

Blessed carries the thought of God like joy. When Jesus spoke of blessedness He made reference to a joy that is complete.

James spoke of the poor in spirit, not referring to materially poor, but poverty of spirit. Poor in spirit is an attitude which recognizes its own hopelessness and is utterly dependent upon God. When we realize we cannot feed ourselves spiritually, we then put ourselves in the hands of the Lord. We find joy this world cannot know. The poor in spirit belong to the Kingdom of Heaven, the society where the will of God is perfectly done.

Those who mourn will be comforted and receive joy. To mourn means to truly be sorry for sins and unworthiness. The person who approaches God in this spirit will be comforted and receive joy. This broken and contrite spirit arouses a response in the heart of the Lord. Joy will remain and be full as you walk with Christ daily. Is the Kingdom of Heaven yours? Are you comforted? Come to the Savior and let Him comfort and love you as you make Heaven yours.

DAILY PRAISES	DAILY PRAYER REQUESTS
1.	1.
2.	2.
3.	3.
4.	4.
5.	5.

June 22
Read II Corinthians 1:3-11

II Corinthians 1:10

"He has delivered us from such a deadly peril, and he will deliver us. On him we have set our hope that he will continue to deliver us,"

Can you count the number of known times that God has delivered you from danger, evil, trials, temptations, or even death? What about the unknown times He has delivered you? Have you praised Him and thanked Him for those deliverances He has provided?

He is able to deliver from everything. God is the deliverer right now. God delivered in the past. God will deliver in the future. God will deliver right now. God is our hope in time of pressure. Human strength is not enough to escape the evil force that is so great in the world today. God will direct us through it all. He is our only hope for deliverance. He will give abundance, if we put our full trust in Him and let Him deliver us.

What has God done for you recently? What have you done for God? What have you not let God do for you? He stands at your heart's door waiting for you to let Him deliver whatever you need.

DAILY PRAISES	**DAILY PRAYER REQUESTS**
1.	1.
2.	2.
3.	3.
4.	4.
5.	5.

June 23
Read II Corinthians 2:12-17

II Corinthians 2:14

"But thanks be to God, who always leads us in triumphal procession in Christ and through us spreads everywhere the fragrance of the knowledge of him."

Oh, how we should praise God for the many triumphs He has brought us through! He helps us to fight our conflicts. He is speaking to us in every part of our lives. We can handle everything that God allows to come our way, if we remain in Christ and allow Him to help us triumph.

We have a spiritual warfare to fight because we have chosen to walk with Christ. It is the good walk. It is the good fight that Christ will help us to win.

Christ will walk beside us and help us win our victories in everything. We only have to continuously ask Him for help and rely on Him as we praise Him for the victory.

Let His knowledge and victory permeate your heart and soul. We owe our all to Jesus. Give Him all the thanks.

DAILY PRAISES   **DAILY PRAYER REQUESTS**
1.   1.

2.   2.

3.   3.

4.   4.

5.   5.

June 24
Read II Corinthians 3:7-18

II Corinthians 3:17

"Now the Lord is the Spirit, and where the Spirit of the Lord is, there is freedom."

We were made free by Christ dying on the cross at Calvary and rising from the dead. If we serve Christ and have His Spirit, we will be at liberty. When we serve Him, we are no longer a slave to sin. We must grow in His Spirit and not become entangled in the world of unrighteousness again.

We must continue to be obedient to God's Word and do the things it teaches. We must also be motivated by love to do the deeds instructed in the Bible. If we are living in love, we will be doing well and our deeds will be a blessing. When we do not have love our deeds will be in vain.

We are free from fear, when we have the Spirit of the Lord. We will be led by love. Love is given to us by the Father to cover all and conquer all. Through love we will give and do for others without selfishness. Love leads to growth in Christ. As long as we remain in the Spirit we are free. If we remain in the Spirit and abiding love of God we will not be lead astray.

DAILY PRAISES	**DAILY PRAYER REQUESTS**
1.	1.
2.	2.
3.	3.
4.	4.
5.	5.

June 25
Read II Corinthians 5:11-21

II Corinthians 5:17

"Therefore, if anyone is in Christ, he is a new creation; the old has gone, the new has come."

There is a plea for all people to come to God. There is a void in everyone's life until they come to Christ and let Jesus take His rightful place in their lives. Wealth, fame, honor, and recognition in this world will not satisfy that hunger that is deep inside the soul. It is honorable to be well thought of and receive honors in this world. Regardless of the many accolades we receive in this world, they cannot replace the need of Christ.

All must repent and be sorry for their sins. Jesus forgives and forgets our sins. Man must let Jesus do the forgiving by calling on Him and asking for forgiveness. Allow Jesus to Change you. You cannot do it yourself, no matter how many times you try. Allow God to love you and show you the way to a better life. He will help you become a new person through Him. He will help you put your old way of life and old things aside.

Let God's will take place in your life by submitting to Him today. All things are new through Him.

DAILY PRAISES	**DAILY PRAYER REQUESTS**
1.	1.
2.	2.
3.	3.
4.	4.
5.	5.

June 26
Read Galatians 5:1-15

Galatians 5:7

"You were running a good race. Who cut in on you and kept you from obeying the truth?"

Many people begin a good race. Some fall by the wayside from discouragement or defeat. Perhaps they did not receive the proper training after accepting Christ. Whose fault was it? Maybe they were glorying in themselves and letting pride slip in thinking they could do it all on their own.

Many people love this present world too much to follow Christ. This world will perish and all its contents along with it. What will those people do then?

Many people begin their Christian race and are so easily distracted by the world, that they lose the love that Christ gave them when they were first saved. We are instructed to do the first works over if we lose our first love. Go back and start anew with Jesus. He is always there for you.

Many people love to make excuses for not following Jesus, such as: family, personal goods or property, other people's faults, jobs and on and on they will go. None of these excuses will be valid on the day we stand before God and tell Him why we did not obey His word of Truth.

DAILY PRAISES	DAILY PRAYER REQUESTS
1.	1.
2.	2.
3.	3.
4.	4.
5.	5.

June 27
Read James 1:2-18

James 1:12

"Blessed is the man who perseveres under trials, because when he has stood the test, he will receive the crown of life that God has promised to those who love him."

This verse can be thought of as a judgment or a verdict. James offers consolation to Christians for suffering through trials and temptations. He offers us a reminder that God has rewards prepared for those who are faithful under trials. The reward is the inner blessedness the believer possesses and then we will receive a crown of life when we get to Heaven.

The blessing comes to the believer in enduring trials of life. When the believer stands firm in the very face of temptation he will have the peace of God as well as the promised Heavenly home.

Temptations can be overcome by facing them squarely in reality; then committing them in their reality to the Lord. Realize the power of God is able to help you overcome. His power and promises are real. He is able to help you stand and keep you safe. There is a great reward of Eternal Life for those who are true to the Lord.

DAILY PRAISES	**DAILY PRAYER REQUESTS**
1.	1.
2.	2.
3.	3.
4.	4.
5.	5.

June 28
Read John 15:1-17

John 15:17
"This is my command: Love each other."

It is so easy to generalize one's love, but so very important that we specify it as well. To love like Jesus means we must personalize our love. Personalized love means there are no faces, names, or addresses that we refuse to love. If there is one person we cannot love, we do not love like Jesus.

Criminal investigators use uniqueness of finger prints for personalization. We need to concentrate on the uniqueness of every person and the situation in which they are involved. We need to let them know we love them and they are special.

Jesus is mindful of the lilies, sparrows, and the very hairs of our heads are numbered. He views each of us as special individuals, unique, and precious in His sight. We also have the opportunity to love and care for those we come in contact with, as Jesus loves and cares for us. Let us repay the love of Jesus by loving others.

Our love breaks down when we try to force a person in conformity with our ideas. Conformity will never lead to love, but a personalized love will exert a conforming influence. Because God loved us, therefore we loved Him and we have changed. Love will result in change. Do you love as Jesus loved? Try it.

DAILY PRAISES	**DAILY PRAYER REQUESTS**
1.	1.
2.	2.
3.	3.
4.	4.
5.	5.

June 29
Read Ecclesiastes 12:1-14

Ecclesiastes 12:13

"Now all has been heard; here is the conclusion of the matter: Fear God and keep his commandments, for this is the whole duty of man."

Solomon learned from experience the utter vanity of trying to live without reverence for God and obedience to His word. Solomon, the wisest of men, became a fool and learned painfully that he could find the purpose for his life only in returning to God. Without God, life was vain and unmeaningful.

God wants us to learn the lessons that come with pessimism and discouragement. If we can learn the lesson, we can avoid the attitude of pessimism and discouragement.

People's effort to find happiness without God is futile. There is no profit in the search for wisdom, for the solution to one problem raises another question. Worldly wisdom cannot save us from our sins, but God can. The knowledge that begins with true reverence for God and the wisdom that comes from above instructs us to look beyond ourselves to God. Jesus is our Redeemer and He has already paid the price for our Salvation.

Let us look at the entire matter. Life will go beyond this world. Let us prepare to live in Heaven after this life is over. Praise God for preparing the way for entry into Heaven.

DAILY PRAISES	**DAILY PRAYER REQUESTS**
1.	1.
2.	2.
3.	3.
4.	4.
5.	5.

June 30
Read II Corinthians 4:1-18
II Corinthians 4:17, 18

"For our light and momentary troubles are achieving for us an eternal glory that far outweighs them all. So we fix our eyes not on what is seen, but on what is unseen. For what is seen is temporary, but what is unseen is eternal."

There are times when we are so burdened that friends and family cannot help. Only through calling on the Savior can we get relief from those burdens. Burdens seem to be a tremendous load and strain, but they are really an 'eternal weight of glory'.

We must put our minds toward Heaven and not think of our afflictions here, because they are so small and of such a short duration. They will soon pass away. We will have a home prepared in Heaven if we will just endure all the troubles that come our way. We should count them as joy and realize that they are a growing experience, making us closer and more ready for Heaven. We can take troubles to Jesus. He will help us bear our burdens and lead us through those which seem to be unbearable. He will not allow us more than we can stand. When it appears that we cannot undergo another trial or problem, we should bow to God and pray for deliverance and guidance. We are promised His help and love. He wants to comfort us. Let Him love you.

DAILY PRAISES	**DAILY PRAYER REQUESTS**
1.	1.
2.	2.
3.	3.
4.	4.
5.	5.

JULY

July 1
Read Luke 14:15-23

Luke 15:23

"Then the master told his servant, 'Go out to the roads and country lanes and make them come in, so that my house will be full.' "

The underlying theme is the mission of God to bring people into the Kingdom of God through the Salvation message. This solemn and tragic story shows us how reluctant sinful humans are to yield their lives to worship God. But God will have people of His own possession, if He has to go to the highways and byways to reach them. When some resist, He will widen the invitation to include others.

To compel, means to urge irresistibly; to obtain by force; to force to yield; to overpower. Compel is a very forceful word. We must be forceful witnesses and pray for an opportunity to witness to the lost. The Spirit has a powerful force to draw people to Jesus.

Let us be filled with that Spirit as we daily minister. God will not violate the human will by forcing Salvation on people. God will have people to serve Him. He receives and fills all that come unto Him. The Father's house is open. There is room for all.

God calls us to repentance and then to evangelism. We are all to witness for Jesus and go out to compel others to come to Jesus. It is our responsibility to minister to our portion of the world. Our part of the world is where we live, work, and play. We are not to make excuses. If God leads you to it He will lead you through it. As He gives you opportunity to witness, He will give you words to say.

DAILY PRAISES	**DAILY PRAYER REQUESTS**
1.	1.
2.	2.
3.	3.
4.	4.
5.	5.

July 2
Read Psalm 23:1-6

Psalm 23:3

"He restores my soul. He guides me in the path of righteousness for his name's sake."

Jesus is our compassionate shepherd. He provides for us. He gave His life for the sheep (us). He renews us. He knows each of us by name and calls us unto Him. He gathers us into the fold. He cares about our earthly and physical needs. He has very clearly made the provision for our spiritual needs which is more important than any physical needs.

Christ provides the food and water of life for us. He leads us in the path of righteousness for the honor of His Name. He restores our soul, our very source of life. He is still restoring souls today. God will supply all our needs (not our wants). One of the greatest dangers the church faces today is materialism. We tend to work overtime or get a second job to get the extra material things in life. We often over-commit ourselves toward the physical and material so that it interferes with our spiritual lives and our involvement in the church to do the work of the Lord.

We must be on guard and make Jesus Christ our first priority because He is all sufficient. He is strong and mighty. He is at our side. We are more than conquers through Jesus. Let us keep our heart open to Him as He renews us and leads us along life's way.

It is necessary to work and make a living to support our families and ourselves. The danger is in over doing for our selfish reasons. We must give the Lord the prime time and season of our lives.

DAILY PRAISES	DAILY PRAYER REQUESTS
1.	1.
2.	2.
3.	3.
4.	4.
5.	5.

July 3
Read Deuteronomy 4:1-14

Deuteronomy 4:5

"See, I have taught you decrees and laws as the Lord my God commanded me, so that you may follow them in the land you are entering to take possession of it."

God gave Moses the Law and words of knowledge and instruction for the Children of Israel. They were instructed to keep the Laws and write the words of God in their hearts. They were also told to teach their children the Laws and ways of the Lord.

We are also to follow the instructions contained in God's Word. It will help us to prosper in everything we do, if we keep His Commandments. We definitely are to hear and obey the Word of God. We hear by attending Sunday School and church. We hear by reading the Bible, which is filled with commandments, promises, hopes, and instructions. We hear through prayer and meditation upon the Lord, through the Holy Spirit. We hear through Mothers and Fathers who have walked upright before Christ and believed on Him. They have experienced much more than we have so far.

Our very life hinges on our ability to hear and obey the Words of God. He has given us His Word to teach us and help us increase in love and knowledge. His Word will keep us from evil. It will stand when all else fails. His Word will satisfy that emptiness in a longing soul. His Word is sweeter than honey and to be desired more than pure gold.

Are you hungry for God's Word? It will give you security that you are unable to find any other place in this world. God is love and safety. Put yourself in His hands.

DAILY PRAISES	**DAILY PRAYER REQUESTS**
1.	1.
2.	2.
3.	3.
4.	4.
5.	5.

July 4
Read John 8:31-41

John 8:31-32

"To the Jews who had believed him, Jesus said, 'If you hold to my teaching, you are really my disciples. Then you will know the truth, and the truth will set you free.' "

Jesus seeks to deliver everyone from the error of their ways. He offered mankind freedom from slavery to sin. This freedom does not mean we are free to do 'our own thing', but it means free to serve the Lord in righteousness. No one is free until Jesus comes into their life. Then there is freedom to live and be ruled by love and justice. His call to freedom rings loud and clear to all humans. He calls each of us individually. Jesus is interested in bringing followers into a full and complete relationship with Him. He does not want to just gain a following but to lead people to a deeper spiritual experience in which their faith will be based on truth.

As we celebrate the independence of our nation from tyranny rule, let us give God the glory that He helped us gain freedom from slavery and abuse of others. Thankfully, we are a free nation to serve God as we read in the Bible.

When we see ourselves as not needing God's help, we are lifted up in pride. Pride comes before a fall. We need to see ourselves as needing more of the teaching of Jesus. When we accept Jesus and become free, we can grow and become what He wants and what He intended us to be. He wants us to be a worshipping, joyful, and inspiring people.

Just as our ancestors fought for our physical freedom, let us fight to keep our Spiritual freedom.

DAILY PRAISES	**DAILY PRAYER REQUESTS**
1.	1.
2.	2.
3.	3.
4.	4.
5.	5.

July 5
Read Matthew 12:1-14

Matthew 12:11

"He said to them, 'If any of you have a sheep and it falls into a pit on the Sabbath, will you not take hold of it and lift it out?' "

The Pharisees had posed the question to Jesus, about healing on the Sabbath. Jesus used an example with which they were familiar, the missing sheep. Sheep meant money to most of the people in that day. They could relate to going after a lost or injured sheep on the Sabbath. You see, people should value the souls of others much more than sheep. If it was all right to rescue a suffering, lost lamb on the Sabbath, surely it would be fine to end the suffering of a fellow human being on the Sabbath.

We must allow Jesus to be Lord of our lives every day of the week, as well as on Sunday. He must also be allowed to be Lord of our attitudes, feelings toward others, and toward worship. We must let the Lord guide our feelings toward others. Christ is the Supreme Authority figure in our lives. We should follow Him as closely as His disciples. We may not always be without persecution or criticism, but the Lord, with whom we walk, has the answers for every critic. He will not uphold wrong doings, but will bless us in every necessary action that does not break His commands. Jesus proved himself Lord on the Sabbath. He asserted Himself as a miracle worker. He is Lord over sickness. Let us accept His authority and rededicate our lives to Him on every day of the week.

DAILY PRAISES	**DAILY PRAYER REQUESTS**
1.	1.
2.	2.
3.	3.
4.	4.
5.	5.

July 6
Read II Timothy 1:3-18

II Timothy 1:7

"For God did not give us a spirit of timidity, but a spirit of power, of love and of self-discipline."

Fear is a very wide term. It may mean fear for personal safety and health or concern for others' welfare. It may range from a mild alarm to an extreme terror. Terror is the most extreme fear and may cause people to be unable to act or it could result in wild, panic rage which can be unhealthy. Dread is a type of fear which makes one afraid of future events and suggests that the person has no control over what is approaching.

Praise God, we do not have to have the spirit of fear, because He has given us the spirit of "power" which is the ability and strength to exercise control over every situation. We have competency through Jesus. He has given us the spirit of love, which is adoration and affection for God, and the kindness and charitableness that we show to others through our devotion to God and others. Love is the strongest term used to describe the warmest, most intense regards of one person for another. It also implies a spiritual quality. It means loyalty and service given because of love. Jesus gave us a sound mind, which means it is free from injury flaw, defect, decay or mutilation. It is founded on truth, legal and valid. It is solid, stable, firm and trustworthy. It is based on good judgment.

Memorize this verse to use when Satan wants you to fear things. God will release you from fear if you will trust in Him and believe His Word.

DAILY PRAISES	DAILY PRAYER REQUESTS
1.	1.
2.	2.
3.	3.
4.	4.
5.	5.

July 7
Read I Corinthians 2:6-18

I Corinthians 2:9

"However as it is written: No eye has seen, no ear has heard, no mind has conceived what God has prepared for those who love Him."

The Lord is the very strength of our life. We should obey Him and receive the blessedness of His love. We need the Holy Spirit's infilling to help us love God as we should. Jesus promised us the Holy Spirit to lead us into all truth for work in our lives. He will not leave us comfortless, but is with us through the Holy Spirit.

If we love Jesus we have joy and delight in Him. He is our shield and glory He is our strength and support. He has done great things for us while we reside on earth and serve Him. He is our Salvation and we should give Him praise. He is greatly to be praised and when we praise Jesus He is glorified.

We can live with blessings from God upon our life in this earth, but with expectation we look forward to being ushered into the presence of Heaven where we shall have an eternal rest. Heaven will be a place of many mansions, whether separate apartments or condominiums, we don't know. We do know Heaven will be a secure abode. We will always be safe there. Heaven will be a far better country than we can imagine, because God prepared it for us. Heaven is described as the New Jerusalem. The light will be as precious stones of Jasper and crystal. The city is pure gold, like glass and the walls have all manner of precious stones. God will be the light of Heaven; therefore, we will not need the sun or moon. Words cannot describe the beauty of what is to come or the comfort and happiness God will give us. We must remain faithful to the Lord in order to enter Heaven.

DAILY PRAISES	**DAILY PRAYER REQUESTS**
1.	1.
2.	2.
3.	3.
4.	4.
5.	5.

July 8
Read Ephesians 5:1-21

Ephesians 5:14

"For it is light that makes everything visible. This is why it is said: 'wake up O sleeper, rise from the dead, and Christ will shine on you.' "

The death and resurrection of Jesus established the Church as a new covenant body. By the blood of Jesus, we are saved, cleansed, forgiven, justified, and given a new beginning before God, as if we had never sinned. He breathes on us to give us life by His Spirit.

Everyone has a special part in building up the Body of Christ. God has chosen each person for a special job. We must learn to receive from the Head of the Body, Christ. Sometimes we fall back into the old ways of thinking and that delays the work of Christ. We must guard against grieving the Holy Spirit. Do not give way to evil. Please the Holy Spirit by showing kindness, happiness, generosity, forgiveness, and compassion. By doing this we become imitators of Jesus. We act the way children who are loved should act. Psychologist say children who are loved pattern themselves after their parents. The older we become the more like Christ, we should become. God requires that there be a difference in His children and the people of the world.

We need to stir the potentiality within our soul. The Holy Spirit is for all and through our cooperation with Him the fruit of the Spirit will grow and develop into a mature Christian. Enjoy the benefits of being a child of God. Help awaken those who have fallen asleep spiritually.

DAILY PRAISES			**DAILY PRAYER REQUESTS**
1.						1.

2.						2.

3.						3.

4.						4.

5.						5.

July 9
Read I Peter 2:1-12

"I Peter 1:2

"Like new born babies, crave pure spiritual milk, so that by it you may grow up in your salvation,"

Our world is filled with a plague of selfishness or me first attitude. People tend to go to any length to satisfy self. They even destroy fellow humans or families to gain their satisfaction. Peter explained that we are to use the Word of God to grow and mature. He says we are to get rid of some old things and to put on some new other things as we read in I Peter 2:1.

We are to get rid of malice, which wants revenge, wanting to see that person suffer harm in payment for harm. The Word says to put off guile, which is treacherous or disloyalty. It also has a deceptive appearance. As Christians we should show forth loyalty, truth, and trustworthiness. We are to put off hypocrisies, pretending to be what we are not. Hypocrisy is the most extreme word. It denotes the feigning of admirable qualities, such as goodness, sincerity, and honesty by those who actually have the opposite qualities. Sooner or later the real person will show through. Put off envy, a feeling of resentment or discontent toward another because of their good fortune. Lastly, get rid of evil speaking, which destroys people and does not accomplish any good thing.

Peter emphasized the positives and he tells us to eat the proper food, the Word of God. We are to eat with a healthy appetite, have hunger for learning the Word, and we will grow becoming a lively stone in the building of God's Kingdom.

DAILY PRAISES	**DAILY PRAYER REQUESTS**
1.	1.
2.	2.
3.	3.
4.	4.
5.	5.

July 10
Read Psalm 119:17-24

Psalm 119:17

"Do good to your servant, and I will live: I will obey your word."

The Word of God is to be obeyed. God, Himself, exalted His Word and our emphasis should be on it and the power and use of God's Word. God's Word is powerful. Consider what it will do: cleanse, keep the heart from wandering from God's commandments, give victory over sin, delight our souls, remember, respect, meditate, and rejoice within us.

The Psalmist's future efforts were based on past experiences and the results of those experiences. Because he already knew what the Word would do, he was motivated to study further.

No substitute has been found for the Word of God. Although the Bible was written centuries ago, it is still relevant to our present lives. The men who wrote the Bible were inspired by the Spirit of God and that is why the message is timeless. Any answers you need are in the Bible.

It is a natural response to desire to live and enjoy the blessings of the Lord. There are wondrous things in God's Word which we have not seen and will not see unless He opens our eyes and reveals them to us. We, too, should pray as the Psalmist, "Lord, open my eyes and let me live by your Word."

The Holy Spirit is ever revealing to us the wonders, riches, and blessings of God's true love. The need for the Word is great. It is our food, our guide, and our shield. We must read the Bible and feel its impact on our lives. We must apply the truth of the Word in living out our personal lives.

DAILY PRAISES	**DAILY PRAYER REQUESTS**
1.	1.
2.	2.
3.	3.
4.	4.
5.	5.

July 11
Read Mark 14:27-31

Mark 14:27

"You will all fall away," Jesus told them, "for it is written: I will strike the shepherd, and the sheep will be scattered."

Jesus had been the Shepherd for the disciples and they were very dependent on Him. He warned them of the prophecy of Zechariah 13:7 that said when He was taken they would all scatter as seeds in the wind.

The disciples did not seem to realize the Holy Spirit would be with them, even during those trying hours. Often we, as Christians, walk by sight rather than by faith. There are times when we may feel Jesus is far away, but He is as close as we let Him be, in the presence of the Holy Spirit.

Jesus knew of the coming ordeal. He knew He would be killed and rise again to victory. Although He taught and told His disciples, they failed to comprehend the meaning of His teaching while they were with Him. We must comprehend the meaning of the Word and take hold of it, apply it, and be able to stand on it. We do not know how we will react when certain trials come our way, but we do know that we can overcome and be kept from falling (Jude 24) when we face adversity. God holds the future and we need to face it with His strength and wisdom instead of ours alone.

Turn your eyes and look on Jesus. We should desire His Spiritual strength in glory and grace. He is able to keep us, if we do His will and honor Him by believing on Him.

DAILY PRAISES **DAILY PRAYER REQUESTS**

1. 1.

2. 2.

3. 3.

4. 4.

5. 5.

July 12
Read I Peter 1:13-25

I Peter 1:23

"For you have been born again, not of perishable seed, but of imperishable, through the living and enduring word of God."

The Christian's true and sure foundation is Christ Jesus and His Word. Jesus is the Living Word. He is the only reliable foundation upon which to build one's life. Christ is sustainable, solid, and eternal. We must stand on His promises and we will not fall.

We are born again of the Spirit of God. He puts a divine and incorruptible seed in our hearts through His Word. He brings newness of life, fullness to our beings, and everlasting life to our souls. As the Word of God abides forever, so shall we abide with Him forever. His truth will outlast all eternity, much less all earthly things, for the Word is based upon God Himself.

Our life is part of the living stones, part of God's Spiritual house. Our life is not our own, but is derived from the source of God. Jesus is the cornerstone of our Christian faith. If we believe and accept Him, we become willing to be used in His service for Him. He breaks our stony heart and makes it new. It is the sign of a wise human, who accepts the Word of God and adheres to its commands.

Every person has a choice to accept or reject the Word of God. Those who accept it shall be saved. Those who reject it shall receive damnation.

Which have you chosen? Do you know for sure that your name is written in Heaven? You can know today, by accepting Jesus. Make sure you are saved.

DAILY PRAISES	**DAILY PRAYER REQUESTS**
1.	1.
2.	2.
3.	3.
4.	4.
5.	5.

July 13
Read Ecclesiastes 2:10-16

Ecclesiastes 2:13

"I saw that wisdom is better than folly, just as light is better than darkness."

Solomon was a man who asked God for wisdom instead of riches. God granted him wisdom and thoroughly blessed him with riches, also. Solomon eventually turned from divine wisdom to natural resources and reasoning. His life got off course and away from the highest ideals and noblest purposes to the depths of folly and devastation. He was out of fellowship with God and turned in all directions to see what his heart could find for pleasure and satisfaction. Solomon began to look at life and all he had done, all of his possessions, and his self-indulgence. He said he had everything his heart could desire and found it all vanity.

There was no lasting pleasure for Solomon away from God. His conclusion was that wisdom is of more value than foolishness of this world. Just as light is better than darkness for people to see, the wise man sees wisdom as the most important asset. The fool is still searching for happiness in ways of the world.

Only the Lord Jesus Christ can give life. He gives the most rewarding, meaningful, beautiful kind of life. He gives purpose, establishes values in our souls, and teaches our hearts the way of righteousness. If we fully commit ourselves to the Lord, He will develop us into stronger, more loving Christians, who can share our relationship in Jesus with others. We need God's help in everything. Remember we cannot do it alone.

DAILY PRAISES
1.
2.
3.
4.
5.

DAILY PRAYER REQUESTS
1.
2.
3.
4.
5.

July 14
Read Matthew 28:1-10

Matthew 28:2

"There was a violent earthquake, for an angel of the Lord came down from heaven and going to the tomb, rolled back the stone and sat on it."

The fact that Jesus arose from the grave is what our entire faith and hopes are built upon. The apostle Paul staked his entire life unto the faith. Our hope of life after death is rooted and grounded in the certainty of the Resurrection of Jesus. It is not speculation, but reality, a known fact. Oh, how joyful is this Resurrection story! We are certain it took place. We know it is true, because Jesus lives. There is an empty grave where Jesus was laid. Because He is alive we will also live forever.

The most sensible person should dedicate their life to the Lord. It is the sanest thing anyone could ever do. He is our clear hope for survival in a world that is ruled with fear, misery, emptiness, loneliness, and no purpose.

Imagine the joy as the women arrived at the empty tomb of Jesus! How they must have rejoiced that God was at work and the tomb was empty.

We know that we cannot suffer defeat when we ally ourselves with the Lord and His purpose for our lives. This is just what Jesus had done. He came to do the will of God, His Father. He arose from the tomb and shed the grave clothes as a moth sheds its cocoon. The Resurrection power of God assures us victory in our daily living. We have victory over sin and can live a joyful spiritual life. All we have to do is trust Jesus.

DAILY PRAISES	**DAILY PRAYER REQUESTS**
1.	1.
2.	2.
3.	3.
4.	4.
5.	5.

July 15
Read Judges 16:1-22

Judges 16:18

"When Delilah saw that he had told her everything, she sent word to the rulers of the Philistines, 'come back once more; he has told me everything.' So the rulers of the Philistines returned with the silver in their hands."

We all have our weaknesses and the devil is taking advantage of them. We are to resist temptation. Often that means not going places where we will be tempted. We have to pray for the Lord to keep us during temptation and make a way for our escape.

Samson judged Israel twenty years and he had to have a good knowledge of God's law. Samson was a humorous person who knew a lot about human nature. He was very brave and fearless. His downfall appears to have been women. He did backslide and let a woman know the secret of his strength. How sad to see someone abandoning himself to the lawless indulgence of his appetites and passions. What a disaster one strong man made of his life. He became a fool for the love and desire of a woman who was using him for her advantage. One more fool thought he could dally with evil and get away with it.

God raised up a man to serve Him and he ended up serving himself in the end. It is unwise to take our life into our own hands. We should pray and ask God for directions. We cannot expect God to guide us when we do not seek His help or when we go against His direction or purpose.

The story of Samson illustrates the progression of sin and the effects of sin in a life. Sin tends to grow and get stronger if it is not checked. Through repentance and prayer, we find forgiveness and are united with the Lord.

DAILY PRAISES
1.
2.
3.
4.
5.

DAILY PRAYER REQUESTS
1.
2.
3.
4.
5.

July 16
Read Exodus 12:21-28

Exodus 12:28

"The Israelites did just what the Lord commanded Moses and Aaron>"

Moses had approached the Pharaoh many times, asking for the release of the children of Israel. Each time the Pharaoh refused to lose them. Ten plagues fell on the Egyptians because of the hardness of Pharaoh's heart. The plagues were:

1. Water turned into blood.
2. A vast amount of frogs.
3. Lice, sand flies, and fleas appeared.
4. There were swarms of flies.
5. Murrain on the cattle.
6. Boils and blain on men and beasts.
7. An enormous hailstorm.
8. Locusts occurred everywhere.
9. Dense darkness over the country.
10. The death of all first born in Egypt.

The Pharaoh had a willful stubborn heart. Each time Moses encountered him it hardened his heart even more. His attitude was for his will and his way. God cares for His people. Those who love Him and serve Him will be well taken care of. This teaches us that when we ask God for something, He moves hearts to give us our prayer. We need to learn to ask and rely upon the sufficiency of God. God makes a difference between His people and people of the world. We need to be watchful and careful that we live for Christ and walk after His commandments rather than after our selfish way or ways of the world.

Christ shed His blood for the remission of our sins. His sacrifice is sufficient for all eternity. He can and will deliver us from sin. We must be willing to obey Him. He is our hope. We must place our faith in Him and understand our place of service and know our calling and worship at the center of God's will.

DAILY PRAISES	**DAILY PRAYER REQUESTS**
1.	1.
2.	2.
3.	3.
4.	4.
5.	5.

July 17
Read Genesis 3:1-7

Genesis 3:3

"But God did say, 'You must not eat fruit from the tree that is in the middle of the garden, and you must not touch it or you will die' "

The tempter entered the Garden of Eden for the purpose of deceiving mankind. We do not know a lot about the serpent other than it was an instrument of Satan. If it was a real snake or Satan took the form of a snake does not appear clear, but the purpose for the snake being there is clear and its mission was accomplished.

The devil uses various instruments as his agent to work for him as he used the serpent with Eve.

God selected this tree for a moral test of man. It was a test of obedience for the occupants in the Garden. The real test was God's way or man's way. How many times do we have to pay for doing things our way instead of God's way? Satan is still at work setting out to lure people away from God. He attracts our attention. He begins to talk to us. He raises doubts in our minds. He contradicts Divine authority and the Bible. He undermines God's motives. What a lie and illusion the devil is! Nothing outside of God's will is a blessing or good for us.

The consequences of sin are:
1. We are separated from God.
2. It brings suffering, pain and sorrow.
3. It brings death, which is an eternal separation from God.

We have victory over Satan and through Jesus. We can use the Word when we are tempted, as Jesus did. Praise Jesus for the Word! Make sure you know enough of the Bible to rebuke the devil and don't be deceived. Read the Bible daily.

DAILY PRAISES
1.
2.
3.
4.
5.

DAILY PRAYER REQUESTS
1.
2.
3.
4.
5.

July 18
Read Luke 2:41-52

Luke 2:52

"And Jesus grew in wisdom and stature, and in favor with God and men."

Jesus must have been a model adolescent and teenager. He submitted to parental discipline and carried out routine duties of the household. He continued to learn the skills of carpentry from Joseph.

Jesus matured physically, socially, spiritually, and intellectually. Our children can have a balanced adolescent and teenage growth period if we provide an atmosphere at home, school, and church which contribute to intellectual maturity and emotional stability. These must be accompanied by wisdom as well as love and discipline. Physical maturity comes by proper diet, rest, and a schedule of well-balanced activities to promote physical exercise. Social interaction with adults and peers will develop when our children are properly supervised and treated with love. Spiritual growth takes place as we provide Bible study, worship, prayer, and other Christian activities within our home and church of which the children are a part. When adolescents and teenagers acknowledge parental authority it is a blessing because the Bible instructs children to obey and honor their parents.

It is important for a child to receive Spiritual nurture in the home and church. The experiences a child goes through from infancy and early childhood prepare them for their behavior throughout life. As Christian parents we have the guidance of the Holy Spirit to aid us in directing and leading our children.

It is our duty as parents to show love to our children. Tell them you love them. Show them affection by hugging them and kissing them good night or good bye when they leave for school, etc. Affection provides security for children as well as for older people.

DAILY PRAISES
1.
2.
3.
4.
5.

DAILY PRAYER REQUESTS
1.
2.
3.
4.
5.

July 19
Read Mark 6:30-44

Mark 6:41

"Taking the five loaves and the two fish and looking up to heaven, He gave thanks and broke the loaves. Then He gave them to His disciples to set before the people. He also divided the two fish among them all."

Several of the miracles of Jesus were miracles of provision. The Lord is all power and He has the ability to meet every human need through the interworking of human and divine resources. This miracle speaks directly to the whole range of human needs. Jesus could have spoken the word so the food would have appeared miraculously, but He chose to combine the natural with the Spiritual and make a miracle multiply. Jesus divinely multiplied something that was natural, thereby making sufficient provisions for all those in need.

In the same way Jesus multiplies natural energies and gifts to meet the needs of people today. There is no way natural provisions would ever be sufficient to meet needs, but when the divine and natural are blended together under the anointing of Heaven, there is sufficiency. God shows us that He has everything we need and more. A great multitude witnessed the miracle of the loaves and fishes. They also participated in it by eating the food Jesus provided. Only bread of God satisfies the deepest longing in our souls. Let the Lord feed your soul today. He has exactly what you need.

DAILY PRAISES	**DAILY PRAYER REQUESTS**
1.	1.
2.	2.
3.	3.
4.	4.
5.	5.

July 20
Read Mark 3:13-15

Mark 3:15

"And to have authority to drive out demons."

Jesus appointed the apostles to complete and do the work He had begun. He gave them power much like His own, the ability to cast out unclean spirits and to heal all manner of sickness. Jesus was moved with compassion while He was here on earth. He looked upon the needs of a suffering sinful world. He directed His close associates to do as he had done for the suffering world.

Although Jesus ascended to Heaven, He sent the Holy Spirit to comfort and quicken our hearts. The Spirit is ever present with us. The apostles have died, but we can still have healing and cast out devils through the Holy Spirit and by the power and in the Name of Jesus. Jesus shed His blood at Calvary for us to be able to receive healing. At the Name of Jesus, Satan has to flee. In the Name of Jesus, by the blood at Calvary, we rebuke the devil and his power. Jesus is more powerful. Praying in His Name really works.

Healing is a reality in this present day. I personally suffered from Hypoglycemia and was told by my doctor that I would always have the disease. I was told to stay on a special diet all of my life. I am, by nature, a lover of sweets and you can imagine my dismay when I was told I could not eat sweets. I realized that if I felt better and it was better for me not to eat them I would do it. For two years I followed that diet, eating six small meals each day, no white flour, sugar, caffeine or additives in food. I prayed to be healed and let my faith take hold. I believed for healing. I was healed. Praise God, I am able to eat anything that I want now. I know His healing power is real. I know if the Lord will heal me, He will heal others.

What is your need today? Is it healing? Open your heart, pray and believe and let the Lord meet your need.

DAILY PRAISES
1.
2.
3.
4.
5.

DAILY PRAYER REQUESTS
1.
2.
3.
4.
5.

July 21
Read John 5:1-15

John 5:8

"Then Jesus said to him, "Get up! Pick up your mat and walk." At once the man was cured; he picked up his mat and walked."

Jesus is here to meet the needs of persons. People may have given up and have no hope that they can ever be well or free from what is gnawing at them. In reality, Jesus came to meet the despair, discouragement, and disappointments of humans with positive love and acts of mercy. He gives courage to the fearful, cleanses the sinner, hope to the hopeless, and life to the dying. Christ is here, in Spirit, to lift you from your despair. He is asking you, "Do you wish to be made whole?" You can be through Jesus Christ.

Jesus can stimulate your faith and give you hope and the desire to live. He can give you a renewal of expectancy and keenness of desire. How badly do you need to be healed in body or spirit? Jesus is Lord of all. He does not want people to suffer. His authority to command, grants us the authority and responsibility to obey.

The man in today's reading obeyed Jesus and was healed. He believed he could walk when Jesus told him to do so.

Many times I have been healed. It has not been a cloud clapping, earth shaking experience, but it has been in the quiet solitude of God, with faith believing and reaching toward His promises. There is power and reward for the faithful who serve the Lord. There is joy and achievement for those who love Jesus and believe in Him.

Have you personally experienced the healing of Jesus for your needs? He is here to meet you.

DAILY PRAISES
1.
2.
3.
4.
5.

DAILY PRAYER REQUESTS
1.
2.
3.
4.
5.

July 22
Read Luke 2:21-40

Luke 2:27

"Moved by the Spirit he went into the temple courts. When the parents brought in the child Jesus to do for him what the custom of the Law required."

The dedicated parents of Jesus were intent upon performing every duty prescribed by their religion. The infant, Christ, was dedicated in the Temple at Jerusalem.

The instruction recorded in Scripture is applicable to us today, as a model for Godly behavior. We have the responsibility of presenting our children to the Lord.

Today we see the morals and values of people deteriorating. We seek guidelines by which we can rely and raise our children so they will develop into strong and happy adults. We must look to the Bible as God's source of communication with our children. We will find it contains wisdom, knowledge, and valuable information for meeting life's tasks and processes.

The Spirit of the Lord will lead us in rearing our children if we are sensitive to Him. God has a plan for each life. We are responsible to help our children develop according to God's plan. As we obey the Spirit and are led by His guidance we can see the unfolding of God's plan and will for our children. Praise God for our children! What a blessing they are to lives of all ages. There is a value in dedicating children to God. It helps them to grow physically, mentally, and spiritually. Dedicating a baby does not save them, but it is a time when the parents show outwardly that they agree to raise the child by God's standards.

DAILY PRAISES	**DAILY PRAYER REQUESTS**
1.	1.
2.	2.
3.	3.
4.	4.
5.	5.

July 23
Read Hebrews 2:9-18

Hebrews 2:9

"But we see Jesus, who was made a little lower than the angels, now crowned with glory and honor because He suffered death, so that by the grace of God he might taste death for everyone."

Jesus was willing to lay aside His divine nature and take upon himself all of human nature. Jesus, who never sinned, died for all sinners and their sins. He came to live as a human among men. He was born in a lowly stable, raised in the peasant class of society, and trained to perform a common trade. He dwelt among men and women and ministered to their needs. He died a humiliating death to bring about redemption of men and women. He arose from the dead and ascended to Heaven where He sat down at the Father's right hand. He is now our intercessor. He is crowned with glory and honor.

Jesus took the bitter sting of death for us. He experienced the full horror of dying. He took the burden of guilt of all mankind and total estrangement from His Father at that time. Because He underwent such a death, the Christians death will be the mere cessation of physical activity. We will just pass from this life to Heaven. Spiritually, we shall never die. (John 11:26).

The name of Jesus is above every name and He is over all humans, who voluntarily bow before him and do His will.

Have you acknowledged Him as Lord of your life? He is the Lord of all. Let Him be your Savior today.

DAILY PRAISES	**DAILY PRAYER REQUESTS**
1.	1.
2.	2.
3.	3.
4.	4.
5.	5.

July 24
Read Luke 1:26-38

Luke 1:37
"For nothing is impossible with God."

God's power is limitless in every situation. So often we limit what we allow God to do. If we would just stand on His promises and believe through unwavering faith, we would see so much more done by the Lord.

God is in charge of the universe. He chose a handmaiden, Mary, to give birth to the Second Person in the Trinity, His Son. Mary accepted, with faith, the task of God. She performed it without question or complaining. She presented herself in total submission and accepted God's plan for her life.

God can use only yielded vessels. We need to surrender all to Him so that He can use us as instruments in His service. As we consecrate our will to His will, we unloose the forces of Divine omnipotence in our lives and make possible our increasing cooperation with God's plan and purpose for our lives. Those purposes lead to the flow of His Spirit and to evidence of the Supernatural Spirit when our need arises.

God dwells among us through the person of His Son, who brought God's message of hope to humans during His life and through His death and resurrection. His death spoke a message of deliverance to us. Because of His death we have life.

Does God's Spirit dwell within your heart? Do you have the faith to believe in the promises of the Lord?

DAILY PRAISES	**DAILY PRAYER REQUESTS**
1.	1.
2.	2.
3.	3.
4.	4.
5.	5.

July 25
Read Exodus 3:1-15

Exodus 3:4

"When the Lord saw that he had gone over to look, God called to him within the bush. "Moses! Moses!" And Moses said, "Here I am".

God calls to us in our everyday life. Sometimes He has to use drastic measures to reach us and teach us that His way is best. Our stubborn will must be broken so that God's will can operate in our lives. To be used of God, we must yield to Him completely. We must acquire those qualifications such as humility, faith, and patience. These qualities are necessary before God can use us.

God got Moses' attention by using the burning bush. When He had Moses' attention He spoke to him by name. God makes His way into the depths of our hearts by getting our attention. He often has a message we need to hear and He has a way of communicating that message to us when He is able to get our attention, just as He did to Moses.

We need to be like Moses and reply to God immediately, "Here I am, Lord". We need to have a teachable mind and attitude. We should be open to receive whatever instruction the Spirit speaks to us. We need to be prepared to obey the Lord. We need to be willing to follow the instructions of the Lord. We need to stand before the Lord in reverence and awe and say, "Lord send me, I am willing to go."

Are you willing to let the spirit speak to you? Do you have a teachable attitude and mind? Are you listening to the Lord, as He speaks to you?

DAILY PRAISES	**DAILY PRAYER REQUESTS**
1.	1.
2.	2.
3.	3.
4.	4.
5.	5.

July 26
Read Genesis 1:1-31

Genesis 1:1

"In the beginning God created the heavens and the earth."

God was living and active in the beginning of time. God is everlasting. He always was and always will be God. God is a person. He is not a lonely God. He is all powerful and loving. God said, "Let us make man." He could have been speaking to the angels or to the Trinity. God does have a personality. We can see the tender love He had as He created the six creative days.

The work of the six days in Genesis chapter one:
1. Light and dark in verses 3-5;
2. Sea and sky in verses 6-8;
3. Land, sea, and vegetation in verses 9-13;
4. Sun, moon, and stars in verses 14-19;
5. Marine life and flying creatures in verses 20-23;
6. Land animals in verses 24-25.

Creation is a miracle performed by our omnipotent God. If you believe in God you must believe and know the possibility of His ability to create. We must realize that Genesis is the inspired Word of God and it is without error. It establishes the order of His creative activity. We know God created man 'in the image of God'. So there is something in man which is akin to God. Man is not satisfied until he accepts God and walks, talks, and communicates with God. Man's life is empty and void until God fills that vacant spot, which is meant for God. Have you filled the void in your life with the Lord Jesus Christ? He is waiting for you today.

DAILY PRAISES	**DAILY PRAYER REQUESTS**
1.	1.
2.	2.
3.	3.
4.	4.
5.	5.

July 27
Read Isaiah 58:6-14

Isaiah 58:11

"The Lord will guide you always; He will satisfy your needs in a sun scorched land and will strengthen your frame. You will be like a well-watered garden, like a spring whose Waters never fail."

Someday God will reward the faithful. We must get our priorities in order. According to the Word we need to be concerned about the lost, once we become Christians. There is rejoicing in Heaven when one soul is saved. The angels rejoice more over one sinner being saved than over ninety-nine righteous persons.

Souls are valuable to God. God values each person. We should also value the lives of the lost as assets to be brought into the Kingdom of God.

There is a price to pay for gaining lost souls. It is through prayer and fasting. God's kind of fast touches people. Souls are born again; the hungry are filled, and fed. The naked are clothed, the homeless are given a home and the sick are made well. The glory of God will go before us, as we fast, He will also be our rear guard.

When we do God's will, we are pleasing to Him. He will reward us for every act of kindness performed through love. People respond to people who do the will of God first and foremost in their lives. We must show love and let people know and see Jesus in us. We will be blessed as we bless others.

Where are your priorities? Are they operating according to God's Word?

DAILY PRAISES　　　　　　**DAILY PRAYER REQUESTS**

1.　　　　　　　　　　　　　1.

2.　　　　　　　　　　　　　2.

3.　　　　　　　　　　　　　3.

4.　　　　　　　　　　　　　4.

5.　　　　　　　　　　　　　5.

July 28
Read Colossians 3:1-11

Colossians 3:1

"Since, then, you have been raised with Christ, set your hearts on things above, where Christ is seated at the right hand of God."

Put away the 'old man' by letting Christ help you as He fills you with the Holy Spirit. We must be led by His Spirit. We must put 'old things' aside and serve God as a new person.

We know that Jesus has ascended to Heaven and we are seeking those things which are above. All good things come from the Father above.

We should all honor the Son of God, who was sent to this earth to save sinners. He gave His life on Calvary for sinners to be saved. He is real. Believe on Him today.

We need to look up because our redemption is near. Be strong in grace. Put on the whole armor of God and be able to stand against evil.

It is time to share the cross of Jesus and then someday we will share Heaven with Him and His Father and the Holy Spirit, as well as the angels and our loved ones.

Let us put those things above as our first priority. Jesus will supply all of our needs. He desires to be first in our lives.

DAILY PRAISES	**DAILY PRAYER REQUESTS**
1.	1.
2.	2.
3.	3.
4.	4.
5.	5.

July 29
Read II Thessalonians 1:3-12

II Thessalonians 1:12

"We pray this so that the Name of our Lord Jesus may be glorified in you, and you in Him, according to the grace of our God and the Lord Jesus Christ."

A person's name used to be valuable. It meant what a person was. The Name of Jesus is still the one we can call on or turn to for whatever we need. He never changes.

Jesus will lift up those who recognize Him and call on His Name. His love for all mankind is so great we could never measure it or put a price tag on it.

He has been merciful to us and we should give Him the praise and glory. Let us continue to magnify His Name.

He has given us health and for that let us tell the world about Him and the fellowship He can give us.

Let us be glad and rejoice for what Christ has done for us. Let us give Him praise, testimony, and daily rejoicing. We should continue to pray and seek His leading, knowledge, wisdom and understanding.

Thank and praise God always for everything. Let us glorify His Name above all names. Let him be first and foremost always in our lives. We will never be sorry we have let the Lord be first and revered His Name.

DAILY PRAISES
1.
2.
3.
4.
5.

DAILY PRAYER REQUESTS
1.
2.
3.
4.
5.

July 30
Read Psalm 34:1-22

Psalm34:18

"The Lord is close to the brokenhearted and saves those who are crushed in spirit."

Jesus is as close as we let Him be. He wants to help us in every situation. He can make the hard and heavy situations seem easy and light. He bears us up in His arms in time of great troubles and burdens, if we will only let Him. He wants to walk side by side with us each day. He wants to talk with us, as we listen for His voice and obey Him. He gives that great peace, for which everyone is seeking.

He saves those who are truly sorry for their sins and desire to be forgiven. He never remembers those sins again. Today is the day to be forgiven.

No one is promised tomorrow, so we cannot be sure of having the opportunity of getting sins forgiven tomorrow. Do it now, while you have time. Begin to love and praise God for His love and grace. He is just as near as you want Him to be. He helps as much as you will allow Him to help you. Open your heart and life to Him.

DAILY PRAISES	**DAILY PRAYER REQUESTS**
1.	1.
2.	2.
3.	3.
4.	4.
5.	5.

July 31
Read Matthew 25:14-30

Matthew 25:23

"His master replied, "Well done, good and faithful servant! You have been faithful with a few things; I will put you in charge of many things. Come and share your master's happiness!"

We have the responsibility of occupying our position until Jesus returns. To occupy means to use what is possessed. We should carefully consider our responsibility to put our talents and abilities to good use. We should make them as effective and profitable as possible for the kingdom of God. The signs of the end of time are real. The need for preparation is serious. There is a call from Jesus for consecrated service.

All of us have been given talents to use for the Lord. We are responsible for what we do with these special abilities. How wonderful to be able to stand before Jesus and say, "I have used what you gave me and I have gained souls for the kingdom!"

We must be obedient in the application of our abilities. Obedience is a condition of the heart. It is also a reflection of one's attitude and character. If we focus on the Lord's gain first and realize that our gain will come from the Lord. We will truly be rewarded in the end.

We should serve Jesus with joy. We should be joyful when we render fruit of our labor to the Lord. Then what a joyous wonderful day when we are asked by the Lord to enter into His Kingdom! For being faithful servants of Christ, we will rule and reign with Him during the Millennium. We will attend the Marriage Supper of the Lamb! Oh, what a wonderful time! Praise Him!

DAILY PRAISES　　　　　　　**DAILY PRAYER REQUESTS**
1.　　　　　　　　　　　　　　1.

2.　　　　　　　　　　　　　　2.

3.　　　　　　　　　　　　　　3.

4.　　　　　　　　　　　　　　4.

5.　　　　　　　　　　　　　　5.

AUGUST

August 1
Read Psalm 103:7-22

Psalm 103:17

"But from everlasting to everlasting the Lord's love is with those who fear him and his righteousness with their children's children."

It is hard for us, as humans, to imagine something being everlasting. But that is how God's mercy works. We are to be respectful, worshipful, and standing in awe of His wonderful everlasting mercy. When we do that, it will be well with us. There will be a reward for our righteousness if we follow and live for God.

He will not keep good things from His children. He will continue to bless those that serve Him and walk before Him. He will also continue to bless the children of those that serve Him. We know that we will not labor in vain. God has promised us mercy, love, and deliverance if we seek and serve Him.

I see the evidence of the Lord working in the lives of my children and grandchildren continuously. I see Him blessing them and doing great things for them. I am holding onto the Lord to save the ones outside the Lord's Kingdom. I know He will save as He promised. I love the Lord with all my soul, mind, and strength. My greatest desire is to please the Lord with my life and for my children and grandchildren to serve this great One and only God.

DAILY PRAISES	**DAILY PRAYER REQUESTS**
1.	1.
2.	2.
3.	3.
4.	4.
5.	5.

August 2
Read Philippians 1:15-30

Philippians 1:29

"For it has been granted to you on behalf of Christ not only to believe on him, but also to suffer for him."

When we come to Christ, we agree to serve Him but sometimes it means we must suffer for His Name. If we are suffering because we are Christians we should praise God, because His Spirit is in us and we are worthy to suffer for Him.

This suffering will bring with it patience, experience, and growth. We grow closer to God as we encounter and suffer through every trial.

This suffering is only for a short time because we will soon be through the trial. These earthly trials only last for a short time. We must be patient during the suffering as we trust Jesus to deliver us. Later we will be taken to Heaven where we will never be persecuted or suffer trials again.

Do not be ashamed to suffer for the one who died for you. Glorify His Name and be glad. Very soon we will be reigning with Him. Everything we suffer now is to teach us to reign with him and live eternally.

DAILY PRAISES	**DAILY PRAYER REQUESTS**
1.	1.
2.	2.
3.	3.
4.	4.
5.	5.

August 3
Read I John 2:1-14

I John 2:2

"He is the atoning sacrifice for our sins, and not only for ours but also for the sins of the whole world."

We know Jesus gave His life for our sins. He arose again that we might have life. He is waiting to forgive and forget our sins.

Though your sins are as crimson and many, Jesus is waiting to forgive them and receive you as a child of God.

I was collecting shells on a beach in Florida. I took some conch shells from the ocean that were covered with barnacles and badly discolored from the salty water and the elements. I began to clean those shells and get rid of the foreign materials that had attached to them. As I cleansed them and saw the foreign particles come off the shells and fly away or just drop off. I thought of how Jesus cleanses us and helps us get rid of those weights which we have collected. Jesus forgives our sins and casts them far away from us. He will never remember them again or hold them against us.

He can bring you back to your original luster and purpose. He can help you live a natural life for Him in honor of what He has done for you.

DAILY PRAISES	**DAILY PRAYER REQUESTS**
1.	1.
2.	2.
3.	3.
4.	4.
5.	5.

August 4
Read II Corinthians 5:1-10

II Corinthians 5:10

"For we must all appear before the judgment seat of Christ, that each one may receive what is due him for the things done while in the body, whether good or bad."

We Christians will be judged by the works we have done as Christians. An unwilling Christian will not receive a reward. The person who has an undisciplined body or mind will not qualify for a prize. This verse tells us seven certainties:

1. The judgment is certain for Christians.
2. We must all appear, as believers.
3. Christ, Himself, will conduct the judgment.
4. Each believer will be judged individually.
5. This judgment will be concerned with the works Christians perform while on earth.
6. The works of the believer will be bare. All that we have done will be brought to judgment.
7. Christ will evaluate all the works we have done and they will be categorized as either good or worthless.

They will stand the test or be consumed.

Let us prepare for this judgment by doing good works that will stand. They will stand if the following is true:

1. They are performed in obedience to the Lord.
2. They are performed in the Spirit and by the power of God.
3. They are done for the glory of God and not for self-glorification.

DAILY PRAISES
1.
2.
3.
4.
5.

DAILY PRAYER REQUESTS
1.
2.
3.
4.
5.

August 5
Read II Corinthians 5:11-21

II Corinthians 5:20

"We are therefore Christ's ambassadors, as though God were making his appeal through us. We implore you on Christ's behalf; Be reconciled to God."

To be reconciled is to do away with an enmity. Sinners are enemies of God. An enemy is someone who is on the opposite side. He is altogether opposed. God is vigorously opposed to everything that is evil.

An ambassador for the Kingdom of God means we must first have been born into the Kingdom. We are now new creatures and complete in Christ. When we are in Christ, we are new, living a new life at its fullest. We should see ourselves as a representative of God. We should carry the good news to the lost people in the world.

It is only possible to be an ambassador for God because He has reconciled us to Him. When we are reconciled to God we are also reconciled to one another.

God gives us peace when we come to Him. We also have peace with each other and are able to live together in peace and contentment as we serve the Lord.

We must spend time in prayer and time in God's Word in order to witness to the lost. We are each responsible for our ambassadorship which Christ has entrusted to us to minister to our friends and acquaintances.

DAILY PRAISES	**DAILY PRAYER REQUESTS**
1.	1.
2.	2.
3.	3.
4.	4.
5.	5.

August 6
Read Matthew 10:22-33

Matthew 10:32

"Whoever acknowledges me before men, I will also acknowledge him before my Father in Heaven."

We appear to be living in the last days on this earth. People seem to be doing their own thing. If they have a few moments to recognize God, it is okay. If they do not have time for God, they seem not to be concerned.

We know that today is the day of Salvation and we need to take a stand for our Savior. We should seek Him first and He will add all the other things. We must have the right relationship with the Lord by putting our priorities in the correct order. We need to be honest with God and with others. Our relationships should be in a way that is loving and caring toward all humans.

Our conversation should be Holy. Our life should be a witness to others. We are to be real. We need to strive to be like Christ. We should be led by the Holy Spirit to do the will of the Lord.

As we live and do the things pleasing to God we will be confessing Him before others. Jesus will confess us before His Father one day. It is a very simple act to live for the Lord. There is nothing complicated about it. It is the natural way to live. Christ created us to worship Him. Sin entered into us. We must confess sin and be born anew into the family of God. We must continue to walk beside the Lord as He guides us into His will.

DAILY PRAISES **DAILY PRAYER REQUESTS**
1. 1.
2. 2.
3. 3.
4. 4.
5. 5.

August 7
Read Matthew 5:13-16

Matthew 5:16

"In the same way, let your light shine before men, that they may see your good deeds and praise your Father in Heaven."

We, as Christians, should be so very thankful. Christ has saved us and given us His Holy Spirit to help us live for Him. He provides us glory by being with us continually.

Jesus is Lord over all. He has all power of Heaven and earth. He is the mediator between God and man. He loves us so much and desires that we serve Him.

We should adorn ourselves with the whole armor of God. We should let our light shine to this lost world. God has given us His greatest gift of love. We are to share that love with others so they will be born again into the Kingdom of God. Our mission is to bring others into the Kingdom so God may be glorified and pleased with our earthly works.

Christ is in us and we are in Him. We have a Spiritual help in this life. We are no longer controlled by the flesh, but by the Spirit. In Christ, we are victorious and when we have victory we have peace. Let us praise and glorify Jesus Christ. Let us be as a beacon shining out for the entire world to see that we have something special in Jesus. Let your light always shine.

DAILY PRAISES	DAILY PRAYER REQUESTS
1.	1.
2.	2.
3.	3.
4.	4.
5.	5.

August 8
Read Romans 8:18-27

Romans 8:18

"I Consider that our present sufferings are not worth comparing with the glory that will be revealed in us."

It is easy to say, "I am a Christian," as we relax with family and friends. But when we are faced with grief, a giant trial, or tribulation, are we willing to let God lead and guide? Through trials, temptations, and heartaches, comes growth in Christ.

When we are not encountering troubles we need to stop and listen to what the Lord is telling us. Let us not wait until troubles come to our door to listen to the Lord.

We know Heaven will truly be worth everything we have to suffer in this life. God has not given us all the details of Heaven. He has given us enough to know that it will be a dynamic, wonderful, beautiful experience, far above anything our finite minds can comprehend. Heaven will be the essence of joy, satisfaction, and a song. We look forward to forever being with the Lord and loved ones.

Yes, Jesus is the answer for all problems and fears. He will comfort and give peace in this life, then reward us in Heaven. Think of the worst thing you could ever suffer in this life. Heaven will certainly be worth so much more than that miserable suffering you imagined. When we do suffer, we have the Lord to go with us through each trial and trouble. We have double coverage with Jesus. Praise him.

DAILY PRAISES	**DAILY PRAYER REQUESTS**
1.	1.
2.	2.
3.	3.
4.	4.
5.	5.

August 9
Read Isaiah 59:12-21

Isaiah 59:19

"From the west, men will fear the name of the Lord, and from the rising of the sun, they will revere His glory. For He will come like a pent-up flood that the breath of the Lord drives along."

Salvation is only from God. His Name is to be praised from the rising of the sun until the setting of the sun. Those who serve the Lord will reverence and love His Name. Those who worship the Lord will be kept when the enemy comes against them like a mighty flood. The Spirit of the Living God will put the enemy to flight as it tries to flood out the love of Jesus.

We are assured that "greater is He that is in us than he that is in the world." The enemy cannot destroy us if we stand on the Word of God and believe the promises in the Bible.

When the flood comes to you quote the Bible to it. Pray in the Name of Jesus against the flood of the devil. Praise the Name of Jesus in the midst of the flood. Ask another Christian to help you pray. Talk to your pastor about the flood if you cannot seem to overcome it on your own while praying and praising. Two or three gathered together and praying will be able to conquer the flood. Believe God's word for deliverance.

DAILY PRAISES	**DAILY PRAYER REQUESTS**
1.	1.
2.	2.
3.	3.
4.	4.
5.	5.

August 10
Read II Corinthians 5:11-21

II Corinthians 5:15

"And he died for all, that those who live should no longer live for themselves but for him who died for them and was raised again."

We know that the New Covenant was brought into existence so that all of mankind could be saved. God loves everyone and desires that all come unto Him. In Him we will find new life, hope, comfort, peace, and happiness.

Life seems difficult when we live for ourselves. There is a better way of life than living for self. We find happiness that we never knew existed when we live for Christ.

Jesus gives us the power to live for Him. He helps us to become a new person through Him. He puts His Spirit within us and helps us to walk according to His Word.

Jesus desires everyone to come to the knowledge of the truth of Salvation and know Him in a personal way.

We who are Christians do not have a monopoly on Christ. He is free to all who will come and deny themselves and follow Him. He is ALIVE! He is still in control. He still REIGNS! Come to Him today and accept Him and live the new life.

DAILY PRAISES	**DAILY PRAYER REQUESTS**
1.	1.
2.	2.
3.	3.
4.	4.
5.	5.

August 11
Read Luke 17:20-37

Luke 17:21

"Nor will people say, "Here it is' or "There it is,'" Because the kingdom of God is within you."

People have always been looking for an easier way to serve God. They are looking for some kind of scheme to be equal to God or to be above God. There is no easy, quick scheme. The way is so simple and royal. Look to the Lord for real Salvation. There is no substitute.

What a wonderful day and age in which we live. We have the Holy Spirit within us to teach, quicken, guide, and direct us. Jesus does not walk with us in a physical body, but He has put the Holy Spirit in us to walk with us in all wisdom and knowledge. Isn't that exciting? Jesus is always with us. We are never alone.

It is a real blessing to experience the new life which Christ provided for us. It is a life that cannot be bought with silver or gold. It is a life that is obtained when we allow Jesus to be Lord of our life. It is a life that will give us understanding, wisdom, knowledge, and love. This life with Christ will give good gifts because He loves us more than we love our own children, even more than we can realize the extent of love, He loves us.

Oh, what a blessing in this new life with Christ leading us. The indwelling of the Holy Spirit makes us able to withstand all of the attacks hurled against us.

DAILY PRAISES	**DAILY PRAYER REQUESTS**
1.	1.
2.	2.
3.	3.
4.	4.
5.	5.

August 12
Read Matthew 1:18-25

Matthew 1:21

"She will give birth to a son, and you are to give him the name Jesus, because he will save his people from their sins."

Jesus is the one whom Isaiah prophesied would be given as a sign. The name of Jesus is hope for all for now and for the future as well as for Eternity. Jesus washes away sins. Sinners are the object of His love and affection. He came willingly to be sacrificed for sinners. He suffered for us. He understands our needs.

Although Jesus was never guilty of sin, He was tempted as we are. He overcame temptation by using the Word of God and so can we overcome by proclaiming Jesus. He comes into our lives to help us do the things we cannot do. He is our Savior and Counselor. He is the Right Hand of God. He is also in our hearts. He is the Light of the World. He is our Intercessor with the Father. He really loves us. He desires to wash everyone's sins away and put shattered lives together again.

Today whatever is wrong in your life can be remarkably cured. Oh, it might not be as you would have it to be, but it will be peace and love. Life will be worth living. Things can be good in your life and so much better in your heart.

DAILY PRAISES	**DAILY PRAYER REQUESTS**
1.	1.
2.	2.
3.	3.
4.	4.
5.	5.

August 13
Read 16:7-18

I Chronicles 16:10

"Glory in his holy name; let the hearts of those who seek the Lord rejoice."

Oh, what a privilege and a joy to be a child of the King of Glory! How happy we should be as Christians. It is an honor to have sins forgiven and be able to praise our Savior and Lord.

It is our duty to sing praises and rejoice for what the Lord has done in our lives. We should rejoice because we have the faith to trust in His Name. We are to praise him continually for His marvelous works. He truly has done great things. He made the earth and all things that are in it. He prepared heaven for His people. He gives strength and gladness to His children.

Let us give the Lord the glory which is due Him. We should talk of all His wondrous works and deeds. Make all the deeds of the Lord known to all people. Let us be glad and rejoice because the Lord is in control. He reigns in Heaven as well as on earth. Praise the Name of the Lord.

DAILY PRAISES	**DAILY PRAYER REQUESTS**
1.	1.
2.	2.
3.	3.
4.	4.
5.	5.

August 14
Read Psalm 103:1-23

Psalm 103:3

"Who forgives all your sins and heals all your diseases."

We know that recovery is of God. The body is often afflicted with various hurts and diseases, but Jesus made the provision for healing and recovery from those hurts and diseases.

You must come boldly to Christ and cry out to Him in time of distress. He is aware of our needs. He wants us to tell Him what we need, in faith, believing that He will deliver us from our troubles.

Often our hearts need to be healed from heartache and pain that we have encountered along the way of life. Jesus desires to remove those hurtful scars if we will allow Him to love us and we will love Him in return.

There were times when I thought my pain would never ease from the sudden, accidental death of our eighteen-year-old daughter. Jesus, the healer, delivered us from the gnawing pain of grief. He has given us peace and comfort as we look toward Heaven with anticipation of meeting our daughter again.

How I thank the Lord because He does forgive and heal. It is for you, just as it is for me. He is true and faithful to His Word. Believe Him for your healing. Trust Him to do what He said. Do the things that the Bible instructs us to do. The Lord cares for you.

DAILY PRAISES   **DAILY PRAYER REQUESTS**
1.   1.
2.   2.
3.   3.
4.   4.
5.   5.

August 15
Read John 4:4-26

John 4:10

"Jesus answered her, "If you knew the gift of God and who it is that asks you for a drink, you would have asked Him and He would have given you living water."

People everywhere are starving for the gospel of Christ. Jesus has all the answers. The world needs someone to lead them to Christ. Jesus met the people's needs at every opportunity, as He ministered on earth. He had a deep compassion for the lost, sick, and lonely. As followers of Jesus, we also need to be aware of the needs of our fellow humans.

Jesus was void of sin and harmful bias and prejudice. We should strive to be like Him and not condone talk about fellow believers or others.

One of the most exciting examples of Jesus' ministry to the lost was the Samaritan woman. She tried to change the subject but Jesus responded with a positive aspect of God's relationship of loving and caring and dealing with people. Christ continued to turn negatives into positives by telling the woman about the "Living Water". God continues to satisfy that thirst for the 'Living Water'. By contrast the thirsting the world produces continue to grow and will never be satisfied. Christ introduced a topic close to her lifestyle of sin, which got her attention. She recognized the supernatural power of God through Christ and became excited. We must do as the woman at the well and release the area of our life that needs healing. We must let go and let the Lord minister to us.

DAILY PRAISES	**DAILY PRAYER REQUESTS**
1.	1.
2.	2.
3.	3.
4.	4.
5.	5.

August 16
Read Luke 14:25-35

Luke 14:27

"And anyone who does not carry and follow me cannot be my disciple."

The cross is an example of ultimate sacrifice. Jesus wants us to be totally committed to Him. Every person has burdens, responsibilities, grief, illness, and sadness. When we become a Christian it does not cause all of these things to go away. But we have someone to help us with all of our problems and burdens. We can cast them on Jesus. The devil will use problems and burdens to hinder our walk with Christ, but 'greater is He that is in us than he that is in the world'.

When we take up the cross for Christ we must often deny ourselves. The cross also represents glorious communion as we give ourselves to the service of the Lord. We must die out to self in order to have eternal life; suffer in order to triumph; and surrender in order to gain victory.

Our Christian life is warfare against Satan. We must know where our resources are for doing battle and be prepared. We must let Jesus have full power over our lives and render full service to Him.

Jesus invites all persons to salvation, service communion, and celebration. He holds forth a rigorous standard, taking up the cross. Jesus knows the nature of the course we are to follow, the sacrifices we must make, and the hardships we will have to endure. He knows the enemy we must subdue before reaching our final celebration, THE MARRIAGE SUPPER OF THE LAMB.

DAILY PRAISES	**DAILY PRAYER REQUESTS**
1.	1.
2.	2.
3.	3.
4.	4.
5.	5.

August 17
Read Jude 17-25

Jude 20

"But you, dear friends, build yourselves up in your most holy faith and pray in the Holy Spirit."

When people desire to build themselves up physically, it takes work daily, repeating the work over and over. Adding more time in working up to the physical capacity desired is a must to get where you want to be. We must take time to be with God and His Word. We must spend time in prayer, serious prayer, steadfast prayer, and zealous prayer.

Let us cleanse ourselves from all things that are unlike God and work toward holiness as God would have us to be.

The Holy Spirit was given to bring comfort. It also quickens our spirit so that we may know God's will. The Spirit gives peace in this life. We are to be led by the Spirit. The Spirit will lead us to goodness, righteousness, and truth.

As we build a strong relationship with God, we are to pray in the Holy Spirit. When we do not know what to pray for the Holy Spirit takes over and does the interceding for us.

Are you spiritually strong? Have you started a program toward Spiritual growth? It is very important to get started. It is the only thing that has lasting value. It is great to be in good physical condition, but it will only last as long as you work at it. It is marvelous to be in the proper Spiritual condition. The right Spiritual condition is a great way to live each day. It will even be better as we leave this world. It will last throughout eternity. Grow each day by adding a little more Spiritual work to your exercise with God.

DAILY PRAISES	**DAILY PRAYER REQUESTS**
1.	1.
2.	2.
3.	3.
4.	4.
5.	5.

August 18
Read John 14:15-31

John 14:16

"And I will ask the Father and he will give you another Counselor to be with you forever."

Jesus was explaining to His disciples the nature of His changed relationship between them. He promised to send them the Comforter, after His physical absence. The Comforter is the Holy Spirit, the third person of the Trinity. Just as Jesus promised the Holy Spirit to the disciples, He promised Him to us also.

The indwelling of the Holy Spirit is the Spirit of truth. He leads the obedient believer more deeply into truth and helps to translate the truth into practical living. The Christian knows the gentle voice of the Holy Spirit and how to respond in obedience at the sound of the voice of the Spirit.

The Holy Spirit is our friend, counselor, and helper as He dwells within us to enable us in our Spiritual warfare. He intercedes for us to the Father and the Son.

Even before conversion, the Holy Spirit was active as He urged repentance upon us, as sinners. The Spirit is active in conversion, Himself and does the work for supporting and strengthening the saved person.

When believers are baptized with the Holy Spirit they begin to experience fullness of the Spirit in His supernatural ability. As the believer yields to the Spirit, his life becomes more enriched and full.

We can experience the presence of Jesus through the Holy Spirit. The Holy Spirit is our teacher and Comforter. He is always present as He dwells in our heart. We have no excuse for defeat. We have the WINNER with us at all times. Praise the Lord for giving us the Holy Spirit.

DAILY PRAISES	**DAILY PRAYER REQUESTS**
1.	1.
2.	2.
3.	3.
4.	4.
5.	5.

August 19
Read Deuteronomy 4:15-31

Deuteronomy 4:29

"But if from there you seek the Lord your God, you will find Him if you look for Him with all your heart and with all your soul."

Have you been promising yourself and others that tomorrow or later you will serve the Lord? Today is the day of Salvation. Today is the day to begin to seek the Lord. Call upon Him in faith and He will hear you and come into your heart. Our only hope is in the Lord. We are to trust in Him with our whole heart.

Our hope comes from the Lord. We can come boldly to Him in prayer and ask for whatever we need according to His will. He answers prayers offered in faith and security by a born again believer.

We must believe that He will meet our needs as we come to Him. If we believe we have the petitions for which we pray, we will see our prayers answered.

Jesus will satisfy the emptiness and longing in souls. Without Him people are not satisfied. Something is missing from their lives. When we accept Jesus our life is made full and complete. We are to commit our daily lives to Him for direction and guidance. We are to offer praise to God for what He has done for us.

Praise Him because He saved us. Praise Him continually!

DAILY PRAISES	**DAILY PRAYER REQUESTS**
1.	1.
2.	2.
3.	3.
4.	4.
5.	5.

August 20
Read Psalm 9:1-11

Psalm 9:1

"I will praise you, O Lord, with all my heart; I will tell of all your wonders."

All praise is due God. We were created to praise God. God will have praise if the rocks and mountains have to cry out in praise to Him.

I have prepared a place in my heart for God. I will praise Him. He is my Savior. He is my strength, my happiness, my comfort, my salvation, and my righteousness. I glorify God because He has prepared a place in Heaven for me, which is one of His marvelous works. I will give Him praise for His creation, the earth, in all of its splendor and glory. I will praise the Lord for His wonderful people, who offer fellowship and love. I will praise Him for my spouse, children, and grandchildren, who are a joy from Him.

I will praise the Lord because He is God of all. He is glorious and majestic. He is love and honor. He is peace and security. The Lord is everything we need.

It is a joy to sing praises to such a wonderful Lord. Our Lord gave everything for us. The least each of us can do is offer Him our praise and glory because it is due Him. Sing and praise the Lord! Exalt him as the One and only God! Praise Him with your whole heart.

DAILY PRAISES	**DAILY PRAYER REQUESTS**
1.	1.
2.	2.
3.	3.
4.	4.
5.	5.

August 21
Read Deuteronomy 6:1-9

Deuteronomy 6:5

"Love the Lord your God with all your heart and with all your soul and with all your strength."

How much do you love the Lord? Do you love Him enough to follow where He leads you? Do you love Him enough to trust Him and not worry? Do you love Him more than the world?

So many times we hear people say they love the Lord, yet they spend all of their time with things of the world rather than spending daily time with Jesus. If we truly love Jesus we will spend time with Him and keep His commandments. We will love others and have a desire to see them come to Christ.

To love the Lord is to read His Word daily and write it in our hearts for safe keeping. We must communicate with the Lord daily. If we love Him, we will want to talk and pray to Him and listen for Him to speak to us. We willingly obey His leading. He will deliver us in time of trouble and affliction, because we love Him and serve Him.

We cannot imagine the things God has prepared for us because we love Him and serve Him. 'Eye has not seen them, nor has the ear heard them'. Our love for God is proven as we daily live for Him in awe and love.

Let us love with all of our soul, mind, and strength today. It is such a peaceful good life when the love for God is the number one priority of our lives.

DAILY PRAISES
1.
2.
3.
4.
5.

DAILY PRAYER REQUESTS
1.
2.
3.
4.
5.

August 22
Read psalm 32:1-11

Psalm 32:8

"I will instruct you and teach you in the way you should go; I will counsel you and watch over you."

When we accept the Lord we are not left alone to struggle and find the way. God will teach us and lead us in the way that we will be pleasing to Him. We must be willing to be taught. We must be willing to let the Spirit lead, guide, and instruct us. Our way is not necessarily God's way. Our stubborn will must be broken to let Christ guide us His way.

God will give us inspiration in our spirit and understanding. He will give us wisdom if we walk upright before Him. We are to seek God for that wisdom and He will give it liberally. Wisdom is a principal ingredient in our Christian walk. Whenever we receive wisdom we obtain knowledge and understanding. We have a pleasantness and peacefulness when we receive wisdom from God. Wisdom is to be desired above all gifts. When we have wisdom we are instructed by the Lord and guided by Him. We are blessed because we hear what the Spirit is saying to us.

Give your heart to the Lord so that He might teach you wisdom and knowledge. We should desire knowledge from above so that Jesus may guide us on life's pathway. Be willing to be taught by the Holy Spirit. He has a plan for each life. Let that plan become a reality by being taught by Him. Let the Holy One guide and lead you. His eye is always on you and me. He knows us by name. He even knows how many hairs are on our heads. He desires that we walk with Him.

DAILY PRAISES **DAILY PRAYER REQUESTS**
1.   1.

2.   2.

3.   3.

4.   4.

5.   5.

August 23
Read Psalm 1

Psalm 1:3

"He is like a tree planted by streams of water, which yields its fruit in due season and whose leaf does not wither. Whatever he does prospers."

The Bible tells us that the child of God is to be like a tree planted where it will grow with plenty of water and light. Trees grow upright toward the light. They must have a source of water to reach their roots. God's children are to grow toward Him, as trees grow toward the light. God's children are to have the source of the Word of God to reach their roots in their heart. We are to strive to be like Jesus in our conduct, thoughts, and attitudes.

Trees are used for many different things. It would take pages to list all of their uses. The Christians have many different talents which are to be used for God. Again it would take a book to tell the many uses of the talents of God's children. Whatever abilities we have, we should dedicate them to the Lord to be used for His glory.

Trees are symbols of beauty, strength, rest, and bearing many fruits. As Christians we are to shine to the lost world as beautiful believers who are strong and produce fruits that cause the world to want what we have.

Trees have roots which penetrate to great depths underground. Because of a strong root system, they are able to withstand attacks of winds and storms. We, as Christians, are to be rooted and grounded in the Word so we can stand against the enemies.

Trees produce fruit when nourished with the sun and water. We are to produce fruit as we are filled with the Spirit for the benefit of others and to worship the Lord. The fruits are: love; joy; peace; longsuffering; gentleness; goodness; faith; meekness; and temperance. When we let our souls be fed and we reach up to the Lord to be led by Him, we will grow and abound in faith that is pleasing to the Lord. Our lives will be a witness of great strength to those who are looking for comfort and satisfaction.

DAILY PRAISES	**DAILY PRAYER REQUESTS**
1.	1.
2.	2.
3.	3.
4.	4.
5.	5.

August 24
Read Isaiah 59:1-21

Isaiah 59:1

"Surely the arm of the Lord is not too short to save; nor His ear too dull to hear."

Do you need to talk to the Lord? He is as close as your call to Him. Do not think He will not hear you. His Word is true and settled in Heaven. He will hear you and save you when you call on Him. No matter how far sin has taken you, God loves you. He sees you in your lost and miserable condition and waits for you to call out to Him. He will not force Himself on anyone. You must want Him to help you and come to you.

In His Word, God says that He wants everyone to be saved. That includes you! It is your responsibility to reach out to the Lord. He is there, waiting for you to call, "Jesus, I need you now."

Our Lord does not change. He is the same today, as yesterday, and will be the same tomorrow. His understanding is infinite. He is of great power. His eyes are on everyone. He sees the good and the bad. There is no place to hide from God. Even in the darkness of the night we cannot hide from God. The ways of all humans are open before the Lord.

Is your heart condemning you? God knows all things. Ask Him for forgiveness and have a wonderful and workable relationship with the Lord and those around you.

DAILY PRAISES   **DAILY PRAYER REQUESTS**
1.   1.

2.   2.

3.   3.

4.   4.

5.   5.

August 25
Read James 3:13-18

James 3:17

"The wisdom that comes from heaven is first of all pure; then peace loving, considerate, submissive, full of mercy and good fruit, impartial and sincere."

This verse is contrasting the wisdom of the world with the wisdom of God. True wisdom comes from God. Notice the wisdom from above is first pure. Purity is the foundation for an effective Christian life. Everything else is built upon purity. A holy life is one that knows how to control the tongue as well as every other part of the physical and mental body through the active work of the Holy Spirit.

We are peaceable people, free from violence and anxiety because we have the wisdom of God. We are gentle, mild and amiable by nature through Christ. We are easy to be entreated. We are submissive and open to reason. We are filled with mercy because we love and are forgiving, compassionate, caring, and helpful due to the wisdom of the Lord. We produce good fruits because we are filled with love, joy, goodness, faith, longsuffering, meekness, and temperance. These things are the fruits of righteousness because they are based on the holy wisdom that is ours through Christ Jesus. A holy life should be a pure life that produces peace.

The wisdom of God is available to us as we allow Him to control every aspect of our life in the power of His Holiness. Give Him control today and receive the pure and peaceful life that is available.

DAILY PRAISES
1.
2.
3.
4.
5.

DAILY PRAYER REQUESTS
1.
2.
3.
4.
5.

August 26
Read Psalm 85:1-13

Psalm 85:6

"Will you not revive us again, that your people may rejoice in you?"

To revive is to repent and be aware of God's presence. Oh, how we need to be revived. We need to be joyful and rejoice before God. Because our sins are forgiven we are told by Jesus to rejoice. We are no longer bound by sin. We are free, so rejoice!

We rejoice because our lives will not end at physical death, but we will live forever with Jesus. What joy awaits us! We are filled with the Holy Spirit now and that means we have joy. Be glad and rejoice because He has filled you with His Spirit.

Our faith is in the Word of God and our joy should be full because we have been given the Word of God to live by. We should be so happy because God's Words are so sweet and satisfying to our souls. To be a Christian is to have joy.

Search yourself. Where is your joy? When do you rejoice? Why do you rejoice? Joy comes as we possess Jesus in our hearts and as we grow in Him it will develop joy.

People who are born again are on their way to Heaven and we will have everlasting joy there. Do not let unconfessed sin rob you of joy. Confess, claim victory and rejoice in the Lord.

DAILY PRAISES	**DAILY PRAYER REQUESTS**
1.	1.
2.	2.
3.	3.
4.	4.
5.	5.

August 27
Read John 17:6-26

John 17:20

"My prayer is not for them alone. I pray also for those who will believe in me through their message."

We live in a world that caters to sin and worldly lusts. We cannot leave this world to live, but we must learn to live here with the other inhabitants in which sin is so rampant. Christ resisted the temptations of this world when he was living in the physical body on earth. We can also resist temptations. We certainly will have challenges. It is the devil's desire to challenge and tempt us as much as possible. We must put forth every effort to overcome temptations.

We have to use the Word of God to overcome temptations, as Jesus did. The Lord has the power through the blood of Calvary to keep us from evil, if we have the desire to be kept from the evil one.

We are transformed from this world by the renewing of our minds. We are not to lust after vain things, but set our affection on things above. If we love the world we do not really love the Father. This world will pass away but if we love the Father and do His will we will abide with Him forever.

We are to use prayer to overcome temptations. Our conversion gives the right to approach our Heavenly Father in prayer. Put on the breastplate of faith, love, and hope to defeat the enemy. Be armed and ready for battle when the enemy comes. The enemy is defeated in the Name of Jesus. Temptations will abate in the Name of Jesus and by His blood on Calvary. Just remember He prayed for all believers in today's Bible reading.

DAILY PRAISES	**DAILY PRAYER REQUESTS**
1.	1.
2.	2.
3.	3.
4.	4.
5.	5.

August 28
Read Proverbs 29:17-27

Proverbs 29:18

"Where there is no revelation, the people cast off restraint; but blessed is he who keeps the law."

Here we see the righteous and the wicked contrasted. We, as Christians, need to reach the lost. We need a vision for the people who do not know God. These people are walking at a fast pace into eternity, lost forever. Look at those lost people from God's perspective. He gave His son to die for all sinners. Let us get concerned about those we know that are traveling on in sin.

How long has it been since you wept over lost souls? Jesus did. He was burdened for Jerusalem. He had heaviness, a weight upon His heart for a lost city. How long has it been since you had a real concern, heaviness, and weight upon your heart for the lost souls you know in your family or town?

It is time we start to pray for the lost and to be concerned. If you do not have a burden for lost souls, ask God to give you a burden and a desire to see people saved. Let us pray for the Lord to awaken people that they may be aware of the presence of God.

List the names of people who need to be awakened and concerned about their eternal future. Pray for the power to bind the evil spirit which controls lost people. We can do this as Jesus did, by the authority of Jesus as Savior and Lord through the power of the blood.

Let us pray for witnesses and workers to be sent to the lost. Let us seek God's guidance in what we should do to help win the lost. It is time to get out and get busy ministering to the lost.

DAILY PRAISES	**DAILY PRAYER REQUESTS**
1.	1.
2.	2.
3.	3.
4.	4.
5.	5.

August 29
Read James 5:13-20

James 5:16

"Therefore confess your sins to each other and pray for each other so that you may be healed. The prayer of the righteous man is powerful and effective."

How long has it been since you confessed your faults to another? It takes a modest person to be able to admit their faults to someone and discuss how they can best overcome those faults. We must be free from pride and vanity and confess what we have trouble with, so we can be healed of our faults. We are required to humble ourselves so the Lord will lift us up in due time.

In Proverbs, we are told that humility and the fear of the Lord are riches, honor, and life. This is also wisdom.

After we confess, we will have the power through prayer to reach the desire of our hearts. We will seek God with enthusiasm and our prayers will be of value.

Do not think others are not having problems. All of us have problems of some kind in this world. There is always something to contend with in this world. We live in an age when we try to hide our troubles instead of confessing them.

We should confess and overcome. Confess and be free. Confess and be victorious.

DAILY PRAISES	**DAILY PRAYER REQUESTS**
1.	1.
2.	2.
3.	3.
4.	4.
5.	5.

August 30
Read II Kings 6:8-23

II Kings 6:17

"And Elisha prayed, "O Lord, open his eyes so he may see," Then the Lord opened the servant's eyes, and he looked and saw the hills full of horses and chariots of fire all around Elisha."

How many times have we been protected by God? We cannot count the times He has sent angels, chariots, and horses to protect us. He has supplied our needs by someone bringing the needed food or money. There is no way to explain, other than God, the way my needs have been met.

I praise the Lord because he opened my eyes and let me see that He is the provider. He is on my side and that makes me the majority. Many times we fail to open our eyes and see the good things that God is doing for us. We miss out on so many blessings because we do not look for the good in every situation.

We should awaken from that negative attitude and begin to look positively at all situations. We need to see the good that can come from all internal or external stimuli. If we look for the good, we will find it. God will provide it. We should turn the adverse situation into a positive circumstance. Yes, it is possible. All things are possible through Jesus Christ. Even the most painful experience can be used for glory if we look for the good rather than dwelling in self-pity or guilt. Look for the GOOD IN EVERY SITUATION!

DAILY PRAISES	**DAILY PRAYER REQUESTS**
1.	1.
2.	2.
3.	3.
4.	4.
5.	5.

August 31
Read Proverbs 28:9-20

Proverbs 28:13

"He who conceals his sins does not prosper, but whoever confesses and renounces them finds mercy."

Nothing can be hidden from God. We might think it is hidden because He does not speak to us regarding our sins immediately, but He knows. He will bring it to our memory and give us the opportunity to ask for forgiveness. You may find it necessary to ask others to forgive you for things you have done or said.

God wants each person to be dedicated to Him. In order to do that we must ask daily for forgiveness and ask God to show us how to improve our relationships with others. We must ask Him to help us improve. He wants to help us. Just ask.

Let us meet the sins that beset us head on. If we do, we can grow and mature and prosper in Christ. Be sure, your sins will find you out. Get rid of them today. Do not get caught in an embarrassing situation because you failed to rid yourself of sin. Our God is able to deliver you from anything that has you bound or burdened. **Remember that God hates sin.**

DAILY PRAISES	**DAILY PRAYER REQUESTS**
1.	1.
2.	2.
3.	3.
4.	4.
5.	5.

SEPTEMBER

September 1
Read I Peter 3:1-7

I Peter 3:4

"Instead, it should be that of your inner self, the unfading beauty of a gentle and quiet spirit, which is of great worth in God's sight."

Christianity restores marriage to what it is meant to be. There is nothing more wonderful than a Christian home, with both husband and wife working together for Christ and working to be happy in their home.

I have not always had a total Christian home. After nineteen years my husband was saved. It did not work well before my husband began to love the Lord. When there is one partner going one way and the other partner is pulling in the opposite direction it makes a difficult life.

I did not always treat my husband as Peter tells us to do. I would pray for him and then get so discouraged because the work was not done immediately. (A trick of the devil to make us discouraged.) Sometimes I would become angry and feel like giving up and never praying for him again. These feeling were the wrong attitude. When I became determined to fast and pray and have a gentle, submissive, and loving attitude toward my husband, God did the rest of the work.

We wives must be careful to respect the authority of our husbands, who are the priests of the home. The power of gentleness is much more persuasive than anger of or controversy.

Our lives reflect the inner qualities of peace and the Spirit of God as we live for the Lord. We are to minister to our husbands in this peaceful spirit. Women are models of faith and we can gain our husbands for the Lord and for our homes if we determine to be gentle, loving, caring, and filled with the Holy Spirit.

It is easy to obey Peter's words to us if we have a husband who truly loves us as Christ loves the church. They will treat us with respect and desire the best for us. This makes it easy to honor our partner.

DAILY PRAISES	**DAILY PRAYER REQUESTS**
1.	1.
2.	2.
3.	3.
4.	4.
5.	5.

September 2
Read Isaiah 43:1-13

Isaiah 43:2

"When you pass through the waters, I will be with you; and when you pass through the rivers, they will not sweep over you. When you walk through the fire, you will not be burned; the flames will not set you ablaze."

God has promised the righteous protection in this life. He has prepared a defense for us. He is our shield and strength. He is our Shepherd that tends our needs. He will give us peace during the time of distress. We can put our trust in the Lord because He is our refuge. The Lord is our shelter from the enemy. The Lord is our helper; He will hold us up so that we do not slip. The Lord is on our side, so we have the majority; the winning team.

The Lord surrounds us with His protecting power. We are safe from what people would do to us. The Lord goes with us to protect and cover us with His mighty sheltering wings. When trouble comes, He gathers us into His arms and caresses us into His breast and cares for us, because we belong to Him. He is a gentle Savior, who loves and cares for His children.

We just need to put our trust in Jesus because He will be our strength and comfort in time of despair. There is no need to be confused, because the Lord is on our side as our Helper. He will be with us. He has designated Guardian Angels to be with us. We have favor with the Lord, because we live for Him.

Bring your problems to Jesus, commit them to Him as you name them and He will bring you through your trials to victory.

DAILY PRAISES	DAILY PRAYER REQUESTS
1.	1.
2.	2.
3.	3.
4.	4.
5.	5.

September 3
Read Titus 3:1-11

Titus 3:5

"He saved us, not because of righteous things we had done, but because of His mercy. He saved us through the washing of rebirth and renewal by the Holy Spirit."

There is no way that we can earn our Salvation through works. God gave His Son to die on Calvary to redeem us. It is by the mercy of God that we can be saved. All it takes is faith, believing that Jesus loves us and took our sins. As we believe and receive Him, He gives us power to be His children, by putting His spirit in us and causing us to walk in His statues and to keep His commandments.

We have a new life in God. We love others. We are concerned about the lost, sick, distressed and downhearted. We are to be a light to a lost world as Jesus is our light. We are to care for people as Jesus did. Love is doing. When we become new persons in Christ, we will desire to be like Him. We can and will be overcomers of the world because we have the Spirit of Jesus. Jesus overcame the world and we are to have faith and believe that victory is ours. Everyone that is born of God can be victorious. Are you evidencing victory in your Christian life? Should you submit your will to the Lord and allow Him to lead and guide you to victory?

DAILY PRAISES	**DAILY PRAYER REQUESTS**
1.	1.
2.	2.
3.	3.
4.	4.
5.	5.

September 4
Read II Peter 3:1-10

II Peter 3:9

"The Lord is not slow keeping His promise, as some understand slowness. He is patient with you, not wanting anyone to perish, but everyone to come to repentance."

It is not the will of God for anyone to be lost. He does not get pleasure from the death of a sinner. He calls everyone to turn to Him and live eternally.

God is not slow concerning His promises. Some people are impatient, as I am, for God's promise to meet the present need. He is not waiting just for the sake of waiting. All things are in His time plan and we are to work diligently and faithfully as time allows. God is patient toward us. He loves us. He seeks to give all an opportunity to repent and serve Him. We need to make room for God in our life.

The longer God delays the return of His son to earth, the more people will be able to be saved and come to Salvation. Let us make room for the power of God in our lives, so that we can let Him apply His promises to our lives. He came that we might have life. He deserves our praise and our life a dedicated to Him. He has done so much for us. He is worthy.

He desires for all to have life through Him. The foundation of the Lord is sure with peace. It will stand when all else fails. God knows those who serve Him. He knows the very intentions of our hearts. We cannot hide our motives from Him. Is God satisfied with you? Do you accept His promises as true? Do you rely on Him to fulfill those promises? He will meet your need if you will only let Him.

DAILY PRAISES	**DAILY PRAYER REQUESTS**
1.	1.
2.	2.
3.	3.
4.	4.
5.	5.

September 5
Read Philippians 4:10-20

Philippians 4:13
"I can do everything through him who gives me strength."

Often we are determined to do things our way and in our own strength, but they just do not work out. We get so frustrated, disappointed, and depressed in our strength. But when we let go and let God help us do things His way we are so joyful and happy.

God's answer to problems of worry is to trust in His strength. Let the Holy Spirit intercede for us as we trust Him. We can think of the good and pure things. Look for the best in all people and situations. Do not look for mistakes but look for the good that is being done. God is in control of all things, so do not worry. God is with us always and knows our every care and problem. He wants to be our strength and help us, so let us let Him do His job. We are to set our minds on things above. Do not worry. Commit all things to Christ in prayer. Present your petitions to God with confidence, in prayer, expecting Him to answer and meet the needs. Keep praying for a petition until it is answered, it might not be the answer you had in mind, or the way you think, but the answer will come. Praise God for the answer. If we keep our hearts and minds on God, He will give us the peace we desire.

Let us trust the Lord for strength during those trying times and in the good times. God is all powerful. Yes, He is able.

DAILY PRAISES	**DAILY PRAYER REQUESTS**
1.	1.
2.	2.
3.	3.
4.	4.
5.	5.

September 6
Read Jeremiah 1:4-19

Jeremiah 1:5

"Before I formed you in the womb I knew you, before you were born I sat you apart; I appointed you as a prophet to the nations."

If God knew Jeremiah before he was born, why would the Lord not know us today, before we were born? I believe God knows each baby that is conceived. What a sad fate that our modern society has brought to millions of babies that were conceived to be murdered by abortion. I believe people who perform abortions and who get abortions will have to answer to the Lord for their sins of murder. God is forgiving, if we have sinned, He will forgive us our sins. Now is the time to call on Him for forgiveness. Children are to be raised and taught about the Bible. We have the responsibility to lead and guide them into a profession for which they are suited. We should teach them to pray and read the Bible, to seek God's guidance in their life. Also to see guidance as to friends and marriage as they get older.

We need to pray for our children continually and encourage them to take part in church activities as they serve the Lord. Children will know the right way, only if they are taught the right way. It is our duty as parents to teach our children the Bible standards of what is right.

It is a parental responsibility to teach morals, ethics, and God to our children. We do not need to leave the correct teaching of our children to the church or the schools. Other people may not teach the correct information. If we teach our children what is right, we will know that they have a good foundation. God has called our children for special services. Let us teach them to listen, obey, and be responsive to the Spirit of God.

DAILY PRAISES	**DAILY PRAYER REQUESTS**
1.	1.
2.	2.
3.	3.
4.	4.
5.	5.

September 7
Read Proverbs 14:26-34

Proverbs 14:34

"Righteousness exalts a nation, but sin is a disgrace to any people."

We are to seek God and not evil, that we may live. The Lord blesses those nations that honor Him and uphold righteousness. As Christians we are to stand against sin. Sin is death and destruction to our youth, middle aged, old age and our nation.

It is time the Christian population stands on the Word of God and declares that sin is wrong and we will not tolerate it being accepted as an alternate way of life.

Biblical history tells us what happened to those who accepted sin as a way of life. The end is destruction. People are being destroyed at a vast rate because of sin practices that need not be. Illegal drugs are killing our people. People are looking for something to make them feel good. If they would only turn to God, they could have that good feeling in their soul.

We must enlighten this nation, as well as the world, and try to awaken them to the truths of God's Word. Sin practices result in ruin of the body and the soul. Righteousness exalts a nation. Let us proclaim righteousness and live a life that others see Christ in us. Let us pray that peoples' hearts will be stirred and hungry for the right way. Let us seek God's help in turning the world around.

DAILY PRAISES	**DAILY PRAYER REQUESTS**
1.	1.
2.	2.
3.	3.
4.	4.
5.	5.

September 8
Read Hebrews 2:1-13

Hebrews 2:12

"He says, 'I will declare your name to my brothers; in the presence of the congregation I will sing your praises.'"

We are to be obedient to Christ and give Him our praises. Praise is due the Lord. Often we do not feel like praising the Lord, but we must overcome that feeling and praise Him anyway. When we begin to praise the Lord, we have a different outlook. We begin to feel better and rejoice within. Praising the Lord brings a blessing to us, because we are blessing the Name of the Lord.

The Lord desires to give us good things and a spiritual blessing from Him is the best thing we can have. It renews and revives us. It gives us courage and strength to continue in our walk. It drives our "blues" away. It gives us a positive outlook.

Let us continually declare the Name of Jesus before the people of this world. Let us sing praises unto our God. He is Lord over all. He is worthy of our praise. We will be overcomers as long as we continue to praise the Lord of earth and glory.

DAILY PRAISES
1.
2.
3.
4.
5.

DAILY PRAYER REQUESTS
1.
2.
3.
4.
5.

September 9
Read James 1:2-18

James 1:5

"If any of you lacks wisdom, he should ask God, who gives generously to all without finding fault, and it will be given to him."

When difficult circumstances come we are to seek God's wisdom, as we do for the daily decisions of life. If we ask God, believing for wisdom, He will give it to us. He will not scold or reprove us for asking, but will liberally give to those who ask in faith.

Praise God, because you belong to Him and He will see you through every situation. Rejoice in the Lord! Believe you can, you will and you are able to overcome. As you believe you will receive.

Read the Bible. The Bible is our Spiritual food. We need to know what the Lord is saying to us. We read the newspaper to see what is going on in the world. We need to read the Bible to see what the Lord wants us to know and do.

As we name our problems and seek the will of the Lord, the answers and solutions will come with wisdom. We must be faithful to the Lord. Let us believe and never doubt the Word of the Lord.

DAILY PRAISES	**DAILY PRAYER REQUESTS**
1.	1.
2.	2.
3.	3.
4.	4.
5.	5.

September 10
Read Acts 3:11-26

Acts 3:19

"Repent, then and turn to God, so that your sins may be wiped out, that times of refreshing may come from the Lord,"

When the refreshing presence of the Lord overshadows us, we see that we are nothing, without the Lord. The Holy Spirit must take over and draw people to Christ and make them an instrument of blessings to others.

The more we allow the refreshing presence of the Lord into our lives the more clearly we see God and His purpose for our lives.

There is a world of lost people who need to repent and be converted. We are responsible for praying and witnessing. We need to let God's Spirit penetrate our very soul so we would have the courage and spirit to witness.

People need to see the Spirit of God within our lives, as we allow love, prayer, and humility to flow through us. We can sense the great presence of the Lord as we allow Him to guide us.

Let the Spirit speak to you as you are refreshed by His wonderful presence.

DAILY PRAISES	**DAILY PRAYER REQUESTS**
1.	1.
2.	2.
3.	3.
4.	4.
5.	5.

September 11
Read Ezekiel 37:1-14

Ezekiel 37:5

"This is what the Sovereign Lord says to these bones: I will make breath enter you, and you will come to life."

To be alive is to show signs of life. One sign of life is to be an effective Christian and let the results speak for us.

A dead person cannot accomplish anything. A Christian that is dead is not effective. Are they even Christians if they are dead in the Lord? We need to let God breathe on our bones and bring them to life. When He renews our hearts, we are cleansed. We are filled with love. Faith is overflowing in us and we do not stagger at God's promises. We praise God spontaneously. Our souls are filled with singing praises to our King.

Jesus gives us victory over every temptation and trial. He sweeps over us with a peace so sweet. We walk in unity and oneness with our brothers and sisters.

Let us continue to live in this "lively" state and enjoy God's blessings.

DAILY PRAISES
1.
2.
3.
4.
5.

DAILY PRAYER REQUESTS
1.
2.
3.
4.
5.

September 12
Read Ephesians 6:10-20

Ephesians 6:13

"Therefore put on the full armor of God, so that when the day of evil comes, you may be able to stand your ground, and after you have done everything, to stand."

We must be committed to the Lord to be able to stand. We cannot serve two masters. We must make a choice for God or against Him. When we chose God, He made provisions for us to withstand everything that comes against us.

We are to have our mind filled with the truth of God's Word. We are to apply faith, love, and grace to our lives. We are to live according to the Bible. The helmet is God's banner of Salvation over us.

He has given us weapons to use in our fight. The Bible is our offensive and defensive weapon. We are to constantly use it against the attack of the enemy.

Prayers are to be prayed to God through His Son Jesus. We pray general prayers and we pray in the Spirit. Prayers are weapons against the enemy. We also have the fellowship of other Christians to unite in prayer and intercession for needs. Oh, what tools we have to use against the enemy.

Let us be strong in the Lord and stand firm through Jesus Christ.

DAILY PRAISES
1.
2.
3.
4.
5.

DAILY PRAYER REQUESTS
1.
2.
3.
4.
5.

September 13
Read John 4:1-26

John 4:24

"God is spirit, and his worshippers must worship in spirit and truth."

We must get our priorities in order to worship God in the Spirit. God must be first in our hearts, minds, and lives. The desire to do God's will should be above all other people or things in our lives. When God is first, He puts everything else in its proper place. The Bible tells us this.

Fear is removed when we worship God in spirit. God is love. Love is doing, giving, caring, and sharing with others. Fears move us away from others. We can be free of fear by worshipping God in the Spirit.

We have liberty and freedom when we worship in the Spirit. This is real worship. There is no desire for make believe or false worship. When we have committed our priorities to God, we are free to serve Him only. We can worship in Spirit and truth.

We can pray and sing in the Holy Spirit as the Spirit directs us to worship through Jesus.

DAILY PRAISES	**DAILY PRAYER REQUESTS**
1.	1.
2.	2.
3.	3.
4.	4.
5.	5.

September 14
Read I Peter 3:8-22

I Peter 3:12

"For the eyes of the Lord are on the righteous and his ears are attentive to their prayer, but the face of the Lord is against those who do evil."

What comforting words for the believer and doer of God's Word. The ways of the Lord are watching over us! Praise God! His ears are open to our prayers. He wants us to come to Him with our requests. God hears us and answers our prayers. If we keep His commandments and serve Him faithfully, He will hear and answer His children.

We have so much to praise the Lord for. God is so good. He loves us so much. How easy and simple to trust Him wherever we are or whatever we need. It is a child-like faith.

God sees and hears us when we call upon Him. He knows our situation before we ask Him. He wants us to honor Him by asking Him in faith for what we need. We are to have a prayerful heart always, continuing in instant prayer.

Believe in faith and receive from Christ Jesus whatever you are seeking. He sees and hears our prayers. Wait patiently on Him to answer. He is always with us as our guide and comforter.

DAILY PRAISES	**DAILY PRAYER REQUESTS**
1.	1.
2.	2.
3.	3.
4.	4.
5.	5.

September 15
Read Hebrews 9:15-28

Hebrews 9:28

"So Christ was sacrificed once to take away the sins of many people; and he will appear a second time, not to bear sin, but to bring salvation to those who are waiting for him."

Are you looking for Christ to return? When He returns in the clouds we will meet Him in the air and accompany Him to Heaven. That will be a glorious reunion with Christ, angels, and loved ones. We shall be with Him and rejoice. No one can take that joy or heavenly home away from us. What a glorious time!

Christ died for everyone's sins. All persons can ask for forgiveness and receive Christ. Maybe you started with Christ, failed, and then gave up for Christ. Do not quit. Christ shed His blood for you, the same as for me. He will pick you up when you fall or fail. We learn by trial and error sometimes. When we make a mistake, we must ask for forgiveness, regroup, and try again.

How many people are perfect as they try something for the first time? How many are perfect after the one hundredth time? We will never be perfect in this life. Come on now, Christ will help you as you get ready for His second coming. He wants everyone to be saved and go to Heaven. He wants you! He purchased your salvation on Calvary.

DAILY PRAISES	**DAILY PRAYER REQUESTS**
1.	1.
2.	2.
3.	3.
4.	4.
5.	5.

September 16
Read Psalm 63:1-11

Psalm 63:1

"O God, you are my God, earnestly I seek you; my soul thirsts for you, my body longs for you, in a dry and a weary land where there is no water."

How wonderful to belong to God. To say to Him, "I am yours, Lord; I seek your blessings and your will for my life. I long to commune with you. You are the greatest thing in my heart, soul, and life."

When we are thirsty for spiritual blessings, He gives us a drink of His love and mercy. He extends His hand of kindness to us to meet our needs. He sends us His light and truth to lead us to Him. Oh, how we desire the beauty of the Lord. How marvelous to see His glory and power at work in a dry land!

Seek God early in your lifetime. Youth, seek God's guidance. Seek God early in the day. Let Him minister unto you the first hour upon arising each day. If we will seek Him early, we will know Him better and grow to be more like Him.

Blessed are those who seek Him and dwell in His loving kindness.

DAILY PRAISES	DAILY PRAYER REQUESTS
1.	1.
2.	2.
3.	3.
4.	4.
5.	5.

September 17
Read Ephesians 4:1-16

Ephesians 4:7

"But to each one of us grace is given as Christ apportioned it."

The ministering gifts of Christ are given according to His sovereign will. When Christ gives us gifts, He gives us grace for which to perform those gifts.

The Christian lives by grace through Jesus Christ. The gift of Christ to every believer is grace. Grace is unmerited divine favor by which we are saved. Grace is His divine presence working in us to accomplish Christ's will in our lives.

Grace is the divine enablement for doing all that Christ called us to do as Christians.

The supply of grace is sufficient for every believer to fulfill our calling to follow Christ we must keep our eyes on Christ and not on humans.

We do not all receive the same measure of grace because we are not all called to do the same things in the body. We receive from Christ the measure of grace needed to fill our place in God's kingdom. The more responsibility Christ calls us to do, the more grace is given to do it.

Do not be discouraged, seek grace to help you. Ask the Lord to give you sufficient grace. He is waiting for you to ask Him, so He can help you. The grace is there for our receiving. We only have to ask, believe, obey, and receive from the Lord.

DAILY PRAISES	**DAILY PRAYER REQUESTS**
1.	1.
2.	2.
3.	3.
4.	4.
5.	5.

September 18
Read Revelation 1:1-8

Revelation 1:7

"Look, he is coming with the clouds, and every eye will see him, and even those who pierced him; and all the peoples of the earth will mourn because of him."

If you saw Jesus coming in the air, would you be able to welcome Him?

The Son of Man will judge with a true and fair judgment. People will judge after the flesh, but Jesus will judge according to the Word of God. Everyone will receive their reward according to the Bible.

The Day of Judgment will come to us all at the return of Christ. Jesus is not slack concerning His promises, for one day with the Lord is as a thousand years. The Lord will come back as a thief in the night. We should be ready and always watching for His coming. We should have our hearts prepared for His coming. We are to be Holy and Godly as we live our daily lives. We should be without a spot or blemish as we wait for His return.

Be in the Word of God, praising, and glorifying Him continually. Love your fellow humans in the church, so as to produce unity and win the lost for the Lord. Witness God's love to the sinners around you by being a doer of the Word. Be ready for the righteous reward at Christ's appearing.

DAILY PRAISES	**DAILY PRAYER REQUESTS**
1.	1.
2.	2.
3.	3.
4.	4.
5.	5.

September 19
Read Psalm 28

Psalm 28:7

"The Lord is my strength and my shield; my heart trusts in him, and I am helped. My heart leaps for joy and I will give thanks to Him in song."

Can you list the many times the Lord has helped and strengthened you as your heart trusted in Him? Oh, how we should rejoice in what the Lord has done for us!

Joy is simply the fullness of God's Salvation. We can express spontaneous joy and rejoice in that new life. To rejoice is to express gladness because you feel it. Joy accompanies the gift of the Holy Spirit. It rejoices as miracles are performed by His glory and power.

There is a cause for joy as we are new Christians and see new Christians become part of the faith. Joy may be an outcome of suffering, as we see Christ's power and work taking place and being produced by the Lord, not ourselves. Joy is derived from love, both God's and humans. It is a gift of the Holy Spirit. It can be interrupted by sin, but do not let sin remain there. Ask for forgiveness. We should share in the joy of the Lord by our daily walk of rejoicing in God who made our Salvation possible.

DAILY PRAISES	DAILY PRAYER REQUESTS
1.	1.
2.	2.
3.	3.
4.	4.
5.	5.

September 20
Read Ephesians 5:1-21

Ephesians 5:21

"Submit to one another out of the reverence for Christ."

To submit means to yield to the power or authority of another. Being willing to submit, yielding to submission, and obedient to submitting are all part of humility as required by the Lord.

The importance of submission is that it is like God's character. God is high and great, yet He humbled Himself to take notice of us and our needs.

Jesus submitted to God's will and died on the cross for us. He could have called a legion of angels or He could have come down from the cross. But He desired to submit to the Father's will.

To submit is to willingly serve Jesus. We serve Jesus because we love Him. We give up our will and desire to obey the Spiritual call.

If we submit to Christ and to one another it will allow the Spirit of God to bring the blessing of advancement in all areas. We will develop according to Scripture through the love of nurture of God. Seek genuine submission. Do not get pseudo humility. God is real.

DAILY PRAISES	**DAILY PRAYER REQUESTS**
1.	1.
2.	2.
3.	3.
4.	4.
5.	5.

September 21
Read Exodus 4:1-17

Exodus 4:12

"Now go; I will help you speak and will teach you what to say."

Has the Lord given you a job to do? When God instructs us to do something, it will be done for His glory and according to His will. We must be willing vessels to be used by Him. He will give us wisdom and words to use in doing what He instructs. He will anoint us to speak for Him. He will give us boldness which we never knew we possessed. As we obey the Spirit and witness for Christ we are not to praise ourselves, but give God the glory and honor. Without the Lord sending us we could not go or reach people. He is to receive the credit for what is accomplished. We will receive our reward when this life is over and we go to be with the Lord.

Have you listened to the Holy Spirit to receive instructions? Is He bidding you to step out in faith and do a work for Him? Pray and meditate through the Holy Spirit. Study the Bible and concentrate on what the Word is saying to you. Discuss with your pastor or a mature Christian what you believe God wants you to do. Does the Spirit and the Word correspond with your thoughts and ideas? Praise God for speaking to you and trust Him to lead you.

DAILY PRAISES	**DAILY PRAYER REQUESTS**
1.	1.
2.	2.
3.	3.
4.	4.
5.	5.

September 22
Read Hebrews 9:16-28

Hebrews 9:22

"In fact, the law requires that nearly everything be cleansed with blood, and without the shedding of blood there is no forgiveness."

Jesus shed His blood for us. He paid the price with blood. The Bible tells us the life is in the blood and that is why Jesus gave His life for us.

The blood of Jesus means atonement for us. We can make amends and start anew through the blood of Jesus. There is regeneration in the blood. We can be made alive and reformed by His blood. Jesus paid the price for us once and for all. No further bloodshed is necessary to receive and serve Him.

There is justification in the blood. We can be free from sin and united with God. Sanctification is in the blood. We are made Holy and purified throughout to live a life of holiness and receive spiritual blessings through the blood. Communion is in the blood. Fellowship with our Savior is provided as our faith reaches out to the Lord.

Praise God, because victory to overcome every enemy and opponent is provided in the blood. We will live without end forever in happiness and joy. Have you allowed the blood to cleanse you?

DAILY PRAISES	**DAILY PRAYER REQUESTS**
1.	1.
2.	2.
3.	3.
4.	4.
5.	5.

September 23
Read Romans 8:1-17

Romans 8:13

"For if you live according to the sinful nature, you will die; but if by the Spirit you put to death the misdeeds of the body, you will live."

In the flesh we cannot please God. We must commit the flesh to Christ and be crucified with Him.

The Spirit controls the person who dwells in the Spirit. The person who lives according to the Spirit pleases God. We are to make a home for the Spirit to live within us. He will reveal Himself to us. He reveals Himself to us through the Word and opens our eyes to the Scripture and what it is saying to us. We are able to grow and mature through the Word of God. The hope of God keeps us going as the Comforter dwells inside. To be Spiritual minded is to have the peace of God in our lives.

We must decide what relationship we want with God. If we decide to live after the flesh, it is our choice. We must also realize that eternity cannot be changed. As we enter eternity we will remain there forever. One of the greatest pains of hell will be in knowing that there is "No Hope".

While we are alive we make the choice as to where we will spend eternity. We must choose to serve God and live for Him or to serve the devil and suffer the consequences.

Oh, what a relief to choose to serve the Lord. We can walk in the Spirit and rejoice. We can live a devoted life that is consecrated for Christ and be happy. The Spirit will make your life adequate and fill your needs. You will have peace and contentment in the Lord. His way is easy and His burdens light.

DAILY PRAISES
1.
2.
3.
4.
5.

DAILY PRAYER REQUESTS
1.
2.
3.
4.
5.

September 24
Read II Timothy 2:8-19

II Timothy 2:19

"Nevertheless, God's solid foundation stands firm, sealed with this inscription, 'The Lord knows those who are his,' and, 'Everyone who confesses the name of the Lord must turn away from wickedness."

We belong to God. We are His workmanship and possessions. We are to stand on His promises. He does not like it when the enemy comes against us. People will fail if we put our trust in them, but God does not let us down. We must trust God. We must look to the promises and believe God.

There comes a time when we must lean on the Lord. We must set ourselves to pray and seek the will of the Lord in our lives. It is a joy to seek the Lord, if we love Him. It is our responsibility to pray. We can base our prayers on His promises. We can look to the promises and trust in them. He has promised to remove sin if we ask. He will fill us with the joy of the Holy Spirit if we believe. He will help us with all emotional and physical problems if we let Him. He will meet our needs financially if we allow Him. He is here to meet every need because we belong to Him. We are known by Him personally. He even knows how many hairs are on our head. Believe and receive today.

DAILY PRAISES	**DAILY PRAYER REQUESTS**
1.	1.
2.	2.
3.	3.
4.	4.
5.	5.

September 25
Read I Peter 5:1-9

I Peter 5:8

"Be self-controlled and alert. Your enemy the devil prowls around like a roaring lion looking for someone to devour."

Satan has declared war on us as Christians. We must prepare an offensive battle for Jesus. We must get our eyes on the Lord and trust in His strength, not our own. We need to be motivated by the Word of God through prayer. We must have that secret place to meet with the Lord in prayer every day.

It is necessary to put on the whole armor of God to stand against the cunning and deceitful ways of the devil. This is a Spiritual battle. We must fight until we win. We are to add to our faith. In faith sometimes we must be still and wait on the Lord. We have to live by the truths in the Bible. As we live by the truths we get our priorities in order. We are to spread the good news of Jesus to the world. As we witness, the Holy Spirit will convict hearts and they will come to Christ. We must have our feet shod with the Gospel and we will have peace which will keep our souls and minds. The shield of faith will stop the fiery darts of evil.

We are able to defeat Satan by the sword of the Spirit and the Word of God. Get in the Word and be victorious. If the Bible says it, believe it, because the Bible is true.

DAILY PRAISES	**DAILY PRAYER REQUESTS**
1.	1.
2.	2.
3.	3.
4.	4.
5.	5.

September 26
Read Colossians 3:18-25

Colossians 3:21

"Fathers do not embitter your children, or they will become discouraged."

Praise your children. Look for the good points in their lives. Find things to compliment them about. Build your children up and give them confidence.

Teach your children God's ways. Begin as soon as they are born or before birth. Read the Bible to them, tell them Bible stories, sing songs to them, and talk to them about the love of Jesus. Help them develop a love and respect for the Word of God. Teach your children to begin and end the day with prayer. Teach them that the Lord will bless those who put Him first and recognize that He is God over all. If they keep His commands and honor Him, the Lord will show them His way and will for their lives. The Lord will bless their lives.

As parents we have a great responsibility to teach our children the love of God. To love God and our fellowmen is our responsibility. We have an obligation to love our children. We are responsible for bringing them into this world and we are obligated to do the best we can for them. The ordinary thing is to begin each day with our children by giving them a good morning hug and kiss. We should do the same at bed time every night. We need to show affection by kissing and hugging our children good-bye as they go to school or other places. As we teach love we help to develop respect for others. We are to teach morals and virtues to our children. We are teaching a love that will stay with them when they have grown up and have a family of their own.

DAILY PRAISES	**DAILY PRAYER REQUESTS**
1.	1.
2.	2.
3.	3.
4	4.
5.	5.

September 27
Read Romans 13:8-14

Romans 13:8

"Let no debt remain outstanding, except the continuing debt to love one another, for he who loves his fellowman has fulfilled the law."

When does the Lord speak to you and communicate with you? Often it is during prayer and meditation upon Him or when you are reading His Word. Those are wonderful times of fellowship with Jesus. I love it when the Holy Spirit speaks to me in the middle of the night. That is when this verse was given to me, with special emphasis.

With tears, I rejoice in God's love, that He bestows His love on us so that we can love others. Christianity is based on love. If we don't love our fellowmen, whom we see and know, how can we love God, whom we have not seen?

Love will not fail or cease. Love will be kind, good, meek, truthful, hopeful, faithful, enduring, and satisfying. We are to love one another as God loves us. This is a commandment. It is not a suggestion or an option. We are to put on love above all else.

When we love we act. Love is action and doing. Love is God. Because He loves us, we are to love one another.

Do not be ashamed to show your love for others. We all need more love. We cannot be loved too much. There is always room for more love. Act out the true love of God by doing for others as our Lord did.

DAILY PRAISES **DAILY PRAYER REQUESTS**

1. 1.

2. 2.

3. 3.

4. 4.

5. 5.

September 28
Read Hebrews 12:1-13

Hebrews 12:1

"Therefore, since we are surrounded by such a great cloud of witnesses, let us throw off everything that hinders and the sin that so easily entangles, and let us run with perseverance the race marked out for us."

What is your weakness? Does it hinder you in your walk with Christ? Whatever your weakness is, name it as you pray. Ask Jesus to remove it and He will help you lay it aside so that you may walk like Him. He wants us to travel light, not bogged down with weights. If there is a sin you are keeping in your heart, it is making you miss the mark. You must ask for forgiveness and begin to walk as Jesus taught.

Many times we will stumble and fall. Many times we will fail. But Jesus has patience to help us when we stumble and fail. We must not give up but keep pressing toward the mark, our example, Jesus. If we keep our eyes on Jesus and walk after Him, we will be successful. He has given us the Holy Spirit as a Comforter and Helper. We are to continue in the love of Christ, be unmovable, be steadfast, and work for Christ.

We have a responsibility to run this Christian race the best we can with guidance from Jesus. Let us run with patience, remembering our first love. He will provide the endurance. He has not brought us this far to leave us now. He will be with us as long as we allow Him to be in our life. Trust in the Lord with all your heart.

DAILY PRAISES	**DAILY PRAYER REQUESTS**
1.	1.
2.	2.
3.	3.
4.	4.
5.	5.

September 29
Read Galatians 2:15-21

Galatians 2:20

"I have been crucified with Christ, and I no longer live, but Christ lives in me. The life I live in the body, I live by faith in the Son of God, who loved me and gave Himself for me."

This verse says so much to us. Read it two or three times and meditate upon the message it is conveying.

Christ died for our sins; therefore, we are dead to sin and this world. Christ gave His righteousness to cleanse us from our sins. He purged us from sin that we might not yield our bodies to that sinful life that we lived before we met Christ.

Oh, praise His Name because He redeemed us through His blood! We can now live by faith in Jesus Christ. We belong to Him. We are to walk and live in peace and love after the model of Jesus. We are to do the will of the Father, as Jesus did. We are to come to Christ in prayer, boldly for our petitions. He loved us so much that He gave His Son to die for our sins. He will answer our prayers. He will not forsake us. If we walk in the light, we will have fellowship with Jesus and with each other.

We can say with all surety that God truly loves us. No love can surpass God's love. Yes, He loves you as you are. Let Him love you and cleanse you so that you let Him live within your heart.

Don't forget to praise the Lord. He desires our praise. He is worthy to receive praise for what He has done and what He continues to do. Praise Him continually. God wants our praise. If we don't praise Him the rocks and mountains will praise Him.

DAILY PRAISES	**DAILY PRAYER REQUESTS**
1.	1.
2.	2.
3.	3.
4.	4.
5.	5.

September 30
Read Romans 14:8-18

Romans 14:12

"So then, each of us will give an account of himself to God"

We are each accountable for the choices we make. It is impossible to escape accountability before God because He says in His Word that we will give an account of our life to Him.

Humans can choose their own moral character. They are not born with moral character. We will answer for the choices that we decide upon, whether good or bad.

The model for our character is Jesus. God is love. He gave us Jesus in love. God works toward the good in humans. He lets people choose their own model for character. Intelligence is choosing to obey God and live under God's moral character. God says that you are responsible if you choose to sin. You will answer for it.

Sin is seeking the wrong goals. It is a selfish attitude. Sin is missing the mark. When we sin we have feelings of guilt, confusion, frustration, and even eternal death.

Because God is love, He chose to take our accountability and deal with us in mercy and grace. We can experience forgiveness through repentance and faith. Obedience to the moral law of God brings peace, righteousness, and joy.

Satan makes us think we will never be accountable. We cannot immediately see that accountability is coming. God has acted in love toward us. All we have to do is accept His love. We can stand and be accountable for our lives and never be ashamed because we have chosen the Lord and life instead of the devil and wrong morals.

DAILY PRAISES	**DAILY PRAYER REQUESTS**
1.	1.
2.	2.
3.	3.
4.	4.
5.	5.

OCTOBER

October 1
Read Solomon's Song 4:1-9 (Song of Songs)
Song of Songs 4:9

"You have stolen my heart, my sister, my bride; you have stolen my heart with one glance of your eyes, with one jewel of your necklace."

Who can grasp the love that Jesus has for us? Jesus loved the thieves hanging on the crosses beside Him, enough to honor the plea of forgiveness made by the one thief. While hanging on the cross in the hours of death, one thief accepted eternal life from Jesus. If the sinner will only give one look at Jesus, he will receive love and life in abundance. We only have to look at Calvary to live. By turning our eyes toward Him in prayer and praise, we can hold our Lord dear and He will bless us with His love and presence, if we will come to Him in obedience, submission, adoration, humility, and love He will answer our prayers.

The love of Christ goes out to all. His heart is delighted to see the neck of the Bride adorned with even one beautiful attribute, which He died that we might put on. As we take up the cross daily and walk with Him, putting off the flesh and all that is unworthy. We can be adorned with jewels of His attribution.

He has given us weapons, which refers to the chain around her neck. The great weapon is the Word of God. The Word is the sword of the Spirit which we bring to God through prayer and supplication. God will grant our prayers if we follow His Word and walk according to His will. He demands so little from us for all that He has done and all that He has given us. He wants us to acknowledge Him as Lord of our lives. He wants us to love Him more and unselfishly as we live for Him.

DAILY PRAISES	**DAILY PRAYER REQUESTS**
1.	1.
2.	2.
3.	3.
4.	4.
5.	5.

October 2
Read I John 3:11-20

I John 3:17

"If anyone has material possessions and sees his brother in need but has no pity on him, how can the love of God be in him?"

Compassion is so necessary in this modern day. We seem so at ease with an attitude of let The Welfare Department take care of those who are in need. Compassion means action. The Bible says to have compassion on those who are less fortunate.

A man we scarcely knew and whom we had not seen in many years, stopped at our house the other day. He said, "I have been in the hospital with a nervous breakdown. I have lost my job, because of drinking and going the wrong places since my wife divorced me, I need some money to keep going until I get a payday. I have gotten my job back and I need to buy gas to get to work and back. I have started going to church. I will be there on Sunday morning. I am anxious to see the guest speaker as he used to be a good friend of mine."

Of course, we could not refuse the man and his request for money on which to eat and buy gas. Love will make you give with good intentions. It was disappointing when the man did not show up at church and even more disappointing when we learned that the man had visited several people from church with a similar story. We all gave in the Name of the Lord and for His glory. We gave because we loved the Lord.

This was only one instance of a person taking advantage of Christians. We knew we could not let a person go away hungry. The Bible says to give. We gave believing the Lord would bless this person and the situation. The Lord will bless those who give with a good heart in the Name of Jesus.

DAILY PRAISES	**DAILY PRAYER REQUESTS**
1.	1.
2.	2.
3.	3.
4.	4.
5.	5.

October 3

Read I Peter 4:12-19

I Peter 4:19

"So then, those who suffer according to God's will should commit themselves to their faithful Creator and continue to do good."

We must be totally committed to God. We should pick up our cross and follow Him. We have to be strong in grace as we commit to the Lord.

We should be as committed to the Lord as a soldier and as athlete or a farmer who is committed to his profession. A soldier lays his career aside to work for his country. He must be taught and led by his superior. An athlete deprives himself or certain foods and his own time so that he can train to overcome the hardships and win the contest. A farmer performs exhausting tasks from early morning until night to become a success and have a bountiful crop.

Let us choose Jesus and commit all things to Him. Let us think of the things given up and the tasks that we are to openly perform in order to be committed to Jesus. Jesus will supply our needs. He will keep us. It is a life worth living. It is the blessed hope of life that will be eternal.

We should be willing to put our profession aside, if necessary, to do what the Lord is calling us to do. We should be willing to deprive ourselves of those selfish desires in order to please the Lord. We should be willing to perform exhausting chores for the glory of our Lord. All of these things seem hard, but if we think of the results and not of the effort we are putting forth, we will be blessed as we serve the Lord. We will be pleasing to our Savior.

DAILY PRAISES	**DAILY PRAYER REQUESTS**
1.	1.
2.	2.
3.	3.
4.	4.
5.	5.

October 4
Read John 8:31-41

John 8:32

"Then you will know the truth, and the truth will set you free."

As Christians we have certain liberties. One is the liberty to be free because of the truth. We are free from sin and servants of righteousness. Because we are free from sin we will bear fruits of holiness and the end will be everlasting life.

How will you know the truth? By reading and studying the Bible we can know the truth. His Word contains the truths with which we can be made free. We can know the truth through prayer and meditation upon Jesus Christ, the Son of God. He hears us when we pray. He wants us to speak our prayers in faith believing on His Name. We can know the truth by seeking and doing the will of the Lord; walking according to His Word. We should obey the commands of Jesus that He has given us. We know the truth by witnessing to a lost world. We can be a light wherever we work or to our neighbors, schools or cities. We may be the only light some people will ever see. Jesus told us to minister to sinners. It is our responsibility to spread the truth of God's Word.

The power of the Holy Spirit can drive out all things unlike Jesus and you will be free, if you desire to be free. The Lord will do the work, but you have to desire that the work be done. Claim victory and freedom through Jesus Christ. He came to give you freedom. Take your liberty.

DAILY PRAISES
1.
2.
3.
4.
5.

DAILY PRAYER REQUESTS
1.
2.
3.
4.
5.

October 5
Read James 4:1-12

James 4:7

"Submit yourselves, then to God. Resist the devil, and he will flee from you."

The devil has one principal goal for us and that is to keep us from worshipping God. The devil wants to sever the life line we have with the Lord. He wants to steal our personal relationship with God. The devil is always diverting our attention to get us away from the Lord.

Do not let Satan steal your relationship with God. God gives us grace to withstand the fiery darts and assaults of Satan. With Christ dwelling in our hearts, we are purified by faith, crucified with Jesus, walking with Him, serving Him and loving Him always. Submit yourself to Jesus Christ and resist the devil. He will flee from you as you use the Word of God on him.

Satan is ever tempting us and sometimes we feel condemned or convicted. When we feel that way the devil is seeking to destroy our faith through a sin. When we feel conviction, God is telling us to confess our sins and be cleansed. We can be free. God cast our sins away from us, as far as the East is from the West, never to be remembered again. Do not let the devil bring your sins back to you again. The moment you respond to conviction, the precious blood of Jesus cleanses us and we are free from sin, as we believe on the Lord Jesus.

We should put on the shield of faith, with the Word, and go to prayer to withstand the temptations that come to us. We should use the Bible as Jesus did to overcome Satan. Satan is defeated. We should realize this fact and acknowledge the Word of the Lord. We are overcomers by the Word of the Lord. Praise God!

DAILY PRAISES	**DAILY PRAYER REQUESTS**
1.	1.
2.	2.
3.	3.
4.	4.
5.	5.

October 6
Read Revelation 3:14-22

Revelation 3:21

"To him who overcomes, I will give the right to sit with me on my throne, just as I overcame and sat down with my Father on his throne."

We were created with the purpose of being a companion for the Son of God. We, as the church, will one day become Christ's bride. We are to share the throne with the Lord; therefore, we must be educated, prepared, and trained for our royal role.

We have been commanded, in Scripture, to pray. By praying, we enter into communication with Jesus. Through prayer, we overcome the advances of Satan. Through prayer, we experience on the job training for victory. We must learn to pray and overcome the evil forces in this world. This praying educates us for the assumption of the throne. God has ordained the plan of prayer for human's sake. Prayer is God's plan and way of preparing us to overcome and be ready to accept the throne.

God could remove our adversary, the devil, but we need the practice in overcoming exercise. The Spirit of prayer releases the Spirit of God to confront Satan. God does nothing except through prayer. Prayer is where the action is. God shapes the world through prayer. Jesus has given up power to bind Satan and his forces. When we feel burdened to pray for someone or for something, we are to pray at that moment, believing it will be done. Victory is ours, no matter how long and desperate the conflict appears. We are in a spiritual warfare. Pray and be ready to become one of the Bride of Christ and rule with Him.

DAILY PRAISES	**DAILY PRAYER REQUESTS**
1.	1.
2.	2.
3.	3.
4.	4.
5.	5.

October 7
Read I Peter 1:13-25

I Peter 1:13

"Therefore, prepare your minds for action; be self-controlled; set your hope fully on the grace to be given you when Jesus Christ is revealed."

Jesus is our hope. We look forward to His coming again. We are cautioned to be ready for action and be prepared always. We are to gird up our loins in preparation. In the mind is the place where thinking takes place. It is the place where we make decisions. It is the place that we let decide our disposition and attitude. We should be quick to think about the new life and hope in Christ Jesus.

To be sober, means to be calm. Do not become frustrated, impatient, or angry; but keep on working and serving God as you wait for Jesus to come. The longer Jesus delays His coming, the longer we have to win more people for the Lord.

We are called to trust Him and wait upon Him. Jesus is on our side. We wait and hope for His marvelous grace which is sufficient to keep us until He appears in the clouds of glory.

DAILY PRAISES
1.
2.
3.
4.
5.

DAILY PRAYER REQUESTS
1.
2.
3.
4.
5.

October 8
Read Hebrews 9:11-22

Hebrews 9:14

"How much more then, will the blood of Christ, who through the eternal Spirit offered himself unblemished to God, cleanse our conscience from acts that lead to death, so that we may serve the living God."

The conscience is the faculty by which we distinguish what is right and wrong. Jesus Christ died to let us live with a clear conscience. We can be sure we are doing what is right because Christ made the atonement for us. We can be reconciled to God through the blood of Jesus. We can be totally forgiven for all sins. He has delivered us from guilt and to a new way of life, free from the sin which had us bound. We can walk in the light of love and peace with a clear conscience toward God and others.

Can you really visualize that Jesus has died for your sins? He took your sins to Calvary. He loves each one so much. He would have taken one person's sins to the cross if necessary. But He took the sins of the whole world to the cross and now everyone can be free of sin.

Oh! This is living! This is love! God's love for us is nothing that we have done to cause Him to love us. He took our sins because He loved us.

Praise Him for His love. He has redeemed us from the world. I thank you, Jesus, for a marvelous act of love in taking my sins, as well as the sins of the entire world.

DAILY PRAISES	**DAILY PRAYER REQUESTS**
1.	1.
2.	2.
3.	3.
4.	4.
5.	5.

October 9
Read Proverbs 18:20-24

Proverbs 18:24

"A man of many companions may come to ruin, but there is a friend who sticks closer than a brother."

A friend is a special person. Someone you can love and trust as yourself. A friend is personally well known whom you feel warm regards and affection toward. It is someone to whom you can tell your inmost ideas and plans. A friend is someone who will lift you up in time of trouble.

Friends will be there for you when you are in distress. They will share your grief and sorrow. They will rejoice in times of gladness with you.

Usually everyone has many acquaintances, but very few real true friends. How do you become a friend? It is very simple. You do for people what you would like them to do for you.

    1. Listen to others dreams, plans, heartaches, and disappointments.
    2. Share grief and sorrow with others.
    3. Feel the joy and success of others.
    4. Be available for others to show love and kindness.
    5. Show affection and warmness to people.
    6. Really care about a person's situation.

If you can do these things with true feelings in love, you will truly be a friend. Jesus did all these and more. He is a true friend to each and every one of us.

DAILY PRAISES	**DAILY PRAYER REQUESTS**
1.	1.
2.	2.
3.	3.
4.	4.
5.	5.

October 10
Read II Timothy 3:10-17

II Timothy 3:14

"But as for you, continue in what you have learned and have become convinced of, because you know those from whom you learned it,"

Jesus knows our hearts. He is aware of our desire to continue in service for Him. As we read the Bible we receive the instructions we need to serve Christ.

Do you remember the joy and excitement you had when you first came to Christ? We are to serve Jesus with that joy and enthusiasm as we continue our Christian walk. We are assured of Salvation by believing and keeping the promises of God. We are to walk in Him as we received Him, continuing in love.

Love everyone, knowing that the Father also loves you and me, as well as everyone in the entire earth. By loving we can be steadfast, unmovable, and working for the Lord in faith.

The Holy Spirit will help us face the adversity which the world throws our way. By the Holy Spirit we can overcome the enticing words, temptations, and vain glories which Satan sends our way, hoping to destroy us.

We can uphold the profession of faith without wavering because Jesus Christ is faithful to His promise to keep us as we put our trust in Him. We are to keep our minds on Him and not on the things of the world.

We should continue in our first love in joy and gladness as we give the Lord our best life now. He gave His all for us.

DAILY PRAISES	DAILY PRAYER REQUESTS
1.	1.
2.	2.
3.	3.
4.	4.
5.	5.

October 11
Read II Samuel 22:1-15

II Samuel 22:2-3

"He said: "The Lord is my rock, my fortress and my deliver; my God is my rock, in whom I take refuge, my shield and the horn of my Salvation. He is my stronghold, my refuge and my Savior-from violent men you save me."

The Lord is our hiding place. He is a place of rest and security from the storms of life that rage about us. There is no need to fear. The Lord is with us always, if we serve Him.

He is our keeper in the time of trouble. He will protect us from evil. He will deliver us. In Him we find Salvation which will preserve us with peace and comfort.

Where can we go in the time of trouble and distress except to Jesus Christ? What else is there to comfort and deliver us from violence or fatigue?

Jesus visits us to help renew our spirit and faith in Him, when we seem alone or are depressed. When the enemy comes to us like a roaring lion, Jesus is our defense. We have to not be nervous or anxious because Jesus is our strength. Jesus is the light above the trial. Jesus is the refuge we seek. He will not be moved and neither will we if we trust in the Lord and let Him abide within our hearts. We must patiently pray and read the Bible to stay grounded in Him. He will deliver us. Believe Him to meet your every need today. Let Him deliver you from whatever has you bound.

DAILY PRAISES	**DAILY PRAYER REQUESTS**
1.	1.
2.	2.
3.	3.
4.	4.
5.	5.

October 12
Read Mark 1:14-20

Mark 1:17

"Come follow me," Jesus said, and I will make you fishers of men."

All people become missionaries when they are born again into Jesus Christ. You bring numerous people to Christ when you get saved. You are responsible for others coming to Christ. When you walk with Christ you are a witness to the world and community in which you reside. Your responsibility is to share the gospel through love to those you come in contact with. You may be the only good thing some people come in contact with. You are the only Jesus some people will ever see. What a privilege it is to be a fisher of people's souls. We know some non-Christians, whom we can introduce to Christ. Do not clam up when you get the chance to witness for Christ, use the opportunity. We may have to go where the 'fish' are to witness to them. We may have to go out and meet them on their territory. If we never talk to anyone but Christians, we are isolating ourselves from becoming 'fishers of men'.

Choose someone who is unsaved. Be a friend to them. Get to know them and win them to Christ. It is a joy to win the lost for Christ. He told us to be a witness to the whole world. Go out and communicate to the entire world. Be a fisherman for lost souls. Bring them to Christ in love and compassion.

DAILY PRAISES	**DAILY PRAYER REQUESTS**
1.	1.
2.	2.
3.	3.
4.	4.
5.	5.

October 13
Read James 3:1-12

James 3:2

"We all stumble in many ways. If anyone is never at fault in what he says, he is a perfect man, able to keep his whole body in check."

We reflect what we live and speak. Wisdom is equated with the ability to control the tongue, according to James. We know that all wisdom comes from God. God created the universe and humans. The technical skills of humans are a result of wisdom from God. Experiences give us wisdom which we can use in the future. So God makes all wisdom possible.

Wisdom is a gracious gift. It is either used toward and for God or it is used opposing Him. Wisdom helps us to bridle our tongues. As we seek to be wise and make the proper decision and say the correct words, our life reflects what we verbally confess.

What comes out of our mouth is a great danger to us, especially if it is negative, filled with envy, or untrue. We need to put our tongue under the Lordship of the Holy Spirit to become fruitful, positive, and lovingly useful for Christ.

To control the tongue, we must be pure. If we can control the tongue, every other part will be easy to control. Let us think about our speech. How will it sound to another? Will it heal? Will it edify? Will it comfort? Will it be pleasing to Jesus Christ?

DAILY PRAISES **DAILY PRAYER REQUESTS**

1.

2.

3.

4.

5.

October 14
Read Hebrews 13:1-16

Hebrews 13:6

"So we say with confidence, 'The Lord is my helper; I will not be afraid. What can man do to me?'"

We begin our Christian walk by and through faith. Faith is our legal right to what the Lord has for us, but we have not seen it all yet. You see, we have to believe before we can receive. Faith is the underlying reality of things hoped for. We are linked to faith by God and His Word. Faith comes through the heart.

Just envision what you need from God. Tell Him exactly and be specific. Have a burning desire and strive earnestly for whatever you need. Pray with assurance until it is settled. Peace will come. Just speak and confess to others what God has promised. Claim it and share what the Lord has done.

The Lord is on our side. Instead of being afraid, trust in Him. He is our refuge in times of trouble; especially then. The Lord will bless us with peace and comfort. He will deliver us from our enemies and protect us. When the Lord is on our side we should not fear man and what he can do to us. God is on our side and greater than any other power.

A good idea is to ask the Lord to fight our battles each day. Begin prayer by asking the Lord to fight for you. He has experienced everything we will experience. He will fight for us if we walk upright before Him and if we allow Him to be in charge of our lives and to really fight our battles.

DAILY PRAISES	**DAILY PRAYER REQUESTS**
1.	1.
2.	2.
3.	3.
4.	4.
5.	5.

October 15
Read Psalm 139:1-24

Psalm 139:7

"Where can I go from your Spirit? Where can I flee from your presence?"

Just where do you think God is? God is omnipresent. He is everywhere at the same time. Can you imagine our God being so big and so special? Heaven is His throne and the earth is His footstool. (Isaiah 60:1) He is God and He is close beside us. He is not far away. He does not dwell in buildings or temples, but in humans.

He is the everlasting God. He was from the beginning and will still be God at the end of time. He will endure forever. He is the same always. He will never change. He will reign forever. He is a Living God who has shown great signs and has done mighty wonders.

Do people see God in you? There is but one true God. He has provided a way for us to receive His Spirit through the Son, Jesus Christ. We are to walk upright and serve this One God; the Father of all things.

The Lord knows our hearts. Nothing is hidden from Him. He knows our thoughts deep within our hearts. He sees all we do. He discovers the secret things of the darkness and brings them to light. You cannot hide things from the Lord. He is great in power and understanding. Realize the greatness of God. Know that you cannot escape His presence. He is everywhere.

If you seek the Lord, you will find Him. He is near and is waiting for you to come unto Him. He is close at hand. Just call His Name in prayer and adoration, asking Him to come into your heart. He will hear and enter into your heart to abide with you and help you. Oh, what a magnificent relationship!

DAILY PRAISES	DAILY PRAYER REQUESTS
1.	1.
2.	2.
3.	3.
4.	4.
5.	5.

October 16
Read Judges 5:1-5

Judges 5:3

"Hear this, you kings! Listen, you rulers! I will sing to the Lord, I will sing; I will make music to the Lord, the God of Israel"

God deserves our praise. Although Deborah sang praise to God after a victory in battle, we should also sing praises to God for bringing us through our battles. Our battles may not be physical conflicts in combat. We are to praise the Lord as we are in battle daily with the spirit of the world. Have you given the Lord God the praise for delivering you out of sin and through all the battles of this life? Praise Him for the strength and wisdom you have. Exalt Him above every name. Praise Him for His wondrous works. Glorify Him for salvation. Thank Him for all He has done. It is so exciting to tell of answered prayers, when we have totally relied on the Lord and recognized Him as the Creator, Healer, and sustainer of life. He never fails. We should never fail to praise Him and give Him the honor for what He does. He is pleased with praise.

Sing praises to His Name. It is pleasant to sing praises to the Lord. Sing praises for His mercy and grace. Let us allow our mouth to be filled with praise for Him all during the day and night. God shall bless us as we praise Him. Praise the Lord always!

DAILY PRAISES	**DAILY PRAYER REQUESTS**
1.	1.
2.	2.
3.	3.
4.	4.
5.	5.

October 17
Read Proverbs 22:1-6

Proverbs 22:6

"Train a child in the way he should go, and when he is old he will not depart from it."

Children are such a pleasure and a great gift from the Lord. The Lord looks upon us with great affection as He graciously gives us children. Children keep us young in spirit and make us happy and restore life as we get older. Now that I am older, I realize that grandchildren are a joy and a blessing.

Will children ever become extinct as the dinosaur or the Dodo Bird? People choose to have fewer children each year. They choose to begin their families later in life. The unwanted children mostly get aborted in our society. The homosexual lifestyle does not provide for reproduction of children. Many children are mistreated physically, sexually, and mentally. Lots of couples are saying that they cannot afford children.

Let me tell you the Lord makes a way. He does provide, as long as we honor Him. He makes a way where there seems to be no way. The children may not eat steak every day or wear designer clothes, but the Lord will provide for their physical, material, and Spiritual care of the families.

We raised four beautiful children. They have not had everything they wanted but they never went hungry or unclothed. They were taught the Word of the Lord and trained to follow Jesus. I would not take anything for the experience of holding a new born baby close and feeling the thrill of motherhood. It was exciting to count those tiny toes and fingers of the new born. Parenting is a big responsibility. God is on our side as we honor Him with our children. There is a great excitement in raising and caring for children. It is a challenging job. I praise God for allowing me to be a mother and feel the joy of fulfilling my call to be a mother. God protects and cares for our children.

DAILY PRAISES	**DAILY PRAYER REQUESTS**
1.	1.
2.	2.
3.	3.
4.	4.
5.	5.

October 18
Read Hebrews 11:4-13

Hebrews 11:10

"For he was looking forward to the city with foundations, whose architect and builder is God."

What kind of foundation are you building upon? Is it a foundation that will crumble and fall at the slightest attack of the enemy? Is God the foundation of your building, your faith?

God is able to perform what He promised. We need to put our faith in Him and build on that faith through His Word. We have the same Spirit of faith with which Abraham, Jacob, Joseph, and Paul were filled. Let us exercise that faith, because we do not walk by sight, but by faith. We are not to stagger at God's promises through unbelief, but be strong in faith, giving the glory to God.

Jesus is our pattern to follow. He was longsuffering, merciful, loving, and abounding in faith while He walked among humans. We should look to His example as the road to life everlasting.

We may suffer disappointments and trials. Just as long as our faith is built upon the Word, through the Spirit, given by Jesus, we will have solid foundations that will survive all the evils which come against us. Trust in the Lord and be blessed with a foundation whose builder is God. This builder is Eternal. This builder will never forsake us or leave us. Praise God!

DAILY PRAISES	**DAILY PRAYER REQUESTS**
1.	1.
2.	2.
3.	3.
4.	4.
5.	5.

October 19
Read James 1:1-18

James 1:2

"Consider it pure joy, my brothers, whenever you face trials of many kinds, because you know that the testing of your faith develops perseverance."

God will keep us from falling into temptations of sin. However, we may find ourselves tempted or mistreated in many ways. How should we respond when we encounter difficult circumstances?

First pray and ask the Lord to reveal what we can learn from the situation. Look to God's Word for specific answers, advice, and guidance in the matter. The Bible is our light and guide.

We can seek counsel from mature Christian believers. A wise person will seek counsel and listen to experienced believers. We must be willing to take counsel from our fellow Christians in order to be able to take counsel from the Lord.

We are to praise God because we belong to Him. He is able to deliver us from the present temptation or dilemma. When we begin to praise the Lord, we get our mind off the problems and on what God can do. There is nothing too hard for the Lord.

The Lord wants the best for us. We must also want the best for ourselves by giving the best we have to the Lord. We must praise Him and believe Him. We belong to Him.

Pray, rejoice, read the Bible, and love, especially those who are involved in the present problem you are going through.

DAILY PRAISES	**DAILY PRAYER REQUESTS**
1.	1.
2.	2.
3.	3.
4.	4.
5.	5.

October 20
Read Romans 12:1-8

Romans 12:3

"For by the grace given me I say to every one of you: do not think of yourself more highly than you ought, but rather think of yourself with sober judgment, in accordance with the measure of faith God has given you."

What is faith? How is your faith? Do you believe God can and will meet your needs? Do you believe God without need of certain proof?

If you believe, that is faith to meet your desires and needs. Faith as a grain of mustard seed grows to be a tree in which birds can build their nests to make a home. Use what faith you have. The faith that God has given you will grow. Let it go! Watch it grow! Look up and believe for all things not seen. Faith is confidence, pleasing, and enduring by the Word of God.

Honor God by maturing through trials, heartaches, and problems. Believe He will see you through with others encouraging you. Stand on the faith God gave you when you first believed. Believe without previous experience.

The Bible says it and it is true. We have faith. We must trust and believe. Believe without hurrying to prove it. Faith and works go together. Talk faith to every one you meet. Exercise faith every day. Have a positive attitude and desire to please God first of all.

Faith brings victory. Ask and receive all God has for you. He will provide.

DAILY PRAISES
1.
2.
3.
4.
5.

DAILY PRAYER REQUESTS
1.
2.
3.
4.
5.

October 21
Read Ephesians 4:1-16

Ephesians 4:15

"Instead, speaking the truth in love, we will in all things grow up into him who is the Head, that is, Christ."

Jesus Christ is the Head of the church. We Christians are all members of one body. We do not all have the same office or job. We are to know our office or job and fulfill it.

We are to care for other members, to love and cherish them as our own body, because we are all one in Christ.

We are to follow the example of Jesus. We are His family. He has given each of us gifts to use in the church in unity. We must be willing to let the Holy Spirit lead us.

Our first realm of ministry is to worship the Lord. We worship what is most dear to us; make sure God is first in your life. Next we must minister to our brothers and sisters in fellowship. Then our ministry to the lost world will come as sinners see our worship of the Lord and our fellowship with one another. In doing these things we are forming a spider web of love for catching others, to grow up into Christ.

Make sure Jesus is first in your life. Give Him the number one priority in your life. He will make it worth your while.

DAILY PRAISES	**DAILY PRAYER REQUESTS**
1.	1.
2.	2.
3.	3.
4.	4.
5.	5.

October 22
Read Psalm 62:1-12

Psalm 62:6

"He alone is my rock and my salvation; he is my fortress, I will not be shaken."

What is your defense? Is it God? Is it something or someone that is perishable?

When the enemy attacks us, we need God as our defense. We will be able to endure the attacks of the world if we abide in Him.

I know I will suffer attacks from the enemy as long as I live in this world, but just as surely, I know God is on my side. I will not fear what man can do to me. If God is for me, and He is, who can be against me? God and I make the majority. I know that with God, I will come out victorious every time. It is nothing that I have done, other than call on Jesus and ask Him to be my deliverer and my God.

Today's verse is so dear to me, because the Holy Spirit gave it to me when I needed a Spiritual touch for a defense against the enemy. I have displayed this verse at work and at home to show that God is my defense. When the devil comes against me I use this verse from the Bible.

God truly is my defense and as long as I abide in Him I cannot be moved. I will always be a winner with God. You can also be a winner with the Lord as your defense. Praise the Lord for victory!

DAILY PRAISES	**DAILY PRAYER REQUESTS**
1.	1.
2.	2.
3.	3.
4.	4.
5.	5.

October 23
Read I Peter 1:3-12

I Peter 1:7

"These have come so that your faith-of greater worth than gold, which perishes even though refined by fire-may be proved genuine and may result in praise, glory and honor when Jesus Christ is revealed."

Praise the Lord for rewarding the steadfast Christians. Those who put Christ before everything and serve Him through the good times as well as the bad are to be commended.

We must die out to self in order to serve Jesus. Our wants must not come before our desire to please Christ. Let Him be first in all things. We will never be sorry that we put Jesus first every day and in every way.

This life is of short duration and we need to spend our time witnessing, interceding, and doing satisfactory work for the Kingdom of God. The next life will be forever and we must be prepared and ready to rejoice at the appearing of Christ.

We cannot out do or overdo Christ. Let Him lead you in a work of service. You will not be sorry. You will be forever grateful that you served the Lord.

DAILY PRAISES	**DAILY PRAYER REQUESTS**
1.	1.
2.	2.
3.	3.
4.	4.
5.	5.

October 24
Read Luke 11:14-28

Luke 11:28

"He replied, 'Blessed rather are those who hear the word of God and obey it.'"

The Word of God is so important. It is our road map to Heaven. That is why every Christian should be into the Word, reading and studying it every day, so they do not miss the mark.

It is important for us to have Christian friends with whom we can discuss and share the Word of God. We need to share the wonderful things the Lord is doing in our lives. By sharing we can build up our faith and the faith of others.

We need to go about with a positive attitude, influenced by the Bible and our communication with the Savior. We should share our faith with those less fortunate, by visiting the hospitals, nursing homes, or shut-ins.

When you relax, think on good things, praise the Lord, or listen to positive or spiritual music. Praise the Lord for your Salvation, your health, your mind, your home, or your family. Find something positive to praise the Lord for, even if it is a rainy day. We need the rain. Just admire nature and enjoy the blessings from God.

When the enemy comes to sneak in, crowd him out with praise. Sing songs, read the Bible, talk to Jesus or call a Christian friend to help you pray.

DAILY PRAISES	**DAILY PRAYER REQUESTS**
1.	1.
2.	2.
3.	3.
4.	4.
5.	5.

October 25
Read Romans 6:15-23

Romans 6:23

"For the wages of sin is death, but the gift of God is eternal life in Christ Jesus our Lord."

First, let us look at the positive part of this verse. Eternal life: life without end, a rest, a house of many mansions, fullness of glory and joy, reigning with Christ, likeness of Christ, a secure abode, an inheritance that is incorruptible, a Better Country, a New Jerusalem, praising God, no more sickness, tears, pain, sorrow, always eating from the Tree of Life and drinking of the Water of Life. Who would not desire to spend eternity in such a wonderful place? This is the promise of Eternal Life. All people can have this life if they will come unto the Lord and accept Jesus Christ as their Savior.

On the negative side of this verse, the wages of sin are death. Death without God is: prison, a bottomless pit, the blackness of darkness, a lake of fire and punishment everlasting. We can reject the wages of sin and accept Jesus Christ and Eternal Life. There is no shortcut to Jesus. We must have our sins forgiven and accept the love of Christ. Jesus is the only one who can forgive our sins. It is necessary to know Jesus personally as our Savior.

If you have not made a commitment to the Lord, invite Him into your heart this minute. You can have the gift of Eternal Life now and forever.

DAILY PRAISES	**DAILY PRAYER REQUESTS**
1.	1.
2.	2.
3.	3.
4.	4.
5.	5.

October 26
Read Ezekiel 36:1-12

Ezekiel 36:9

"I am concerned for you and will look on you with favor; you will be plowed and sown,"

God is still for us. He is on our side. We are overcomers through Jesus Christ. We shall bud and blossom through the Holy Spirit and fill the earth with the fruit given by the Holy Spirit. We shall be planted and cultivated by Jesus because of His mercy and His grace. He will not remove His peace from us, but we shall rest in His presence.

We shall sing praises unto God with a voice of gladness and joy. We shall thank Him for His redemption through Jesus Christ, His Son. We shall exalt and honor the One and only God, who cleanses us from all sins. Jesus is the One who fights our battles, speaks comfort to our troubled souls, renews our physical and Spiritual bodies, and who floods our souls with joy so divine. Yes, He is the One who is on our side. He is the One who gives us joy unspeakable and full of glory.

Let the Lord minister to you today. He truly is on your side. He wants the best for you. Allow Him to speak to you. Honor Him through His Word and through prayer and praise.

DAILY PRAISES
1.
2.
3.
4.
5.

DAILY PRAYER REQUESTS
1.
2.
3.
4.
5.

October 27
Read Solomon's Song 4:1-9 (Song of Songs)
Solomon's Song 4:8

"Come with me from Lebanon, my bride, come with me from Lebanon. Descend from the crest of Amana, from the top of Senir, the summit of Hermon, from the lions' dens and the mountain haunts of the leopards."

A fellow teacher sent a student to my classroom one morning to borrow a Bible. The teacher, later explained, that he was showing the students why Lebanon, Ohio, has so many businesses which call themselves Cedar City this or that. The name refers back to the country of Lebanon, which was known for its Cedar Trees.

My colleague made up his mind to marry his wife because of this verse. At the time, he was in the military service. He entered the chapel one day and picked up a Bible. He began to thumb through it and stopped at the fourth chapter of Solomon's Song. This passage confirmed his marriage plans and his plans to reside in Lebanon, Ohio.

Every answer we need can be found in the Bible. We only need to take the time and patience to look for it as we pray and seek guidance from the Lord. We should search the Word for the will of God.

Symbolically, Lebanon is the Spiritual borderland between Heaven and the world between half-heartedness and abandonment to God. Its borders were infested with wild beasts which lurked in the hiding places of the cliffs and mountains. The lion is a symbol of the enemy, going about seeking whom he may devour. He is full of hatred for God's people. The leopard is a symbol of subtle, fierce swift foes against mankind. We should know where we need to look for the enemy. We should know our enemies. Let us examine our place in life. We should know where we need to look for the enemy. We should know where our life lacks victory and watch our steps, because the enemy is lurking in the shadows, just waiting for us to slip and fall.

DAILY PRAISES	**DAILY PRAYER REQUESTS**
1.	1.
2.	2.
3.	3.
4.	4.
5.	5.

October 28
Read II Timothy 2:15-26

II Timothy 2:22

"Flee the evil desires of youth, and pursue righteousness, faith, love, and peace, along with those who call on the Lord out of a pure heart."

Each born again Christian is called to a ministry for God. It might be ministering to our own family, the people with whom we work, our neighbors, some club or organization to which we belong, or to a foreign mission field. We all have a work to do somewhere. It is our responsibility to ask the Lord to show us what He would have us do. Often the life we live is our choice. We should let the Lord direct us to where we will be the most beneficial. Many times our life is our biggest witness to people, without saying a word. We preach a sermon with our everyday life.

We are overcomers of our youthful lusts and desires and follow after a quality life in Christ. We are to put total dependence on the Lord as the one to trust completely, because His truth is recorded in Scripture. We are to love and have compassion for our fellow Christians. Then we are to have compassion for sinners, who are dying without Jesus. The Lord will give us a mental and physical state of quiet tranquility; a calmness for our lives. We can be free from mental anxiety or strain. We can call on the Lord with a heart that is free from the ingredients that weaken, pollute, or impair our lives.

We should be genuine with the Lord and we can be if we put on faith, charity, peace, and follow the will of the Lord. He will lead us by His strength. Are you genuine or is your life a facade? You can be the real deal. You do not have to pretend. God knows all about you any way. Ask Christ to help you become the real person you should be.

DAILY PRAISES	**DAILY PRAYER REQUESTS**
1.	1.
2.	2.
3.	3.
4.	4.
5.	5.

October 29
Read Romans 15:1-13

Romans 15:13

"May the God of hope fill you with all joy and peace as you trust in him, so that you may overflow with hope by the power of the Holy Spirit."

I had a schedule all prepared for today. My list was long and my mind was set on getting things done. The flower beds needed digging and plants replanting. The roses needed to be reset in the sunshine. I needed to go to the nursery for more plants and pots. In my mind, I had it all planned. I was going to get things done on my day off.

The Lord had another schedule for me. I am so used to my husband being well and needing no help, but today he wasn't feeling well. I went to the drug store for medicine for him. I spent time helping him with things he normally did alone. I was getting a bad attitude because my agenda wasn't working out. I am, by nature, an impatient person. I wanted to get my work done. The morning passed and I had not accomplished one thing on my list.

The Holy Spirit reminded me that my love for my husband was to come before my selfish schedule. I love my husband very much and desire to please Him. I love the Lord and it is my pleasure to please Him. I know that when I help my husband I am pleasing the Lord. John reminds us to love one another and to serve each other. We witness by serving and showing love.

As the day passed, I was filled with peace because I knew I was helping and pleasing Jesus. Through the power of God's love and hope we can be filled with joy.

DAILY PRAISES	**DAILY PRAYER REQUESTS**
1.	1.
2.	2.
3.	3.
4.	4.
5.	5.

October 30
Read John 1:1-18

John 1:17

"For the law was given through Moses; grace and truth came through Jesus Christ."

Grace is undeserved favor. No one can do God a favor. He is Ruler and Lord of all. He does not need our favor. Grace came into the world with Christ. There were some examples of grace in the Old Testament, but it is not in the foreground. It is concerned chiefly with Israel. Grace is found in the law the election of Israel to be God's people is attributed in the law to God's free choice and not Israel's righteousness.

Grace involves other substances such as, forgiveness, salvation, regeneration, repentance, and love for God. Mercy, kindness, loving kindness, and goodness are all associated with grace. God gives His grace to humans. We can have steadfast love to another human being and to God through grace.

A new heart can only be a gift of God's grace. Grace is preferred to mercy, because it equips a human to live a normal life. Jesus said He came to seek and save the lost. Many of His parables teach the doctrine of grace. The parable of the laborers in the vineyard (Matthew 20:1-16) teaches that God is answerable to no one for His gifts of grace.

The parable of the great supper (Luke 14:20-24) shows that spiritual privilege does not ensure final bliss and that the gospel invitation is to all.

The prodigal son was welcomed by his father in a way he did not deserve (Luke 15:20-24). Repentance is stressed as a condition of salvation. Faith also has its place because we have to believe to receive salvation. Faith is the human response to divine grace. Faith is the gift of God.

Humans are shown as sinners, but by grace we are justified. God in His grace treats us as if we have never sinned. The believer's position in grace is explained not by anything in himself, but by the will of God. In bestowing favor, God is perfectly free. Every step in the process of the Christian life is due to grace. The religion of the Bible is a religion of grace or it is nothing.

DAILY PRAISES	**DAILY PRAYER REQUESTS**
1.	1.
2.	2.
3.	3.
4.	4.
5.	5.

October 31
Read II Peter 1:3-7

II Peter 3:5

"But they deliberately forget that long ago by God's word the heavens existed and the earth was formed out of water and by water."

The Word of God is compared to water. If you want fresh water, you need to go to the spring or get it at the fountain. I remember when we lived on the farm and had an underground spring. That water was the most delicious and refreshing cold water. It tasted as if it came from the very heart of the earth.

Too many people are content to get their water piped in through a preacher or a television program. The water loses some of its freshness when it is brought from the spring by others. Although we have ministers to bring messages from God, we are to read and research for ourselves.

Take your cup and go to the spring for yourself and enjoy fresh water to the fullest.

By going to the Word of God on your own and reading for yourself you can be certain of the promises God has given you. We will be fresh and be able to give others a refreshing drink from the Word of God.

DAILY PRAISES	DAILY PRAYER REQUESTS
1.	1.
2.	2.
3.	3.
4.	4.
5.	5.

NOVEMBER

November 1
Read Isaiah 44:1-5

Isaiah 44:3

"For I will pour water on the thirsty land, and streams on the dry ground; I will pour out my Spirit on your offspring, and my blessings on your descendants."

People need to be awakened today. The Lord has promised to pour out His Spirit, if we repent and invite Him to bless us.

Our country really needs a revival. We need to pray specifically for a revival in each heart. Everyone should have a desire to see revival sweep this nation as well as the entire world. When we pray for revival we need to pray persistent prayers. Pray, regardless of delays, weaknesses, fatigue, or discouragement. Pray effectively for revival to come. Effective prayers reach the object. They are prayers prayed through the Lord.

We need to pray clean prayers by having our hearts cleansed and speaking to the Lord from the depth of our heart about our serious desires and motives of our hearts. We should pray without ceasing, be earnest, and fervent in prayer.

We should submit to God's will through prayer. We are to keep praying until we have an answer or until we know God's will is revealed for us to pray differently.

When we pray for revival we will not have a spirit of worldliness and indifference, which so often has crept into churches and Christian lives. When we pray for revival we should be willing to shed tears and cry our hearts out to the Lord. We should have strong emotional feelings for the lost and for backsliders, who need to be reunited with the Lord. We should have a burden for the lost and desire above all else to see the sinner commit to the Lord. God will not let the prayers of His children go unanswered. He will hear and give an answer. Begin praying for a revival to start in your heart.

DAILY PRAISES	**DAILY PRAYER REQUESTS**
1.	1.
2.	2.
3.	3.
4.	4.
5.	5.

November 2
Read I Chronicles 17:16-27

I Chronicles 17:20

"There is no one like you, O Lord, and there is no God but you, as we have heard with our own ears."

The Lord is God and there is no other God but Him. He is God of Heaven and God upon the earth. What more do we need?

The attributes of God as a being are unity, self-existence, spirituality, eternal, omnipresence, and immutability.

We have unity with God because He has chosen us to believe in Him and serve Him. He is our Redeemer, our Rock, and our Strength. He is self-existent because He created the world and all the things in it. He gives life to all things. He does not need us, but we need Him.

The Lord is Spirituality because God is a Spirit and we must worship Him in Spirit and truth. He is eternal, invisible, and wise. We owe Him all our honor and glory.

God is eternal because He is everlasting. He will live forever. He was before the earth existed and will endure for ever and ever. He is from the beginning and He is the end.

God is omnipresent because He indwells the earth. We cannot flee from His presence. He indwells those who have accepted Him. He is always near.

God is immutable because His Word is written and fixed for all generations. He is faithful to all who call upon His Name. He is the Lord and He does not change. He gives us these good and perfect gifts which we desire and seek from Him. There is no other God. God is God and we are called to seek and serve Him.

DAILY PRAISES	**DAILY PRAYER REQUESTS**
1.	1.
2.	2.
3.	3.
4.	4.
5.	5.

November 3
Read I John 5:13-21

I John 5:14

"This is the confidence we have in approaching God: that if we ask anything according to his will, he hears us."

There are conditions of acceptable prayer. They are praying in faith, sincerity, in Christ's Name, in righteousness and in the will of God. To know the will of God is by the revelation of His promises, by circumstances, and by His Spirit. We should always pray for God's will to be accomplished and not pray selfishly for our will to be done. God is all knowing and His way is the best way. When we get our way, we will often suffer the selfish consequences of being self-oriented instead of having the mind of Christ.

Praying in faith is belief that God will hear and answer the petitions we put before Him. He has promised to meet the need, if we pray in faith believing according to His will.

We must be sincere when we pray, not just praying because we fear or some other reason. If we will humble ourselves sincerely seeking Him, we will find Him and worship Him in Spirit and in truth.

We must seek Him in righteousness. God hears the prayers of the righteous. If we serve God and keep His commandments, He hears our prayers and answers according to His divine will.

Oh, praises His Name, we have victory through Jesus Christ! Just think, VICTORIOUS PRAYERS ANSWERED FROM OUR LORD!

DAILY PRAISES	**DAILY PRAYER REQUESTS**
1.	1.
2.	2.
3.	3.
4.	4.
5.	5.

November 4
Read Matthew 6:25-34

Matthew 6:33

"But seek first his kingdom and his righteousness, and all these things will be given to you as well."

What more could one ask for than this promise? If we seek God and put Him first in our lives, He will give us all the other things we need in this life. He has promised us an eternal home forever.

What is first in your life? Get honest before God. He knows. If something or someone is first, above God, ask Him to help you get your priorities in order. God should be first. Then He will supply all needs and help us put our lives in order, as is pleasing to Him.

By living a righteous life for God, we receive blessings in this life. He gives us peace the world cannot have. He delivers us from the enemy. He protects us from evil. We have the hope of the glory of God. He has promised us eternal life when this life is finished. We are given joy unspeakable and full of glory because we live for Jesus. We are blessed because we trust in Jesus. We are to cast all of our cares on Jesus, because He cares for us and will take care of us.

If God takes notice and cares for the birds, flowers, and grasses, how much more will He care for us? We are of more value to Him, according to His Word. He will not forsake us. He will take care of us if we will only let Him.

Let us seek Him first and just watch what He adds to our lives.

DAILY PRAISES	**DAILY PRAYER REQUESTS**
1.	1.
2.	2.
3.	3.
4.	4.
5.	5.

November 5
Read Ephesians 3:7-13

Ephesians 3:12

"In Him and through faith in Him we may approach God freedom and confidence."

Jesus Christ is our truth and our life. We come to the Father through Jesus. We know the Father loves us and sent His Son to give His life for us. Jesus is our Mediator. We are to come boldly to Him in faith, asking that our petitions be granted according to God's will.

We are to live in righteousness. That is living above Satan and guilt. We are to carry the Gospel message with boldness. We are to have the knowledge of God's Word and share it. We are to apply the truths' of God's Word to our lives and live by those truths'. We are to live by faith which sustains us in the time of a challenge, sickness, or discouragement.

God has given us weapons to use for our earthly warfare. The Word of God is to be read and remembered. It is to be used constantly. It is both an offensive and defensive weapon. Prayer is another weapon. We can use prayer to defeat the enemy. We can pray a general prayer or pray in the Spirit. We might use an intercessory prayer for others and their needs. God has given us these tools to use to come boldly in faith and receive our needs met. We have the power and the weapons to defeat the enemy. It is up to us to use the weapons God has made available to us. We are in control of our weapons. What is hindering you?

DAILY PRAISES	DAILY PRAYER REQUESTS
1.	1.
2.	2.
3.	3.
4.	4.
5.	5.

November 6
Read Matthew 7:15-23

Matthew 7:21

"Not everyone who says to me, 'Lord, Lord,' will enter the kingdom of heaven, but only he who does the will of my Father who is in heaven."

Obedience to God is required. We must first know God, before we can obey Him. To know Him means we come to Jesus and ask for forgiveness of sins and let Him come into our lives. We live for Him by keeping His commands, praying, reading the Bible, and serving Him. We are to obey the Bible by walking after Jesus' pattern. When sin is forgiven, we belong to Jesus. We are not to commit those sins anymore. We are to look to Jesus and the Holy Spirit for guidance and help, even deliverance from everything unlike Him.

When we receive Jesus we are to seek His guidance, wisdom, and knowledge to apply to our hearts for understanding. We have many examples of obedience by people in the Bible who followed God. Noah is an excellent example, because he did what God commanded him to do. He built an ark, while his friends and neighbors, as well as the entire area, laughed and made fun of him. He was the winner because of obedience. Moses did what God commanded as he led the children of Israel out of Egypt in spite of the stubbornness of the Pharaoh and the Israelites. Moses won in the end. David kept the ways of the Lord and did not depart from them. When God asked David to seek Him, David said, "Thy face, Lord, will I seek." Although David failed God many times, he always returned to seek God and win. The disciples obeyed Jesus. They were winners. Who are we that we should not follow Jesus? There is a reward for obedience. I want to receive heaven and meet Jesus Christ.

DAILY PRAISES
1.
2.
3.
4.
5.

DAILY PRAYER REQUESTS
1.
2.
3.
4.
5.

November 7
Read Philippians 4:2-9

Philippians 4:7

"And the peace of God, which transcends all understanding, will guard your hearts and your minds in Christ Jesus.

Oh, what a blessed promise, the Peace of God! To have peace is to be in a state of physical and mental tranquility, to be calm, and to have order and harmony in your life. It also means to have physical and mental tranquility of the self-existent and eternal creator, sustainer, and ruler of life on this universe. It is so marvelous to have peace.

Do you worry? Why? How does worrying help to change the situation? Worrying only puts you in a bad mood and makes you hurt others. Do not worry. Do not be anxious. God can take care of the small things in life as well as the large ones. Peace is in you when you put your burdens on the Lord. The Lord will not forsake us and leave us without peace. We must allow Him to put peace in us. We should trust the Lord for peace.

The peace of the Lord is so sweet when we meditate upon Him and let peace flood our hearts. We can have peace by loving His laws and walking after Him. He has promised to give us peace if we keep our hearts and minds on Him. We are not to fear and worry because God desires to give us the Kingdom and it will not be of fear and worry.

Who can harm us if we follow Jesus? Who is greater than our Lord? Let us just put our trust in Him and allow Him to fill us with His peace.

DAILY PRAISES	**DAILY PRAYER REQUESTS**
1.	1.
2.	2.
3.	3.
4.	4.
5.	5.

November 8
Read Hebrews 3:7-19

Hebrews 3:15

"As has just been said: 'Today, if you hear his voice, do not harden your hearts as you did in the rebellion.'"

Have you heard the voice of Jesus calling you? How did you respond to the call? Did you answer it faithfully? It is a dangerous thing to resist the call of the Lord. God wants everyone to be saved and walk with Him. He calls and keeps bidding people to come unto Him. When He calls, do not harden your heart against Him. Obey His voice and give your life to Him. Let Him be your God so that life and death may be well with you.

God dealt with hard hearted people of Israel. They kept tempting Him and turning their backs on Him in preference for other gods. They limited His great work because of their selfish desires and rebellion against God. We should learn a lesson from the experiences of the Israelites. We should be open to God's will in our lives. We should be willing to go or do what the Lord wants us to do. We should put the Lord first and follow only Him. He has a plan for our lives.

When the Lord speaks to us we are responsible to obey. He is able to provide all we need. He will take care of us, we need to just be happy and rejoice in the Lord as we answer His call to service. We should receive His instructions and knowledge through His Word. We must desire wisdom and understanding from the Lord.

Those who find the Lord, find life. Those who reject Him reject life and must love death, according to the Bible. Find life and receive it through Jesus Christ. Keep Him in your life always.

DAILY PRAISES	**DAILY PRAYER REQUESTS**
1.	1.
2.	2.
3.	3.
4.	4.
5.	5.

November 9
Read II Kings 20:1-11

II Kings 20:5b

"--------This is what the Lord, the God of your father David, says: I have heard your prayer and seen your tears; I will heal you. ---------"

God has promised to hear our prayers. He has promised to answer our prayers. His answer may not be what we think it should be or when we think it should be, but He does hear and answer.

I remember the first day this Scripture really spoke to me. It was on a Sunday morning that I got up sick and thought there was no way I could go to Sunday School and teach a class, then sing in the choir and enjoy a worship service. I managed teaching Sunday School and singing in the choir. I even went for prayer during worship. I went home feeling as bad as or worse than when I went to church. I spent the afternoon in bed and insisted that my husband attend choir practice and evening worship without me. My husband became my ministering angel as he urged me to attend worship regardless of my feelings. I did my best to go, struggling to stay alert and forget the pain in my body. Sometime during that evening worship service, the Lord healed me. All the pain and anguish left my body.

I praise the Lord because when we go as far as we can and do all we can, then He takes over and does His work. Often we suffer needlessly. We do not relegate our minds, souls, and bodies to the Lord. He is ready and waiting for us to submit to Him so we can be healed.

DAILY PRAISES	**DAILY PRAYER REQUESTS**
1.	1.
2.	2.
3.	3.
4.	4.
5.	5.

November 10
Read I Peter 4:12-19

I Peter 4:16

"However, if you suffer as a Christian, do not be ashamed, but praise God that you bear that name."

In America today, we enjoy more freedom to be a Christian than in any other country and probably in any other decade or century in history.

There are many reasons for rejoicing in this Christian life than any other life style. God has given us a lively hope through the resurrection. He has promised to keep us by His power. He watches over us as faith keeps us in the Holy Spirit. He provides protection by being in front of us and behind us, as well as above and below us. God has taken care of everything we could possibly imagine. What a marvelous source of strength and comfort.

Many believers live in pleasant and safe circumstances, sheltered, they think, from the outrageous attacks of Satan. Satan will attack. Peter reminded us that if Satan attacks us we are to remember God's promises. We are to glory in tribulation because it makes our faith genuine. There is nothing earthly that can compare with our saving faith in Christ Jesus.

Our faith abounds with praise to God. We praise Him because He is the soon coming King! This hope does not fade as the flowers fade. It shines pure and bright every day and night. This is why we can joy and glorify God when we suffer. Let us keep this hope fresh and new in our minds.

DAILY PRAISES	**DAILY PRAYER REQUESTS**
1.	1.
2.	2.
3.	3.
4.	4.
5.	5.

November 11
Read Joshua 1:1-11

Joshua 1:9

"Have I not commanded you? Be strong and courageous. Do not be terrified; do not be discouraged, for the Lord your God will be with you wherever you go."

Isn't it just like the Lord to give us the very Scripture we need for victory in each situation? What a wonderful promise from the God we serve! He has promised to give us victory all the time.

As parents we cannot always be with our children, but we can rest assured that God will be with them wherever they go. What a comfort and strength we draw from His presence and His Word!

When our daughter left for Europe on a student tour, I was anxious and had trouble sleeping the first few nights. I began to pray committing her group to the Lord and for His protection. He gave me this marvelous Scripture, which let me know He was with her and would protect and keep her safe. I was no longer filled with anxiety but had a peace of mind about her safety.

We are not to fear, but take courage and believe the promises of the Lord. He is with us and He will be with our children even when we cannot be there. He is their God, just as He is ours. He loves our children even more than we love them. We must commit our children to Him because He will always be there with them. Praise the Lord for going with us and our children.

DAILY PRAISES
1.
2.
3.
4.
5.

DAILY PRAYER REQUESTS
1.
2.
3.
4.
5.

November 12
Read Philippians 4:12-23

Philippians 4:19

"And my God will meet all your needs according to his glorious riches in Christ Jesus."

What are your needs? Notice the Word of God says "your needs" not your wants. Often we confuse our needs with our wants. We are not promised our wants, but our needs. God is certainly able to supply all your needs as well as your wants, but what good would that be? We may need food to replenish our physical body. Maybe we want a steak to eat, but a hamburger will meet our needs if that is all that is affordable. It is better to eat a hamburger and be sustained rather than starve because we want a steak. Suppose you need a coat for warmth and want a mink coat. A down-filled wool coat would meet the need rather than freezing because you can't have a mink coat.

Jesus will supply our needs whether they are physical, material, or spiritual. Often our wants are selfishly motivated. These wants usually do not benefit us in the end. They satisfy us temporarily. Soon we have other wants, as we seek satisfaction.

Search your heart, as I am searching mine. It is a good idea to list your real needs. Pray for those needs with faith, in the name of Jesus. Stand back and see those needs supplied by Christ Jesus according to His riches in Glory.

Yes, He is able to do whatever we ask. Believe and receive. He is steadfast. He will sustain you. Although you only pray for needs, do not be surprised when He gives more than is needed to satisfy your needs. Praise God!

DAILY PRAISES
1.
2.
3.
4.
5.

DAILY PRAYER REQUESTS
1.
2.
3.
4.
5.

November 13
Read John 1:1-18

John 1:1

"In the beginning was the Word, and the Word was with God, and the Word was God."

Jesus Christ is the Son of God. He was with God from the beginning of time. He is referred to as the Word. God sent His Son to become a human sacrifice for sins. He was born of a woman, which was prophesied by the prophets of old. Jesus lived and represented all people who have ever lived or who live now or in the future. He was hungry for physical food and He ate, as we eat. He became tired and went to a place to rest away from the crowd. He was close to friends and family as we are to ours. He shared their happiness and their sadness as we share with those whom we love and appreciate.

Jesus was tempted in every aspect as we are. Yet Jesus did not sin. He is the Son of God, who is sinless. He has been with God and the world from the beginning of time.

Because we sinned, Jesus came to take our judgment on Calvary. He loves us so much, that He died so we could be forgiven for our sins. He has experienced the pain and disappointments which we experience. He died that we might become the Children of God, the heirs with Jesus Christ.

Just think, if you are a 'born again Christian,' you are a child of God, the King, the Creator of the world and the Word. It is exciting to be a child of God.

DAILY PRAISES	**DAILY PRAYER REQUESTS**
1.	1.
2.	2.
3.	3.
4.	4.
5.	5.

November 14
Read III John 1-13

III John 2

"Dear friends, I pray that you may enjoy good health and that all may go well with you, even as your soul is getting along well."

When we become Christians, life takes on new meaning. We are to love God and our fellow humans. We are to show that love by acts, not by hollow talk. We know we love God because we keep His commands and witness to others to be saved. We love others when we treat them as we treat ourselves. The Bible tells us to love our neighbors as we love ourselves, also. (John 2:8)

We are to have Christian unity by being of one mind and one accord to glorify God. We are to be of the same mind as Christ, having compassion, love, courtesy, and comfort toward one another.

We are to give thanks for one another and rejoice over the joy of others. We can refresh and renew others with Christian fellowship.

Give thanks and rejoice for those who are born anew into the Kingdom of God. Keep praying for them to grow in faith. We praise God for goodness and blessings which He bestows upon others. We joy in the prosperity of our brothers and sisters in health, wealth, happiness, and Spiritual blessings. Rejoice and be generous in praising God for your fellow Christians.

DAILY PRAISES	**DAILY PRAYER REQUESTS**
1.	1.
2.	2.
3.	3.
4.	4.
5.	5.

November 15
Read Ezekiel 22:23-31

Ezekiel 22:30

"I looked for a man among them who would build up the wall and stand before me in the gap on behalf of the land so I would not have to destroy it, but I found none."

God is still looking for men and women who will stand in the gap and intercede for others. It is our duty to pray and seek God continually. We must watch and pray that we are not overcome by temptation. Let us make our prayers to God with holy hands, believing that He will answer our prayers.

When evil comes against us, God moves and delivers us in a mighty way, if we are faithful to believe and pray.

God uses surprising methods to answer prayers. He uses the foolish things of this world to confound the wise. God has the answer. We only have to trust in Him.

God is looking for people who will stand alone with Him. He's looking for people who love Him enough to give up everything, if necessary, to stand by God and before humans. When we are completely sold out to God, we have authority in prayer.

Are you in a place where God wants you? Are you willing to stand in the gap for others? One day, God will reward us for being faithful in this life. He will take care of us if we will be what He wants us to be.

DAILY PRAISES	**DAILY PRAYER REQUESTS**
1.	1.
2.	2.
3.	3.
4.	4.
5.	5.

November 16
Read Romans 10:1-15

Romans 10:9

"That if you confess with your mouth, Jesus is Lord, and believe in your heart that God raised him from the dead, you will be saved."

What are you going to do about Jesus? Have you confessed Him with your mouth and believed in your heart that Jesus is Lord? You have freedom of choice. Only you can make the decision to receive Christ or neglect Him. There are two roads of life that you may choose:

1. The broad road, which many travel, that leads to destruction and Hell.

2. The narrow road, which fewer people travel, but it leads to Life Eternal in Heaven.

Which road are you taking? There is no other way to get to Christ and Heaven, except believing on Jesus. Jesus Christ offers freedom from the chains of sin that have so many bound. He offers freedom from the grave, death, Hell, and destruction.

Repent of your sins by saying, "God, I am a sinner, but I come to you, turning my life over to you. Forgive me and come into my life. I want to live a life pleasing to you," through faith, receive Christ and let Him be Lord of your life. Thank Him for coming into your life. Praise Him for forgiving your sins. You can know you are saved and that you are going to Heaven one day. Christ will live in your heart and all of the emptiness will be gone away. He will fill you with the Holy Spirit to help you.

It is a tremendous responsibility to make a decision for Christ. It may not be easy, but you have Jesus to assist you. He will never leave you or forsake you. You will have more of everything in your life than ever before. **What will you do with Jesus?**

DAILY PRAISES	DAILY PRAYER REQUESTS
1.	1.
2.	2.
3.	3.
4.	4.
5.	5.

November 17
Read Matthew 11:25-30

Matthew 11:28

"Come to me, all you who are weary and burdened, and I will give you rest."

Are you laboring beneath a heavy load? Is it spiritual, financial, physical, mental, worry, or fear? Why not take Jesus at his word and come to Him? Let Him give you rest from whatever burden you have. Let Jesus carry that load. Let Him assume the load by committing your burden to Him. Say, "Here I am, Lord, giving you my heavy burden. I am willing to let you take my burden as I follow and serve you."

When we yield all to Jesus, He will go before us and lead us n righteousness. He will strengthen us and give us rest. We should thirst for a closer walk with Christ as the dry land thirsts for water. We cannot perceive what Christ has in store for us as we remain faithful to God. We may appear poor, but we are rich in Christ. We may seem tired, but we are renewed through the Holy Spirit. Praise God for a refreshing walk with Him.

Who can harm us if we are God's children? As long as we abide in God it is His pleasure to give us the Kingdom. We shall be blessed if we come to the Lord and let Him lead us into rest. He desires to take our heavy load. Let Him take your troubles and help you today and every day in the future.

DAILY PRAISES	**DAILY PRAYER REQUESTS**
1.	1.
2.	2.
3.	3.
4.	4.
5.	5.

November 18
Read Isaiah 41:1-10

Isaiah 41:10

"So do not fear, for I am with you; do not be dismayed, for I am your God. I will strengthen you and help you; I will uphold you with my righteous right hand."

As Christians we have a defense and protection in this life. The hands of the Almighty God are upon us, protecting us. We are not to fear what flesh can do to us. God is our shelter, our refuge, and our strength. Who is able to rise up against God and harm us? The Lord is on our side. Who can be against us? The Lord will take our part and help us when the enemy comes against us. All we have to do is put our trust in the Lord and we will be safe. The Lord gathers us to His bosom as a shepherd gathers the little lambs of his flock in his arms and gently carries them to safety.

Is there any reason to be afraid, if you have given your heart to Jesus? No, there is nothing to fear. The Lord is our helper and strength. We are not to fear the way of humans. The Lord is our confidence. He will keep our feet from being moved by evil. Our Lord will hold us up when fears grasp us.

The Lord is on our side and will deliver us from the unrighteous. The Lord is our shelter from the enemy. Memorize todays verse and claim freedom from fear. Praise the Lord for freedom from fear!

DAILY PRAISES	**DAILY PRAYER REQUESTS**
1.	1.
2.	2.
3.	3.
4.	4.
5.	5.

November 19
Read Romans 13:1-7

Romans 13:1

"Everyone must submit himself to the governing authorities, for there is no authority except that which God has established. The authorities that exist have been established by God."

Did you know that God has allowed the leaders to be elected? They could not be in power unless God permitted it. How do you feel about Christians getting involved in politics? How do you feel about the way things are going in this world today? Are you satisfied with the leadership in the town, state, and country? What would you do to change it?

As Christians, in past decades, we hid and cowered in the corner while prayer was taken out of schools and abortion laws were legalized. Today, I believe, we must get involved. We must stand for what we believe. We have to familiarize ourselves with the issues and candidates before we cast a vote. Often we vote just to vote, because it is our privilege. It is our responsibility to vote and to study the issues and know for whom or for what to vote. We need to read the Bible and pray about voting. We should know the moral issues and vote the correct way.

Do not be afraid to speak out against or for an issue. You never can tell how much good you will be doing by sticking to your convictions. You will cause others to think about their convictions, when you state Bible reasons for yours.

Get to know the local candidates and issues. Express your opinion. Remember the right to vote is a great privilege. We should express that right by being prayerful and seeking God's will. God has a place in our political system. We must give Him the power He ordains and respect His will.

William Penn said, "If we are not governed by God, then we will be ruled by tyrants!" Think about that statement.

DAILY PRAISES	**DAILY PRAYER REQUESTS**
1.	1.
2.	2.
3.	3.
4.	4.
5.	5.

November 20
Read I John 1:5-10

I John 1:9

"If we confess our sins, he is faithful and just and will forgive us our sins and purify us from all unrighteousness."

The greatest need of the people in the churches today is repentance. Most churches and their members have plenty of money, and buildings. People need to return to the Lord with their whole hearts and minds.

We have those who only worship on Sunday morning and do not pick up a Bible or pray any other day during the week. These people need to be awakened. They need to surrender all to Christ. They need to renew their first love for Christ. They need to start anew with Jesus Christ. They need to be willing to be obedient to the Lord. The Lord is calling the church attenders to repentance.

We need to go to the altar for a Spiritual check-up. We need to be separated from the world and filled with the Holy Spirit and let Him guide us.

Numerous times in the Bible, Jesus tells us "to hear". Although we have ears, we are not hearing the call to confession. We go to church and fold our hands while pretending to listen. We do not really listen. Oh, that God would grant us ears to hear His Word and eyes to behold Jesus as the soon-coming King.

It is time to get serious about serving the Lord. There is no time for pretending. There is no time for sleeping on the pew. We must awaken, take our Bibles from the shelf and begin to get instructions through the Word and spend time in prayer, letting the Holy Spirit instruct us.

DAILY PRAISES	DAILY PRAYER REQUESTS
1.	1.
2.	2.
3.	3.
4.	4.
5.	5.

November 21
Read II Timothy 3:1-9

II Timothy 3:1

"But mark this: There will be terrible times in the last days."

What will it take to awaken people to the idea that one day will be the last? Recent movies such as "The Day After" and "The Passion" caused people to think for a moment, but it was soon forgotten. There is a greater crisis today than Atomic or Nuclear war. War only destroys the body. They cannot touch the soul. There are millions of unsaved people on their way to Hell. That is worse than war. There is no hope if they die unsaved.

What are you doing about lost souls? Those times of perilousness are here. We are living close to the end of time. God, help us to alert people to the peril of this hour. It is our responsibility to be the light of the world. We will answer to God if we do not let our light shine.

Are you being led by the Spirit? We need to minister to others in times of trouble. God's people need to be awakened and aroused from slumber. Sinners need to be convicted of their sins before it is too late.

Don't wait until destruction comes to be awakened from luke warmness and self-righteousness. Our unconcern is sending people to Hell. God forbid that we should stand in the door. Today is the day of Salvation, so repent and be refreshed and renewed. Make a vow to tell others about the soon-coming, King. Just ask people if they are born again. That is a huge beginning. Praise God!

DAILY PRAISES	**DAILY PRAYER REQUESTS**
1.	1.
2.	2.
3.	3.
4.	4.
5.	5.

November 22
Read Romans 12:1-8

Romans 12:1

"Therefore, I urge you, brothers, in view of God's mercy, to offer your bodies as a living sacrifice, holy and pleasing to God-this is your spiritual act of worship."

Human's standards often change, but God never changes. A few years ago a certain amount of things were frowned on as wrong, morally, as well as Biblically. Some of those things are abortion, pre-marital sex, homosexuality, unmarried living together, and pornography. We now tend to accept these immoral and sinful deeds. Has God changed? No, He has not. Humans have changed the laws to suit their selfish desires. God's standards have not changed.

When we are saved we become new creatures through Christ. We belong to Him. God can help us solve every problem. We will not automatically become wise, when we are saved. With the help of God, other believers, experience, the Bible, and prayer, we will grow and become what God intends us to become. If we base our standards on the world, we will not have victory. When we base our standards on God's Word we will be victorious and can love and serve faithfully.

God can give us the grace, faith, and courage to repudiate the false standards of the world. Let us, as Christians, embrace the Lord's standards. Let us stand against those things that have penetrated our society as normal, but are not in line with the Bible. God can meet the needs of all those having trouble with God's standards. Through Him all things are possible. Put your trust in Him.

DAILY PRAISES	**DAILY PRAYER REQUESTS**
1.	1.
2.	2.
3.	3.
4.	4.
5.	5.

November 23
Read Ezekiel 37:1-14

Ezekiel 37:4

"Then he said to me, "Prophesy to these bones and say to them, 'Dry bones, hear the word of the Lord!'"

The primary meaning of this chapter has to do with the nation of Israel. We have seen the miracles of Israel as a country and great army come to pass in history. I believe we can apply the secondary meaning of this chapter to our churches today. We have millions of people going to church, but they are dead; a dead army for the Lord. Going to church is great! In fact, we are commanded to assemble ourselves together. What are you like when you leave the church building?

Our witness in the real world is what is important. Do you try to get lost with the crowd at work or play so people will not know that you are a Christian? Do you stand up for Christ regardless of the circumstances?

We need the breath of God to breathe on our dead bones. Yes, there will be noise, rattling, shaking and coming together to praise the Lord. The church will have unity. There will be right relationships and attitudes through the Bible. The breath of God brings life, holy desires, prevailing prayers, and a witness of fire.

We are a great army for the Lord. Let us come alive to engage in this spiritual warfare. He has given us the weapons, the Word of God, the ability to pray and witness. Let us use these by praising God with our mouth; as well as praying and witnessing for Him. Let the breath of God awaken you as you speak to others to encourage and bless them.

DAILY PRAISES	**DAILY PRAYER REQUESTS**
1.	1.
2.	2.
3.	3.
4.	4.
5.	5.

November 24
Read I Peter 5:1-11

I Peter 5:4

"And when the Chief Shepherd appears, you will receive the crown of glory that will never fade away."

Jesus refers to Himself as the Good Shepherd in the book of John. The imagery of Jesus as the Good Shepherd is connected with His return in glory to gather His flock from this evil world.

The crown of life that does not fade away will be conferred upon those who have been faithful to the Lord. The faithful servant is one who is not concerned with recognition in this world, but one who is reflecting the compassion and power of Jesus Christ.

How do we obtain this crown that does not fade away? After we become a Christian, we serve the Lord where He wants us. We are to be eager, with zeal and devotion, in meekness and humility to serve Him. We are to serve in truthfulness, gentleness, and firmness with knowledge and forbearance. As a member of God's family, we are to care for the flock and to feed them. We are not to seek selfish gain, but seek to glorify the Lord in what we do.

Each of us will give an account of our service to the Lord. Begin now to review your account. Will it balance when Jesus appears? Are you overdrawn in selfish deeds? You can settle the account by being willing to serve where and how God directs you.

Oh, how wonderful to have the promise of a crown, when this life has ended. Let us strive to ever be faithful to our Lord.

DAILY PRAISES	**DAILY PRAYER REQUESTS**
1.	1.
2.	2.
3.	3.
4.	4.
5.	5.

November 25
Read Luke 15:11-33

Luke 15:24

"For this son of mine was dead and is alive again; he was lost and is found. So they began to celebrate."

Jesus points to the basic spiritual reality that every person who is estranged from God is spiritually dead. The dead can be resurrected and the lost can be found. That is something to be rejoicing about.

We were all lost and needed to be found; spiritually dead and needing to be made alive. All persons stand equally before the Lord, asking for His grace. His grace flows freely to all willing recipients, leading to Spiritual restoration and to fellowship with Jesus.

Oh, the joy we share as a lost loved one is found! After years of agonizing, praying, waiting, and yearning for that loved one to be saved, we experience earthly joy to the maximum.

If we could look into Heaven, we would see God and the angelic host rejoicing over every lost soul that is redeemed.

God actively seeks to reconcile every lost sinner to a full relationship with Him. God always responds to humans, however weak, frail, or ignorant they may appear. The Lord stands ready to offer salvation, peace, and contentment to every repentant person.

Share in the joy of those who are found. Praise God for those made alive again through His Son, Jesus Christ.

DAILY PRAISES	**DAILY PRAYER REQUESTS**
1.	1.
2.	2.
3.	3.
4.	4.
5.	5.

November 26
Read John 8:31-41

John 8:36

"So if the Son sets you free, you will be free indeed."

We are all enslaved to sin until we accept Jesus. The Son possesses eternal life. When we come to Him and repent He gives freedom from sin. He gives a new dimension to life which we never knew. We are free to become what God wants us to be; a creating, worshipping, growing, loving, and enjoying life person.

To be free is to go from ignorance to knowledge; from uncertainty to truth; from slavery to liberty.

Christ is the Son of God. By that authority He can make people free. Humanity is a slave to sin. Humans are incapable of changing by themselves. They need the power, grace, and mercy of God to help them be freed from sin. Jesus gives freedom which is not attainable any other way. His freedom is genuine. It breaks the bonds of Satan and allows individuals to become heirs of God. It allows them to hear and understand the Father's will.

We find true identity as we walk in the Spirit and produce fruit for the Kingdom of God. Only through Christ and the Spirit can we reach the highest potential and fulfillment of life as God intended.

Begin to realize that you are free through Jesus Christ. Say to yourself, "I am free through Jesus." Live according to His Word and praise Him continually.

DAILY PRAISES
1.
2.
3.
4.
5.

DAILY PRAYER REQUESTS
1.
2.
3.
4.
5.

November 27
Read II Peter 1:3-11

II Peter 1:4

"Through these he has given us his very great and precious promises, so that through them you may participate in the divine nature and escape the corruption in the world caused by evil desires."

These precious promises of God's are of great worth, treasurable, valuable, to be cherished and beloved. The promise certainly relates to redemption. We were purchased by Jesus from darkness into the light. We have escaped the lust of the world. We are free from sins dominion over us.

We are free from moral and spiritual powers of depravity. We are free from the lust that claimed our attention and obedience before Christ came into our hearts. We have overcome corruption by the Blood of Jesus. The greatest promise is, 'we shall be like Him in the Day of Resurrection.' We shall share in the divine nature of Christ as provided for our eternal life.

We are the Creation of God, made to serve Him. When Christ dwells in us, we are transformed into the people we were created to be. Redemption restored us to Christ, that we will be partakers with Him.

We should walk in close fellowship with Him and keep a relationship that is patterned after the very life of Jesus. We have these precious promises to rely upon. God is true to His Words.

DAILY PRAISES	**DAILY PRAYER REQUESTS**
1.	1.
2.	2.
3.	3.
4.	4.
5.	5.

November 28
Read I Peter 4:4-12

I Peter 4:9

"But you are a chosen people, a royal priesthood, a holy nation, a people belonging to God, that you may declare the praises of him who called you out of darkness into his wonderful light."

Today is the day of my birth. I was born into my family as one of them. My name is the same as theirs. I belong to the Phillips family. It is a comfort to belong to a family that loves you and wants the best for you. You have security within that family. They protect you and look out for your best interest. I feel blessed to be born into my earthly family.

When I was six years old, I gave my heart to Jesus Christ. I am a chosen person in God's family. Are you born again into God's family? God has chosen you. You heard the message of the cross and now you must respond in faith through the Holy Spirit. His love and holiness will fill you with new life.

Because we are royalty, we have the opportunity to pray and intercede for others in our world. Because we are holy priests, we have disregarded our righteousness and taken on God's righteousness. Our holiness comes from the Lord. We are holy because He is Holy. Our role of a royal priest means we are children of the One and only King of the universe, God.

We serve the Lord because we love Him. We come to Him boldly in intercession and faith. He is our understanding Father. We live, not by fear, but by the confidence we have in Him and His Supreme Power.

We are a pattern for the world to follow. We are not odd, but we belong exclusively to the Lord. We are to give Him praise for bringing us into the light.

DAILY PRAISES
1.
2.
3.
4.
5.

DAILY PRAYER REQUESTS
1.
2.
3.
4.
5.

November 29
Read Psalm 100

Psalm 100:2

"Worship the Lord with gladness; come before him with joyful songs."

What a nice verse to memorize! It is a joy to serve the Lord. Be glad and thankful for all the benefits He has given us. Be thankful for food, deliverance from trouble, fellow Christians, the Word of God for study and encouragement. The church is for comfort and strength. It brings personal benefits and encouragement.

Praise God for everything He has done. He has done so much for us. We can never realize all that He has done. It is impossible to praise Him enough, but we can try praising Him in joy. Praise Him for the previous things mentioned as well as your own personal praises.

Come to the Lord happy and rejoicing. Let your heart be joyful. Dwell on the good things that God has done for you. Because we trust the Lord, we can sing and be glad. He will delight in our praise and gladness. He has promised us the desires of our hearts if we delight in Him.

Do you delight in the Lord? Is it a pleasure and joy to honor and live for God? If it is, you will be blessed because you give Him the praise He desires. Begin praising Him more and rejoice in the Lord.

DAILY PRAISES	**DAILY PRAYER REQUESTS**
1.	1.
2.	2.
3.	3.
4.	4.
5.	5.

November 30
Read Jeremiah 32:16-27

Jeremiah 32:17

"Ah, Sovereign Lord, you have made the heavens and the earth by your great power and outstretched arm. Nothing is too hard for you."

Are there things you need God to do for you, but think they are too difficult for Him?

Rest assured that there is nothing too hard for God. With men things are impossible, but through God all things are possible.

God is omnipotent in power and authority. God is omniscient about everyone. God is omnipresent always. He has all knowledge of our thoughts and actions. God is irresistible and none can deliver us out of His hands. He will do what He promised.

He is a large God of justice, impartiality, love, mercy, and goodness. His goodness includes truth and compassion. He is no respecter of persons. Not one person that calls on Jesus will be rejected. All are accepted by our Savior.

What do you need from the Lord? Name it to Him. Go boldly to the Lord in prayer, praying for Him to lead you according to His will in the matter. Just tell the Lord in an intimate conversation. Read His Word and meditate upon Him. Continue in prayer until the answer comes. The answer may come right away or it might be delayed. It may be answered in a different way than you planned. Remember we pray for God's will.

Praise God for the answered prayer after you pray. He deserves your praise for all that He has done and all He is going to do. Always praise Him!

DAILY PRAISES	**DAILY PRAYER REQUESTS**
1.	1.
2.	2.
3.	3.
4.	4.
5.	5.

DECEMBER

December 1
Read II Thessalonians 3:6-16

II Thessalonians 3:16

"Now may the Lord himself give you peace at all times and in every way. The Lord be with all of you."

As we come to the close of another year, I lift you up in peace. I desire that God bless you and keep you in His care. I long for Him to put His arms around you and enclose you in His love and peace.

Everyone should realize that the grace of God is sufficient to keep them. Let us direct our hearts to the love of God and the patient waiting for the return of Christ. Until that time our faith in Christ is sufficient to help us serve the Lord as He directs by His Holy Spirit.

Our fellowship is in the Gospel and in unity with one another, with Christ as the Head. Let us continue in unity, loving one another and lifting each other up in prayer.

Let us rejoice and be glad in the Lord for all that He has done for us. Let us praise Him for bringing Salvation to us. Let us magnify His Name.

My prayer is that we can unite and pray for those who have not come to know the Lord. Souls need to be saved. I pray that God will give you the desires of your heart as you follow Jesus. I especially pray for your heart to be at peace in the Lord. May the blessings of the Lord be with your household at this time of the year, even more as we celebrate the birth of our Savior.

DAILY PRAISES	**DAILY PRAYER REQUESTS**
1.	1.
2.	2.
3.	3.
4.	4.
5.	5.

December 2
Read Psalm 61:1-8

Psalm 61:2

"From the ends of the earth I call to you, I call as my heart grows faint; lead me to the rock that is higher than I."

If I wrote an autobiography, there would be many things which would appear overwhelming, but the greatest tragedy in my life was the death of our beautiful, healthy, intelligent, and magnificent eighteen-year-old daughter. I hurt so bad, I thought I could not live. My heart was broken, but Jesus led me to the Rock which was higher than I. He continued to comfort and give me strength. He makes all things possible, when we stand on the Rock.

Jesus is dependable. He causes us not to worry and fret during those overwhelming crises. He will give us peace during the storm. We can rest on the Rock with no fear. We can be secure in Him. He is our Shelter. He is our Foundation. He is the Rock of our Salvation. We can come to the Rock to drink of the Salvation of our Lord. We will never thirst again. There is Honey in the Rock of our Lord.

The Spirit has led me through much growth since our daughter's death. I know the Lord heard and answered my despairing plea for victory in the time of that turning point in my life. My husband gave his heart to the Lord in the crisis. Oh. What a victory! Jesus also led my husband to the Rock. He provided the strength for the family as it was needed. Praise God for His strength and victory. We will meet our daughter again someday because we know Jesus and she did, also.

DAILY PRAISES	DAILY PRAYER REQUESTS
1.	1.
2.	2.
3.	3.
4.	4.
5.	5.

December 3
Read Matthew 6:19-24

Matthew 6:24

"No one can serve two masters. Either he will hate the one and love the other, or he will be devoted to the one and despise the other. You cannot serve both God and Money."

Not one of us enjoys seeing or knowing a hypocrite. Weekly, people come to church and hear the Word of God as they sit faithfully in their pews. But they refuse to let the Word sink into their hearts and soul. They hear with their ears, they speak of love with their mouths, but their hearts are not right with God. They honor God only with their lips. Their hearts are far from Him. We know that we cannot serve God and Satan, too. One spirit is the ruler in our lives. If the Spirit of God does not rule our hearts, then the spirit of Satan is the ruler. We can only serve one master.

Who is the master of your heart?

Do you serve God with lip service, only? Why?

Is God really the ruler of your heart and soul?

The joy of the hypocrite is short lived. But the joy of the Lord is Eternal and forever. Be obedient to the Lord. Serve Him and Him only from the depths of your heart. Let your love for God be real and thankful.

DAILY PRAISES	**DAILY PRAYER REQUESTS**
1.	1.
2.	2.
3.	3.
4.	4.
5.	5.

December 4
Read Colossians 3:1-14

Colossians 3:4

"When Christ, who is your life, appears, then you also will appear with Him in glory."

Oh, what a glorious promise! Just think, we shall appear with Him. Some people get their names in lights for an appearance or starring role. They may feel as if they have accomplished their dream, as if they have made it. But all of this worldly fame will vanish away one day. It is a great accomplishment and I do not wish to take anything away from those who have accomplished great success in this world. However, my goal is to appear with Christ. I will literally have it made at that time. Praise God! Until that time, I have some work to do to prepare for that appearance. As stars of this world must prepare for their roles by learning their lines, practicing their acts, rehearsing their voices and various other chores, we must prepare for appearing with Jesus. I must put off the "old man", which is the sins of the world, and the old life. God does not do it for us, but He helps us. We must desire to put away the worldly things. We must cleanse ourselves of everything unlike Christ. We can do it with the help of the Holy Spirit.

We must put on the "new man", which is: love, mercy, kindness, meekness, long suffering, patience, forgiveness, and humbleness. We must let the peace of God rule in our hearts. We must put the Word of God inside our hearts. We must be without hate or strife. We must be a witness for Christ, letting Him guide us in wisdom and knowledge. In so doing we will appear with Him in Glory.

DAILY PRAISES	**DAILY PRAYER REQUESTS**
1.	1.
2.	2.
3.	3.
4.	4.
5.	5.

December 5
Read Matthew 18:15-20

Matthew 18:19

"Again I tell you that if two of you on earth agree about anything you ask for it will be done for you by my Father in Heaven."

Again and again the Bible tells us of the importance of unity. The Bible emphasizes the importance of agreeing together in prayer. The love which unites Christians to one another is like the love that unites us to God. It is through this love and fellowship that the Spirit can manifest His full power to us.

There must be agreement between believers as to what is to be asked for and received in prayer. It must be a special and specific matter. All must agree in Spirit and truth in prayer. We must ask according to the will of God. Be ready to believe and receive what we ask for in the Name of Jesus. Remember the significance of praying in the Name of Jesus. His presence is with us in fellowship and power.

As a personal experience of agreeing in prayer, I know it is real. I had a migraine headache for three or four days. I went to the home of one of the sisters of the church with the intention of asking her to agree with me in prayer. When I told her I did not feel well, she said, "Let's agree together in prayer for your healing. There is no need for you to suffer." The Lord was already working. I did not have to ask her. She asked me to agree with her. That's the way God's children should be with one another. Feel the need of a brother or sister, agree together in prayer and believe. You guessed it. I have not had another migraine.

DAILY PRAISES	**DAILY PRAYER REQUESTS**
1.	1.
2.	2.
3.	3.
4.	4.
5.	5.

December 6
Read I John 2:15-17

I John 2:17

"The world and its desires will pass away, but the man who does the will of God lives forever."

As Christians we are anxiously awaiting the coming of Christ to Rapture us away. There was a time when I was not ready for the Rapture to take place. Yes, I was a Christian, but I worried about my lost loved ones and friends. No, not all of my family and friends are saved, but now I can truly say, "Come. Lord Jesus".

I don't want anyone to be lost. I am in intercessory prayer daily for all of my family and friends. The Holy Spirit has given me a peace and a readiness about His coming. The Bible tells us to desire to see His appearance. We must love Jesus enough to trust Him. I trust Him exclusively. He has promised to save my family and I have enough faith to believe Him for it. If He returns today, I believe my loved ones will have made a commitment to Him before He returns.

I am doing the will of God and He has promised that He will give me the desires of my heart and I will live forever in Heaven with Jesus and our loved ones. He will do the same for you.

It is a blessing to look for the Lord's return! We have hope in Jesus Christ.

DAILY PRAISES	**DAILY PRAYER REQUESTS**
1.	1.
2.	2.
3.	3.
4.	4.
5.	5.

December 7
Read II Corinthians 3:1-6

II Corinthians 3:5

"Not that we are competent in ourselves to claim anything for ourselves, but our competence comes from God."

The blessedness of the new life is in Christ Jesus. We are not sufficient to live the new life without Jesus. He has given us the Holy Spirit to indwell us. The Holy Spirit teaches us as no other can. He directs our footsteps. He quickens our hearts when we would err. He touches us to pray and when to pray for what we ought to pray about. He even prays through us when we do not know what to pray for specifically.

The Holy Spirit is a wonderful gift to humans, given by our Heavenly Father who loves us so much. He knew we could not live a Christian life without that special strength. He provided that strength through the Holy Spirit.

We are new persons through Him. We can fulfill the requirements of God's Word through Him. We are to love God and one another. We are not an island, but intermingled with many people. We are a light in this new life. We are to beam so others will come to the Lord. This is a new and better way of life. We are to grow in Christ. We are to show our growth through our daily lives in Jesus.

Be confident and secure in Jesus Christ. Through Him we can overcome and accomplish whatever comes our way.

DAILY PRAISES	**DAILY PRAYER REQUESTS**
1.	1.
2.	2.
3.	3.
4.	4.
5.	5.

December 8
Read Proverbs 17
Proverbs 17:22

"A cheerful heart is good medicine, but a crushed spirit dries up the bones."

As I was about to enter the hospital cafeteria, I noticed this verse posted in large letters near the entrance. I rejoiced, because I had just added this verse to my list of favorite verses to commit to memory. I wasn't the only person who believed in having a merry heart. It was posted in the hospital for all to see who entered. Praise God!

God created this earth and He wants us to enjoy life through Him. We are not told to go around frowning and sad and in a rotten mood, but we are to be happy. We have Christ in us and that is something to rejoice about. We, as Christians, should be the happiest, most celebrating people in this world.

Happiness is contagious. We should be able to spread some happiness around. Remember to tell the good news. Do not dwell on the sad or bad. I know we have unhappy times and sadness is in all of our lives, but do not wallow in it. Get through it with God's help. Let your heart be merry and rejoice.

Happiness is a gift from God. Enjoy what He has given you. Give your happiness to others. We can all give a smile, a happy word, and spread the Good News. No one wants to have dried bones and a frown. We are a blessed people. We have received Salvation. Let us rejoice. Show your happiness to the world. Rejoice! Sing! Be merry! Smile! Praise the Lord!

DAILY PRAISES	**DAILY PRAYER REQUESTS**
1.	1.
2.	2.
3.	3.
4.	4.
5.	5.

December 9
Read I Corinthians 2:6-16

I Corinthians 2:14

"The man without the Spirit does not accept the things that come from Spirit of God, for they are foolishness to him, and he cannot understand them, because they are spiritually discerned."

People of the world are often critical of Christians. We know that the world does not understand the Spiritual realm of life. It is impossible for a sinner to understand the Spiritual things of God.

The wonderful news is that sinners can come to God and know Him. Then, He will reveal to them the Spiritual things. God is great, excellent in power, and full of mercy. God's greatness is unsearchable, God is Lord and worthy to be praised. He is never weary or tired. He is the Creator of all things. There are riches in the wisdom and knowledge of God. They can only be known by those who know and love God. Those who obey His will and walk in the Spirit; He will reveal His ways to them. He gives understanding to those who truly walk with Him. He gives the Spirit of wisdom and revelation and knowledge to those walking worthy of the Lord. It is a pleasure to walk in the Spirit and let the Lord lead your life.

DAILY PRAISES
1.
2.
3.
4.
5.

DAILY PRAYER REQUESTS
1.
2.
3.
4.
5.

December 10
Read Psalm 146

Psalm 146:2

"I will praise the Lord all my life: I will sing praise to my God as long as I live."

It is imperative to have time alone with God. He created us to have fellowship with Him. We should choose to have time alone with Him the first thing every morning. This time with the Lord will set the tone of the day. Jesus is waiting for us to enter into fellowship with Him. He wants to teach us as we come to Him for fellowship. He loves us and having redeemed us, He expects to hear us every morning for our time of study, prayer, meditation, and praise. He will reveal such truths, grace, and love to us.

How wonderful it is to spend that relaxed time with the Lord. The enjoyment of just being in His presence and allowing the Holy Spirit to direct us into creative quiet time with Him is a wonderful blessing.

We were created to praise the Lord. I will not be silent; I will praise Him as long as I have breath. I will praise Him for redemption, for His Word, for His healing power, for mercy, for protection, for health, for supplying needs, for my country, my family, and everything else I am and all that I have. The list would be unending for the reasons I will praise the Lord. Praise him! He is worthy.

DAILY PRAISES	DAILY PRAYER REQUESTS
1.	1.
2.	2.
3.	3.
4.	4.
5.	5.

December 11
Read Psalm 91

Psalm 91:11

"For he will command his angels concerning you to guard you in all your ways."

The angels were created by God for His service and glory. They are immortal, superhuman, and they are not to be worshipped. The angels are superior to humans, but they are not gods. They depend on God for their existence. They do not reproduce, but they are an innumerable host. The angels are friends of us, humans. They are interested in our well-being. These holy angels serve God and minister to God's people.

God sends His angels to minister to the needs of His believers. The angels provide guardian care as they en-camp us, that serve God. The angels deliver us from destruction and danger.

The help of angels does not take the place of the Bible or the Holy Spirit in our lives. The angels add to our other Spiritual resources. The promise of care by the angels is made to all who trust in Jesus.

Angels are real. They are active in our world, as guardians and helpers, when we are not aware of it. We should praise God for providing this angelic protection and care. We are not alone. For every evil spirit that would harm us, there is a host of holy angels to protect us.

Praise the Lord for the angels that take charge of us. We are protected daily.

DAILY PRAISES	**DAILY PRAYER REQUESTS**
1.	1.
2.	2.
3.	3.
4.	4.
5.	5.

December 12
Read Romans 8:1-17

Romans 8:16

"The Spirit himself testifies with our spirit, that we are God's children."

We have been adopted into the family of God. He is our Father, because we have received the Spirit of adoption. We can call Him Father and come to Him with every need and always rejoicing.

We are the children of God, because we believe in Him and serve Him. We look to Him as our Savior. He has given us His Spirit and we are led by the Spirit of God, therefore we are the children of God.

Praise the Lord; we are not strangers or alien, but the children of God. God sent His Son and the Spirit into our hearts.

We do not fashion ourselves after the world, but our role model, Jesus, who has such love for us that He died on Calvary for our sins.

We are joint heirs with Christ, because we have been adopted by the Father. We must also suffer with Him in this present world. We will reign with Him in our eternal life.

Thank you, Father, for sending your Son and your Spirit so that we may know we belong to you.

DAILY PRAISES
1.
2.
3.
4.
5.

DAILY PRAYER REQUESTS
1.
2.
3.
4.
5.

December 13
Read Isaiah 43:1-13

Isaiah 43:13

"Yes, and from ancient days I am he. No one can deliver out of my hand. When I act, who can reverse it?"

Our God is irresistible. He can bless and none can hinder. He can give peace and quietness and none can make trouble. There is no power or might to contend with God. When the Lord's hand is outstretched, who can turn it back? In Him is all power. In Him is the beginning and the ending. He is omnipotent and nothing is too hard for Him.

God is from the beginning. He was before the days or before the mountains were in place. He is from everlasting to everlasting.

What a comfort to realize that we can be satisfied when we are safely in His hands. Nothing can deliver us out of His safe keeping. We should not strive against God's will, but gladly submit to obey Him. We are nothing without Him. We need His guiding hand to establish us. We need to receive His commands and be blessed. Let Him make us alive in His Spirit. There is no other to give praise and honor to, except the Glorious Lord.

Always remember He holds you in His hand and will protect and deliver you as you trust in Him.

DAILY PRAISES	**DAILY PRAYER REQUESTS**
1.	1.
2.	2.
3.	3.
4.	4.
5.	5.

December 14
Read Matthew 6:5-18

Matthew 6:8

"Do not be like them, for your Father knows what you need before you ask Him."

What a wonderful Savior, to know what we need before we even ask Him! Don't you see how much He cares for each of us? He wants us to take time to pray, meditate, and speak with Him. He wants us to wait on Him for answers and communication. He hears our sincere, honest, and believing prayers. He wants us to fellowship with Him through prayer and talking.

We are to have our secret place to pray and commune with the Lord. A place for private devotions with Him, if it is the closet, the bedroom or bathroom He will be there. We need a place that will be uninterrupted and where we can get personal with God, as well as where we can tell Him every care and concern. We can pray with our spouse or children if we are sincere and dedicated to concentrating on Jesus.

We are not to use vain repetitions when we pray. We are to believe God, that He will answer our direct prayers. We are to use the example of Jesus when He prayed the Lord's Prayer.

There are many postures to use when praying. The main concern is to be honest and trust God when we pray. God will answer a true believing heart. The answer may not be what we had in mind but it will be God's will. What a promise we have in Jesus!

Just think, the Lord knows what each of us has a need for before we ask Him. What is your need? He knows already. Do not be afraid to ask Him for your needs. He is waiting to hear from you. Prove your faith by asking and believing.

DAILY PRAISES	**DAILY PRAYER REQUESTS**
1.	1.
2.	2.
3.	3.
4.	4.
5.	5.

December 15
Read Philippians 4:1-9

Philippians 4:6

"Do not be anxious about anything, but in everything by prayer and petition, with thanksgiving, present your requests to God."

It is our privilege and duty to pray. We pray because our soul yearns for fellowship with God. We are to seek Him continually, casting all of our worries and cares on Him.

I hear so many parents say, "I worry about my children." This Scripture and others instruct us not to worry. When we have Jesus, we definitely are not to worry or be anxious. God can take care of our children. We cannot be with them all the time, but Jesus can be there. The Guardian Angels are there to protect and oversee our children. God's peace is in you when you put your worries on Him and let Him do the protecting.

Pray, committing your worries to God. Trust in the Lord and let Him take your cares. Praise Him for delivering you from worrying. Tell Him what you are worried about. Continue in prayer until you can give Him all your worries and cares. He wants us to be willing to trust Him to take care of everything and every phase of our lives. We trusted Him for Salvation, why can't we trust Him to take care of our children or trust Him in all other areas of our lives?

Our only hope is in the Lord. Commit your ways to Him, trust Him and He will bring it to pass.

DAILY PRAISES	**DAILY PRAYER REQUESTS**
1.	1.
2.	2.
3.	3.
4.	4.
5.	5.

December 16
Read I John 4:7-21

I John 4:16

"And so we know and rely on the love God has for us, God is love. Whoever lives in love lives in God, and God in him."

What is love? Have you ever truly considered what love really is? Here are some synonyms for love: devotion, affection, passion, attachment, kindness, benevolence, and charity. Do these synonyms describe your feelings of love for Jesus and your fellow Christians?

I want to share an example of love in this modern day. After my father-in-law, who had been incapacitated for a few years, passed away, my mother-in-law got her daughter-in-law, who had been in an automobile accident two years before. The auto accident left her partially paralyzed, unable to walk, think, or do anything for herself. She was very much like a new born other than she could speak a few words. She had suffered a bruised brain along with many other injuries. My mother-in-law devoted three or four years of her life trying to teach my sister-in-law, who has now begun to walk with the help of someone. She can feed herself. She is off medication. She can get in and out of bed by herself. She can take herself to the bathroom in her wheel chair. She can make coffee and stand enough to wash dishes. She was able to give piano lessons with one hand. She was able to live alone for several years, while being monitored and dinner delivered. You see, all of this was possible because of love. My mother-in-law inconvenienced herself to love her daughter-in-law back to a world of reality. If she hadn't done this my sister-in-law would have been living a life like a baby in a nursing home, unable to perform the simplest task. My mother-in-law takes no credit other than love. This is how Jesus loved the world. He gave Himself for us. Let us love in many small acts of kindness. Let the world see Jesus in us.

*Both have now gone to Heaven

DAILY PRAISES
1.
2.
3.
4.
5.

DAILY PRAYER REQUESTS
1.
2.
3.
4.
5.

December 17
Read Romans 2:1-16

Romans 2:11

"For God does not show favoritism."

We have often experienced bosses, friends, or family members who showed partiality to us or others. It hurts when others are chosen over you or taken as a favorite. Our God has no pets. We are all the same with Him. He loves us all. There is no difference.

Praise God that He is impartial. He is God of all and the Lord of all. Everyone has the same chance with the Lord. He is not looking at our personality or to see if we will clash or our size to see if we fit in a certain size. He is not looking at our neighborhood in which we reside or the kind of house in which we live. He is not looking at the type of car we drive to see if we are in a certain social class. He is not looking at the great accomplishments we have made on earth. God is seeking people to love and praise Him. People who are willing to put God first and foremost in their hearts are truly seeking Him. People who will say, "Yes, Lord, I will obey you. I will go where you want me to go. I will follow where you lead. I desire to do your will."

Everyone has the same equal opportunity with God. He is mighty in wisdom and strength; therefore, He does not prefer one person above another. When we come to God and love Him and praise Him, He accepts us and our praise. Whatever good we do we will reap well for it. God is faithful, as He promised in His Word, to communicate and fellowship with us when we believe on Him. He is truthful and without partiality. Let us pattern our lives after Him in all facets.

DAILY PRAISES	**DAILY PRAYER REQUESTS**
1.	1.
2.	2.
3.	3.
4.	4.
5.	5.

December 18
Read Job 14:1-6

Read Job 14:1

"Man born of woman is of few days and full of trouble."

We are not citizens of this world, if we are Christians. Our citizenship is in Heaven. While we are waiting for the return of Christ, we deal with struggles in this world. There are forces trying to gain control of our lives. After we become a Christian, we do not cease to be human, so we are faced with troubles. Just living in this world brings trials and temptations. We do have the power through Jesus Christ to overcome every evil force that comes against us.

We can reduce our strength by living with un-confessed sin in our lives. When sin is allowed to remain, God cannot work in our lives. We are going against Him. As we confess sin and begin to grow and mature in Christ, we encounter many setbacks. However, we must learn and grow into adult Christians that strive to please Jesus.

We must be willing to let God have His will in our lives. He knows what is best for us. He knows the route we should take to glorify Him. We need to listen to Him and follow His directions. After all, He can see the results and we should not try to change God's will for us.

Do not be overwhelmed because our lives are short and filled with trouble. Learn to submit to Jesus and allow Him to work His will in your lives. No amount of worry or panic will lengthen your days or lessen your trouble. Jesus will help to deliver you or give you grace to endure whatever comes your way. Relax in Jesus. We have victory through Him. Although this world is filled with trouble, Jesus is the answer. Look to Him and receive His peace. He is all we need. The answers are there in Jesus, seek Him.

DAILY PRAISES	DAILY PRAYER REQUESTS
1.	1.
2.	2.
3.	3.
4.	4.
5.	5.

December 19
Read I Thessalonians 5:12-28

I Thessalonians 5:18

"Give thanks in all circumstances, for this is God's will for you in Christ Jesus."

It is an easy thing to praise the Lord for the good things and the rich and wonderful blessings He pours out on us. He says to give thanks in "everything". We may wonder how we can thank Him when temptation or trouble or heartaches come. We cannot see the end result of the things that cause us trouble and pain, but we are to praise God anyway, even in the midst of them. We have victory through Jesus. He has delivered us from the powers of Satan and He can deliver us through each trial we encounter.

What did Joseph have to praise God for when He was sold as a slave into Egypt? Just look at the outcome! He was made second in command to the king, eventually. He was able to provide food for his father, brothers and their families during a seven-year famine. He was put there so he could do well, but he suffered many things beforehand. We may be like Joseph in being displaced from our families. We may be suffering. God knows the outcome. Let us praise Him for each situation or obstacle which causes us to pray for God's direction.

Often we wonder why we are in a situation. Praise God for putting you there and look for the positive. God has a plan for us. Give Him thanks always.

DAILY PRAISES	**DAILY PRAYER REQUESTS**
1.	1.
2.	2.
3.	3.
4.	4.
5.	5.

December 20
Read Hebrews 5:1-10

Hebrews 5:8

"Although he was a son, he learned obedience from what he suffered."

How many times have people gotten into trouble because they did not follow orders or obey? Obedience is simply following orders given by a superior. All of us must answer to a superior in some capacity. Jesus obeyed God, although He was and is an equal in the Godhead. We must also obey. Often we are selfish and desire our way. It causes a problem when we go our way rather than the way of Jesus. It is imperative to be obedient to God.

The Lord allows problems to come our way. Often they are to teach us obedience or some other lesson. God can work well through problems. When problems arise, look for and ask the Lord to work them for His glory.

Sometimes problems come to teach us discipline, so we will not repeat the same mistake again.

Other times problems teach us that we can trust Jesus and rely on Him. We need to exercise our faith in Jesus by trusting Him completely. Problems are building, learning, and maturing experiences.

If Jesus learned obedience through suffering, shouldn't we be able to do the same?

DAILY PRAISES	**DAILY PRAYER REQUESTS**
1.	1.
2.	2.
3.	3.
4.	4.
5.	5.

December 21
Read Psalm 27:1-12

Psalm 27:1

"The Lord is my light and my salvation—whom shall I fear? The Lord is the stronghold of my life—of whom shall I be afraid?"

The Lord is everything to me. I have trusted Him since I can remember. Many times I have failed Him and denied Him, but He was always there waiting for me to acknowledge Him again. He has never left me. Oh, what a Savior!

He saved me from sin at the age of six. He has been my best friend, my protector, my strength, and my guide. He has granted me life and health through His Spirit. He has ministered to me continually. He has healed my body physically. He has healed my heartaches. He has blessed me with a wonderful family that follows Jesus. He has comforted me during the death of my parents and our daughter when they were taken to Heaven.

Oh, yes, I will trust in Him and not be afraid. He truly is my song, my salvation, my strength, and my light. My life has not been perfect, but I have Jesus to help me through the trying times.

He will preserve my soul and keep me from evil because I trust in Him. I follow His ways and endeavor to obey His will. I love Jesus and long to meet Him one day. He is my present helper and deliverer. I cannot ask for Him to be more. He is the very breath of life. Oh, that I could express to you, my love and reverence for my Lord! He is ALL AND ALL TO ME.

DAILY PRAISES	**DAILY PRAYER REQUESTS**
1.	1.
2.	2.
3.	3.
4.	4.
5.	5.

December 22
Read Acts 22:6-21

Acts 22:14

"Then he said: 'The God of our fathers has chosen you to know his will and to see the Righteous One and to hear words from his mouth.'"

Jesus Christ who is exalted to the right hand of the Father has sent the promise of the Holy Spirit to us as a helper in knowing His will for our lives. We are to seek the leading of the Lord through the Holy Spirit, prayer, and the Bible. We cannot find the leading of the Holy Spirit through the flesh, because we must be dead to the flesh and alive in the Spirit. We must seek those things which are above, where Christ sits on the right hand of the Father.

Our faith and our hope must be in God, not invested in material or superficial things. We were called for the purpose of praising God and serving as a light to the world. Jesus, who is our example, suffered physical and mental pain as well as harassment as He ministered to the lost world. Should we expect to follow Christ and never be criticized or suffer in this world? Let us get our eyes and mind off people and what they think and begin to please Jesus. Let us see the world as Jesus sees it. Let us have a burden for the lost as Jesus did when He was on earth.

DAILY PRAISES	DAILY PRAYER REQUESTS
1.	1.
2.	2.
3.	3.
4.	4.
5.	5.

December 23
Read John 6:25-40

John 6:35

"Then Jesus declared, "I am the bread of life. He whom comes to me will never go hungry, and he who believes in me will never be thirsty."

Jesus Christ is the bread of life. He is self-sufficient. He is all we need. He is an intimate acquaintance with each of us when we invite Him to come into our lives. He is our protection, provider, and keeper. The enemy has to come through Jesus to get to us, because we belong to Him.

Oh, that we would be as hungry for the Spiritual food as we are for the food that satisfies us physically. If we would only believe and seek more of the bread of life, we would never crave or desire anything else. This bread from Heaven fills our ever longing. It satisfies our desires. It helps us to accept people and things as they are. It lets us see others through the eyes of Jesus. It will cause us to overflow with blessings from Heaven. We will spill out and reach others, who will in turn bless others and be blessed.

Finally, this Heavenly bread will prepare us and cause us to live for life in Heaven. This bread of life is Jesus. Be filled with the Bread of Life today. You will never be sorry. You will never be alone. You will have someone to walk and talk with you.

DAILY PRAISES
1.
2.
3.
4.
5.

DAILY PRAYER REQUESTS
1.
2.
3.
4.
5.

December 24
Read Isaiah 30:1-18

Isaiah 30:15

"This is what the Sovereign Lord, the Holy One of Israel says: 'In repentance and rest is your salvation, in quietness and trust is your strength, but you would have none of it.'"

How happy and how sad is the message of this verse. God gives promises if we will only accept them, for every need and area of our lives. So often we reject the Lord's help. Why? Can we do more than God? Do we have a better plan? The answer to these questions is No! No! No! God's way is the answer. Let us accept it without questions, without doubts, or without complaining.

We will be saved by being restored, rendering everything to Christ and by resting in Him completely.

Our strength shall be in our ability to rest, to remain calm and still to obtain silence and peace in the Lord. We must be positive, assured, certain, and bold enough to stand on these promises as we acknowledge God as Lord of every phase of our lives.

The sad part is to think that we would not accept His rest and quiet. It is so easy to accept His promises. Step out in faith and trust Him. Pray for more faith to claim the promises. Victory is ours through Jesus Christ.

Christians, we live beneath our privilege, because we do not desire more of God and more of His blessings that He has for us. Let us seek the Holy One of Israel in returning to rest, quietness, sacrifice, and confidence in what He will do for us if we let Him be the Lord of our life.

DAILY PRAISES	DAILY PRAYER REQUESTS
1.	1.
2.	2.
3.	3.
4.	4.
5.	5.

December 25
Read Isaiah 9:1-7

Isaiah 9:6

"For to us a child is born, to us a son is given, and the government will be on his shoulders. And he will be called Counselor, Mighty God, Everlasting Father, Prince of Peace."

Oh, what a reason for rejoicing as we celebrate the day of Christ's birth! We have a Savior who is Divine and Mighty. Who came in humility to seek and save the lost. The object of His coming was to save sinners through His great love for them. He proved His love for all humans by sacrificing His life. We are to love others by giving of our time and ourselves. He gave the ultimate sacrifice. Let us pattern our lives after Him. He loves righteousness and desires that all people follow after Him.

The Savior we have been given is forever and ever. His name shall endure always. People who serve Him shall be a blessed people. His name shall be praised continually because He is worthy of praise. Let us magnify the Name of Jesus above every name. He is our most honorable Lord because He came to redeem us and make a way for us to live forever with Him. Praise God for the virgin birth of Jesus. Praise Him for the pureness in life and death and resurrection of Jesus. Through Him we are justified. Through Him we have an abundant life. Praise Him and let every day be celebrated as you celebrate this Christmas Day. Show love and friendship as if each day was Christmas. Let it last all year long.

DAILY PRAISES
1.
2.
3.
4.
5.

DAILY PRAYER REQUESTS
1.
2.
3.
4.
5.

December 26
Read Psalm 31:19-24

Psalm 31:24

"Be strong and take heart, all you who hope in the Lord."

Our hope is in the Lord. We are to look to Him with an uplifted heart and be glad that we have this hope. We have no reason to be cast down, sad or depressed, because our God is our strength and our courage. We are to praise Him and be glad. On the outside we may be hurting and suffering but in our heart we are to give God praise.

We can have hope by reading His Word. There He reinforces our doubts and fears. He gives us His promise to encourage and make us confident in Him.

We have our hope in Him because He is our hiding place and our shield. When troubles and trials come against us, our hope is in the bosom of our Lord. That is where we find rest from the storms.

We were saved by hope. It is a hope that we cannot see, but we can feel and know the surety of that hope.

We have a hope in Heaven which we look forward to and are waiting for that day to come when we will see Jesus and be changed to be like Him.

Let us hope in patience. Let us praise Him as we continually trust in the Lord. He is our God and we have no reason to feel unworthy. We should feel alive and filled with the blessed hope. Praise Jesus.

DAILY PRAISES	**DAILY PRAYER REQUESTS**
1.	1.
2.	2.
3.	3.
4.	4.
5.	5.

December 27
Read I Peter 3:8-22

I Peter 3:14

"But even if you should suffer for what is right, you are blessed. "Do not fear what they fear; do not be frightened.""

God will not forsake us. He is so glad to have people worship and serve Him. He provides our strength in time of suffering and trouble. When we are brought low, He helps us again. He gives us great peace, if we love and serve Him. There is nothing that can uproot us if we truly love the Lord.

He will give us knowledge in our suffering for Him. He will renew us inwardly and give us comfort daily.

We should give our best to the Lord. After all He gave His best for us. What we do for the Lord is so small when we compare it to what He has done for us.

We should not fear because we have God on our side. He desires to give us the Kingdom and we have not seen or heard of anything as magnificent as what He has prepared for us, if we wait upon Him and serve Him.

Jesus forgives and forgets our sins. He dethroned and defeated Satan. His power is greater than Satan's power. We have nothing to fear. Jesus is all powerful.

Our suffering in this life will probably be very little; when we compare it to the blessing we will receive In Heaven. Some people seem to suffer more than others. We do not understand why some have more problems than others. One day we will understand all things. This life is so much better when we have Christ. He helps us through our suffering.

I have tried living both ways; so I know what I am talking about when I refer you to Jesus. No amount of suffering could make up for the glory that will eventually be ours. Whatever your problems, praise the Lord, He will work it out for you.

DAILY PRAISES	**DAILY PRAYER REQUESTS**
1.	1.
2.	2.
3.	3.
4.	4.
5.	5.

December 28
Read John 15:1-17

John 15:13-14

"Greater love has no one than this, that he lay down his life for his friends. You are my friends if you do what I command."

To be a friend is to be personally drawn to another. It is someone with whom we can share the intimate secrets of life. You can speak from your heart and know a friend will understand. A friend respects and regards your feelings as their own. They have an affectionate desire to offer sympathy in time of need. A friend is always ready to rejoice and delight in your happiness.

A friend is precious and to be esteemed above material possessions. It is important to cherish and protect your friendship. We are to maintain our friendships long and hold them close, even though we are far apart physically.

The memories of a friend will last throughout the years. We will cherish the good times as we reflect on our times together. Our friend will be near until the end of our life. We are to value our friends as we would shelter a valuable treasure. A good friend is a valuable treasure to be treated with the most love and respect you can give them.

Jesus called His disciples friends. They were a close knit group. Jesus shared all His secrets with them. They did not always understand what He was telling them. They believed Him and respected Him. The disciples understood more about Jesus after His death on the cross.

It is a pleasure to remember our friends. We may think of their smile or the way their eyes gleamed with amusement. We may think of their bright and fresh personality as we reflect on our friends. It does us good to think on the good times with our friends.

DAILY PRAISES	**DAILY PRAYER REQUESTS**
1.	1.
2.	2.
3.	3.
4.	4.
5.	5.

December 29
Read Romans 10:1-15

Romans 10:9

"That if you confess with your mouth, Jesus is Lord, and believe in your heart that God raised him from the dead, you will be saved."

Life is important. I believe we should begin each day with some type of spiritual worship. For years, I have had the idea to develop a Daily Spiritual Guide for the busy person. By spending a few minutes each morning reading, praying, and meditating on Jesus; they will be equipped for the day ahead. It is necessary to have purpose and meaning to our lives. A good way to have that is to begin each day by being thankful and praising God.

God's power is greater than any power. His love is deeper than any love. Everyone's life can be helped by prayer. They can be healed and made complete through prayer.

The Bible tells us we must be born again (John 3:7; 16). To be born again is to believe on the Lord Jesus Christ according to Acts 16:31. He will forgive you. When you repent you will change because repentance means to change our lifestyle and do the will of the Lord.

We are not to hide Christ but declare Him before the world. We are to witness what He has done for us. He gives us victory over the world. He gives us peace in the world. He gives us so much love that we share that love with others. Our purpose is to win others to Christ, by our daily walk. He will use you as a witness right where you are, if you will only let Him be your guide.

DAILY PRAISES
1.
2.
3.
4.
5.

DAILY PRAYER REQUESTS
1.
2.
3.
4.
5.

December 30
Read II Peter 1:3-11

II Peter 1:4

"Through these he has given us his very great and precious promises, so that through them you may participate in the divine nature and escape corruption in the world caused by evil desires."

Jesus Christ is the Guarantor of all the promises you read in the verses in this chapter. We find our answers in Jesus. A promise is an utterance that goes onward into unfilled time. It arrives ahead of its spokesman and its recipient, to mark an appointment between them in the future. A promise may be a guarantee of continuing or future action on behalf of someone. It may be a solemn agreement of lasting, common relationship. It may be a declaration of coming events.

God's Words do not go out and return void. What He has spoken He will perform. He knows and commands the future. He has spoken it to us in His Word. We can trace His promises throughout the Bible.

What God has promised, He has delivered. All of His promises are confirmed in Him and through Him in worship. The promised Word has become flesh through Jesus. Jesus is the guarantee. The Holy Spirit is our first installment of the Guarantee, after accepting Jesus.

We, as the body of Christ, have a missionary task to spread the news that Jesus died for our sins and to tell that the Holy Spirit has been given, therefore fulfilling the promise of God. The promises of God are open to all who will come in faith, believing in them and on Jesus Christ our Lord.

DAILY PRAISES	**DAILY PRAYER REQUESTS**
1.	1.
2.	2.
3.	3.
4.	4.
5.	5.

December 31
Read II Thessalonians 3:6-16

II Thessalonians 3:16

"Now may the Lord of peace himself give you peace at all times and in every way. The Lord be with all of you."

As I come to the close of my inspirations and ideas at this time, I lift you up in peace. I desire that God would bless you and keep you in His care. I long for Him to put His arms around you and enclose you in His love and peace.

Everyone should realize that the grace of God is sufficient to keep them. Let us direct our hearts unto the love of God and the patient waiting for Christ to return. Until that time our faith in Christ is sufficient to help us serve the Lord as He directs by the Holy Spirit.

Our fellowship is in the gospel and in unity with one another, with Christ as the Head. Let us continue in unity, loving one another and lifting each other up in prayer.

Let us rejoice and be glad in the Lord for all that He has done for us. Let us praise Him for bringing Salvation to us. Let us magnify the Name of the Lord.

My prayer for everyone is to unite in prayer for all people without Jesus. Souls need to be brought into the Kingdom. I also pray that the Lord will increase each of you in the desires of your heart. I especially pray for your heart to be in peace in the Lord. I look forward to meeting each of you in Heaven. May the blessings of the Lord be upon you and your family.

DAILY PRAISES	**DAILY PRAYER REQUESTS**
1.	1.
2.	2.
3.	3.
4.	4.
5.	5.